A Child's life in Wartime Liverpool
Growing up and emigrating to America

By Gladys Thaxton

A Child's life in Wartime Liverpool
Growing up and emigrating to America

Copyright © 2017 by Gladys Thaxton

ISBN   9781549847790

All rights reserved. No part of this book may be reproduced or transmitted in any form or by any means, electronic or mechanical, including photocopying, recording, or by any information storage and retrieval system, without permission in writing from the copyright owner.

This book was printed in the United States of America.

Dedication

To my husband Bill, my friend; my lover; my mentor and to my son John and daughter Susan for their encouragement and patience. Many thanks to my niece Pauline who authored a family history which was instrumental as a valuable resource to write this memoir and in finding my cousin Michael, my Aunt Glady's son. To my sister Vera and her joyful spirit.

And a big thank you to Tom Sullivan for his all-around editing help in preparing this manuscript for publication.

Chapters

	Page
My Birth - Welcome to a topsy-turvy world	6
My musical life - Making my grand arrival	7
A lass from Liverpool	8
The New Boots	10
Eve of War	16
A child's life in wartime Britain	25
The Blitz continues	27
Just looking for shrapnel	37
"All is not lost. Don't give up hope."	39
Life during wartime	40
A delectable chocolate machine	44
The Great Groundnut Scheme	45
Holly and tinsel	59
The Yanks have arrived	61
Jobs carousel	64
Delusions of grandeur	67
The Austerity years	69
Let's go traveling!	72
Doctors and Dating	78
It's time to move on	82
Autographs by the stage door	86
The Great Smog	88
Death, your sting is still with me	89
Time to say goodbye to Liverpool	93
Christmas in Philadelphia	102
Baltimore and Jacksonville	105
Savannah, Georgia - A genteel old city	106
Charleston, South Carolina	112
"One Ringy-Dingy, Two Ringy Dingys"	121
Moving on from Charleston	124
The fabled city of New Orleans	126
So this is Texas	128
Welcome to the Golden State	134
Hello San Francisco!	136
A familiar accent	141
"He's just my Bill"	144
You can't go home again	150
The Swinging 1960s	157
My husband, the actor	163
1970s - Visiting Liverpool	164

Introduction

This is a memoir a small child in wartime Britain and her adventures during the Blitz in Liverpool, England which was second to London in the number of German air raids and bombs dropped on the city. This was never publicized at the time. Liverpool was the only major British port still open which brought in food and supplies from our Allies.

The Germans knew this and tried to destroy the port.

It is a tale of growing up, leaving school at 14-years-old and working in a variety of jobs and a hunger to travel and see all of the places she'd read about in her geography class.

I'd always had a sense of adventure, at four years old, I packed a small case and left the house leaving a message saying, "G.S. is gooin." (I couldn't spell yet.")

I walked to the end of the street and came back.

In her early 20s, she emigrated to America. The voyage took me a month to reach Charleston, South Carolina, due to several docker's strikes her adventures on the voyage and then a temporary first job at an exclusive private golf club where members with names like Rockefellers, Douglas, Claire Booth Luce had their winter cottages/mansions. Travel across America to San Francisco. It's written lightly with a sense of humor.

My Birth - Welcome to a topsy-turvy world!

"Don't let her fall. Don't let her fall!"

Those words were frantically repeated several times by my father as my mother was frog marched out of the bathroom and across to their bedroom.

Dad's large hands were positioned beneath her legs as the crown of my little pink scalp was showing.

I was born in my parents' bed.

Just in time.

My mother, had thought her abdominal discomfort was gas. She sat on the toilet for about an hour patiently waiting to have me.

I kept her waiting. I just wasn't ready to be born yet.

Mine wasn't very glamorous birth.

But who really cares.

I'd made it into this topsy-turvy world.

Now I realize why I never cared for participating in gym class or being upside down.

My father, John Shawcross was born in Liverpool in 1894. He was an apprentice brass finisher with Palatine Engineering in Bootle and on August 4, 1914 he joined the Royal Engineers for the duration of World War I. He served in Egypt, Gallipoli and France and was discharged on August 10th, 1919. He found it difficult to find engineering work in Liverpool at that time and on October 1, 1920, he joined the Liverpool City Police. My Dad served for 26 years and retired in 1946.

My father married my mother Lillian Morrison on May 5, 1922. My older sister Vera, was born in 1923 and I was born in 1932.

My Musical Life - Making my grand arrival

On the day before I was born, my mother told me, obviously hoping she'd induce labor and get me to move, busily pedaled our family pianola for hours, playing all her favorite piano rolls.

I was always a sleepy person and wasn't ready to make my grand arrival into the world just yet.

I've been told that when I was a toddler I always sang and danced along to the radio or my mother singing which she did frequently. In time, I learned all the old music hall songs and I still know most of them.

Many years later, I learned to play the same pianola, a beautiful cherry wood player piano with a mechanical section. You placed a paper music roll into two slots, moved a few levers and then commenced to pedal (like you were riding a bicycle) to bring the machine to life.

The foot pedals operated bellows, which in turn moved the piano hammers. Beautiful music soon poured out. Often, I would pretend to play by moving my hands over the keys.

The piano was in our front parlor of our Liverpool home, and passers-by could look in the window to listen. Of course, I'd pulled the drapes just back a little, in order for this to happen. I enjoyed having an audience.

The family pianola belonged to my grandparents, and was purchased in the 1920s. We had a great selection of popular songs from which to choose from. Ragtime and waltzes. Classics and ballads. A Victorian music hall.

Sometimes, I made up a few of my own tunes, and picked out with one finger on the keyboard.

A lass from Liverpool

Liverpool is over 800 years old. The great city evolved from a small fishing village on the tidal banks of the Mersey River in northwest England. Liverpool appears to have sprung to life when King John granted it a royal charter in 1207. The king needed to establish a port in the north west of England so he could quickly dispatch men and supplies to reinforce his interests in Ireland. By the 14th century it was estimated that the population of medieval Liverpool was about 1,000 people. Over the next few centuries Liverpool started to grow. Today the city's population is 478,000 and the metropolitan borough population is 2.24 million, the fifth largest city in Britain.

The city grew as a major port and was home to both the Cunard and White Star passenger lines and the port of registry too of the ocean liners Titanic and Lusitania.

Liverpool's status as a port city has contributed to its diverse population which historically was drawn from a wide range of peoples, cultures, and religious backgrounds, particularly those from Ireland and Wales. The city is also home to the oldest black African community in the country and the oldest Chinese community in Europe.

Natives are colloquially called "scousers", named after a form of stew introduced by the Scandinavian sailors and enjoyed by the natives. The Liverpool dialect is a mix of Lancashire, Irish, Scottish and Welsh.

The city has been a center of industry and innovations. Inventions, (over 70) and too many to individually list here. They include railways, electric trains, municipal trains which were all pioneered and introduced in Liverpool. In 1829 and 1836 the first railway tunnels in the world were constructed under Liverpool. In medicine and social care came the first School for the Blind; a High School for Girls; 1000's of council built homes; juvenile courts; RSPCA;

NSPCC; age concern; Citizen Advice Bureau and Legal Aid which all evolved from work in the city.

In the field of public health: public baths and wash houses, a medical officer of health, district nurse; slum clearance; a school of tropical medicine, the very first of its kind in the world; free school milk and meals for children; a cancer research center, orthopaedic surgery was pioneered in Liverpool and many modern medical anesthetics all originated in Liverpool.

As well as being a major shipping port and navy base, Liverpool was also home to the headquarters of the Western Approaches Command – A strategic base for the Navy to plan the Battle of the Atlantic Sea. Captain Frederic John Walker masterminded the Atlantic sea battles from Liverpool, and his command destroyed 20 German U-Boats. A statue can be found at the Liverpool's Pier Head in his honour.

Despite being the worst period in Liverpool's history, the War brought people together in a way that perhaps wouldn't happen today. Winston Churchill himself commented after the Liverpool Blitz that "I see the damage done by the enemy attacks but I also see the spirit of an unconquered people."

The New Boots

What a beautiful summer day, said Mum as she stood by the kitchen sink washing the breakfast dishes, her round arms covered with soap suds up to her elbows. She leaned forward and sniffed the warm air coming through the open kitchen window.

"Mum, Mum, can we go to New Brighton I eagerly shouted."

"I don't know," said Mum.

"Please, please," I said.

"Well, it might not be a bad idea." "We don't get too many good days like this one," said Mum.

"Please, Mum." Mum suddenly straightened up and drying down her wet arms on her flowered apron said, "why not. It will take me about an hour to get ready and make some sandwiches to take with us.

"Mum, can I bring Brenda and Nancy and maybe Alan?" I said.

Mum laughed. "I'd better check and see how many pennies I've got in my purse today. Go and tell your friends, Gladys."

I raced out of the house and across the tree lined avenue and knocked on Nancy's front door. Mrs. Allan opened it right away and said it was alright with her if Nancy went to the sea shore and she would give her enough for her fares. And to say thank you very much to your mother, Gladys".

I then raced back across the street to Brenda's house where the same message was relayed by a breathless me, with the same results. Then I went up the street past six houses until I came to Alan's house. Alan was playing in the front garden.

"Hello, Alan," I said.

"Do you want to go to New Brighton with us?"

"Go ask your Mum."

"Oh, yes please," said Alan.

"I can't go past the garden gate, my mum won't let me, in case I mess up my new boots."

Just then Alan's mum, Mrs. Morton opened the front door and said hello.

"Hello, Gladys, how are you?"

"Fine, Mrs. Morton."

"Can Alan go with us to New Brighton? My Mum is taking us. Brenda and Nancy are going too."

I said quite a lot in one very big breath.

"Please Mum", Alan pleaded to his mother.

"No, I'm sorry, Alan, I just don't have the money" she answered sadly.

Gladys knew that Alan's father, Mr. Morton had been out of work for a long time.

Alan didn't get to go to the downtown movie theater like she and her friends often did on a Saturday afternoon.

"That's alright. Mrs. Morton," I said. "My Mum has got the money for the fares and she is making sandwiches to take with us."

At first Mrs. Morton looked like she was going to say no, but she looked down at her sons' rather sad face and instead gave her consent.

"Alright Alan, but don't take your new boots off," understand, do not go near the water."

"Yes, Mum."

"Bring your bucket and spade, Alan. We can build sand castles and things," said Gladys.

An hour later the happy band was skipping up the avenue. Swinging their tin pails and spades. With Mum in the rear, carrying a big, checkered cloth bag filled with sandwiches and bottles of fizzy lemonade. And trying to keep up with the four of us.

"Slow down a little, I can't get my breath," she gasped," there will be plenty of trams along soon." Soon the tram arrived. "Can we go upstairs?" I said. "Alright, but be careful," said Mum.

The four of us scampered up the iron clad steps and raced down to the front of the tram. Everyone's favourite spot. It was a grand view. You could see all around. With no sign of the driver, it felt like you were flying.

The electric tram car careened and clanked along the iron tracks. The upper deck swaying from side to side. The foursome gazing anxiously for sight of the pier, from which the New Brighton ferry boat would sail. Soon we were there and rushing down the sloping floor of the floating deck to which the ferry boat was being tied up. Next to the dock.

With a loud clang, the boat's gangplank was lowered and Mum tried to hold back the four of us saying "Don't go on board until the man tells you." Soon, we were on board and racing for the stairs leading to the upper deck.

The gang plank was raised, a whistle blew and we were off. The smell of tar and rope in our nostrils.

I said, "Look, there's the Gladstone Power Station. My Dad works there." The other three gazed in awe as the giant chimney and buildings glided past.

Nancy and Brenda chimed in with "My Dad works on the docks too."

"My Dad used to work on the docks," Alan said sadly.

They took turns spotting things. Alan was the first one to sight a tugboat. The boat suddenly swung out away from the Liverpool docklands and headed across the Mersey river.

We rushed to the railings. We all wanted to be the first to spot New Brighton. The water grew choppy as the boat came closer to the mouth of the river.

"Look, there's the tower," shouted Brenda, pointing, and soon the ferry was being tied up at the foot of the pier.

Mum got a good grip on all four of us as we impatiently waited for the gangplank to come down and we surged onto the pier. The pier was about 60 years old with wooden planks you could see through to the sand and foam-capped waves hitting the iron supports of the pier. I always felt a little afraid walking on it, and was glad when they reached the street.

"Are we going on the sand first, Mum" I asked.

"Yes, said Mum. The four children jumped up and down, as they hurried to the steps leading down to the beach.

Mum studied the crowds already there and with a curt nod, said "over there quick, that spot will do for us."

We ran as quick as our little legs would go in the soft sand. With Mum coming along behind us more slowly. To spread out the old tablecloth she'd brought. Me, Brenda and Nancy quickly pulled off our shoes and socks, and Mum put them all in a neat row.

Alan started to pull off his boots.

"No, Alan, don't take off your boots," said Mum.

"Why can't I, Mrs. Shaw?"

"We promised your Mum, you wouldn't," said Mum, feeling very sad for Alan.

We four children started to fill our pails and build a sand castle. First, we built up the sand into a big heap and then patted it with our hands until it was much more square-shaped. We took more sand and fashioned four towers, one for each corner. We made two tunnels going crossways and filled the tunnels with water and then decorated the sides of our castle.

Mum called out to Alan.

"Don't go near the water, Alan."

Soon the castle was finished and the foursome sat back on their heels, faces read and shiny, with effort, and gave a loud, collective sigh.

"It's perfect," Mum said.

"Can we have tuppence for flags Mum," I asked.

"Alright," said Mum.

She fished in her purse and brought out two big copper pennies, handing them to me. We four raced across and up on the promenade, where a wooden stall with a blue and white awning stood.

On the counter were bundles of small paper flags with sticks, plus lots of other beach toys. Tin buckets and spades, large rubber balls, inflatable rubber rings, with strange animal shapes.

I handed over the two pennies, and we four ran back to the beach with the flags of all nations to decorate the top of our castle. Without a doubt, it was the smartest castle on the beach, said Mum.

Then it was time to eat. Mum took out the sandwiches and bottles of fizzy lemonade. Everyone was hungry and thirsty from the castle building effort and quickly gobbled down every last crumb of the delicious jam and cheese sandwiches and drank most of the fizzy lemonade, hiccupping after it all.

"Mum," I said, "is it alright if we walk around the beach a little."

"Alright," said Mum, but stay together, and don't go near the water."

"We won't," said the four.

When they got to the edge of the water, Brenda, Nancy and I started to play a little game of dipping our toes in the water and then running up the beach away from the waves. Poor Alan looked miserable not being able to join in because of his new boots and his mother's warning. He started to take little steps closer to the water's edge.

Nancy saw him and yelled, "Don't go near the water, Alan. Remember what your mother told you." Alan looked up at Nancy just as a big wave came in and covered his new boots. A look of horror was on all our faces. Alan ran up the beach crying to Mum.

Nancy, Brenda and I followed sheepishly behind him.

"What on earth happened to you, Alan?" as she took a big handkerchief out of her pocket and wiped Alan's tear stained face.

"Me boots, me boots. They got wet. Ahh, ahh. What will me Mother say?"

Mum looked shocked, then her good hearted nature came to the fore.

"Take them off. Don't worry Alan, we'll fix them."

She helped him with the laces, and pulled the boots off and his damp socks.

"Now you just sit there and let your feet dry off while I see what I can do."

She had brought some old pieces of towel in case of emergencies and started to wipe the boots and laces until they were free of sand. Then she laid everything out on the old tablecloth.

"It's a good thing we have a nice, hot, sunny day. It won't take long to dry this lot."

Alan stopped sobbing and started to smile.

"And when everything is dry, I think I have enough money for five ice cream cones," said Mum.

"Hurray, hurray," we all shouted. Later, we walked around the seaside resort licking our delicious ice cream cones and then tiredly got the ferry back to Liverpool and a streetcar home.

We were a very tired, but a happy band of adventurers.

Eve of War

I was seven years old in November, 1939. The British Government had declared war two months earlier. So far there had been no German air raids. Christmas was only two weeks away.

I came home from school one Tuesday, pushed open the front door and shouted, "Mum, I'm home!"

Walking into the empty kitchen I flung my school satchel towards the coat rack, missed the hook and waited for the usual "Gladys, pick that up!"

This time there was only silence. I searched every room, the house was empty. I know, I thought to myself, today's Tuesday, she's gone to Granddad's.

I wandered about the house for a few minutes, then picked up the satchel, opened it and pulled out a strange looking shape made of rubber with a short tin snout.

I pulled it over my face looking in the mirror. I started to recite out loud. "I'll huff and I'll puff and I'll blow your house down." My voice sounded muffled and far away. The celluloid visor clouded over. I snatched the mask off my face, gasping for air, filled with the same panic that had overpowered me that afternoon in class. Miss Jenkins had said that the civil defense man would come every week and hold a gas mask drill; maybe she could lose the horrid thing before next week.

I went into the kitchen and fixed a snack feeling warmer inside but the quiet of the house was disturbing. "I think I'll walk over to Granddad's; probably meet Mum walking home," I said out loud. I started down the street past the grey stucco houses, privet hedges embracing forlorn gardens; bare of leaf, mounds of naked wet earth with an occasional worm the only sign of life. I wish that summer would hurry back remembering the tar covered road, soft and bubbly from the heat of the sun. Those big tar blisters ready to pop with your thumb. Long summer days that lasted until 10 o'clock at night, days, when I could spend a whole morning lying in the grass making daisy chains.

This time of year, people didn't stroll the streets, but hurried with heads down, coat collars turned up. Already the north winds had made their presence felt. The elms lining the avenue had lost all but one or two of their leaves. The branches seemed to clutch at the sky.

I tried to walk faster but my sturdy legs tingled with the cold. I stopped briefly every few minutes to yank at my baggy, hand-knitted wool knee socks, trying to make them cover my bare legs.

"Ello, Gladys, where yer goin'?"

Tommy Norton, five years old, head barely clearing the top of his garden gate. A huge red and white wool muffler draped over his head and wound around and around his neck; Tommy whose mother never let him venture alone, further than the end of the garden path.

"I'm going to me Granddad, Tommy."

"Yer mother know where yer going?"

"She's there now. I'm going to meet her.

"Ta, ta, Gladys."

"Ta, ta, Tommy."

I was glad I didn't have to stay behind the gate like poor Tommy.

I quickened my footsteps, passing the nearly completed community air raid shelter.

I thought to myself, Old "Shell-Shock" Jones, I hope he doesn't see me. I'll pretend I'm in a terrible hurry.

A tall, bony, middle-aged man appeared from behind a large pile of bricks. Fumbling with his trousers with one hand, in the other a large red handkerchief, into which he sneezed repeatedly.

Keep sneezing, old "shell-shock", until I get by you. I felt my short brown hair prickle the back of my neck as I drew abreast of the man, he suddenly looked up at me, his face in my direction, but his eyes 20 years and 300 miles away, looking up out of a mud-filled trench at black smoke billowing across a Flanders sky.

I counted five houses before I dared look back. Old Jones was still standing there, the red kerchief in his hand, body shaking as if electric currents were coursing through it; the skin tight against the bones; the flesh meager, rendered down from years of shaking.

Suddenly he took off down the opposite end of the avenue in a loping run, his stained raincoat flapping in the breeze. Stopping when the palsy reached a peak, then off once more until his figure grew faint in the distance.

In time, I finally reached the end of the road. Directly in front of me stood the railway embankment on which rested tarpaulin covered gondolas, each one sporting a red flag. Barbed wire had been strung along both sides of the track, as far as I could see.

I turned left and ran under the bridge, holding my breath, hating the dark musty odor, like rotten leaves.

I glanced quickly at the chalk scrawling on the dank walls; reading things I wasn't supposed to know. Ahead on the other side of the road stretched unending, empty flat, wet playing fields; distant goal posts the only thing to interrupt the plane.

The boundaries of the fields obscured with the smoke of a hundred thousand coal fires. I hurried onward.

The rumble of wheels and a clip-clop sound slowed my pace. A cart with a man hunched over the reins. He was dressed in a shabby suit with heavy-shod boots. A sack cloaked his back which was locked in a permanent forward curve from the weight of one hundred pound sacks of coal.

From the top of his cap, which had shaped itself to his skull, down to his boots, he was encrusted with coal dust. Even the whites of his eyes were no more – just a red flush out of which two lumps of coal gleamed dimly.

I could not tell whether he had recognized me or not. All the years he had delivered coal to my home, I had never recalled hearing his voice or seeing any flash of emotion on his coal dust covered face. I shivered as I continued my walk.

Once in a while a tram lumbered by, gently swaying on the tracks. I saw a scattering of passengers downstairs and none upstairs – still too early for the city workers to come home.

I reached the corner of the field and at last turned onto Oak Lane. I stopped to lean over a low brick wall bordering the field. I stood on tiptoe to look down into a small brook, searching the debris with my eyes but no golden flash of fishy scales, not even old tadpoles.

Just rusty tins, a boot with the sole half torn off. Broken bricks and bits of wood. I looked out over the field which was soggy from yesterday's rain. Not one human being in sight, so I started to run and didn't stop until I reached a house. Already the sky was getting darker. A few houses had their blackout drapes drawn, while others were shouting defiance at the oncoming night. In some front parlours Christmas trees with tiny lights winking and shining, casting islands of warmth on the pavement outside.

I wonder what I'll get for Christmas, I thought, maybe something wonderful and different. Another dress, shimmering silk. Every colour of the rainbow banded across it with lace on the collar and cuffs. Dad had bought it three years before at the best store in town.

"If you're going to buy something – buy the best," he had said.

His infrequent gambling wins didn't allow him to do that very often. Her father had said better shop early this Christmas, soon there would be nothing left to buy. I turned onto the main thoroughfare with its many stores, the pavement crowded with heavily- ladened people, most of them seemed to be coming out of grocery stores.

In a few minutes, I will be there. Feeling afraid again, seeing Granddad in my mind's eye. I wonder what he'll think of me, coming here all alone.

I had never said more than a half dozen words to Granddad in my whole life.

But Mum's bound to be there. I just knew it.

I reached up to the big, brass door knocker and managed to pry it away with the tips of my fingers, releasing it, startled by the loud clang it made.

After a few seconds the door was opened by a small woman, with quick, brown eyes, black hair drawn tightly back off of a wrinkled face. A sparrow in a white apron.

"Well, luv. What are you doing here?"

"Is me mum here, Mrs. Ball?"

"No, luv. You better come in and speak to your grandfather. He's in the study. Hurry up now."

I scraped my shoes on the mat that partially covered the whitened doorstep.

"Hurry up now, I have to leave in a few minutes. I'm spending the night with my married daughter across the river and I have to catch the ferry. Lord knows what your mother's going to say, you coming here alone."

The housekeeper showed me into the study saying as she did so "Mr. Anderson, here's your granddaughter come looking for her mother. I'll be leaving now. I don't want to miss the ferry."

There was a chesty cough and then a wheeze from the red faced old man sitting in the big black leather armchair. I shuffled my feet, waiting for granddad to speak, wishing I had stayed home. Finally granddad spoke.

"Well, Gladee, what are we going to do with you. Your mother isn't here, and it's too dark for you to walk back alone. Better stay until your mother comes looking for you. I can't leave the house with this gout."

"Alright child, take your coat off and sit down."

I sat down on the footstool close to the fireplace. Thinking "at least I got out of kissing granddad." I always tried to avoid touching grandfather's big, waxed, yellow-white mustache by giving him a quick peck on the cheek, but sometimes the mustache would touch my face and the smell of wintergreen and wax would make her catch her breath.

"Child, what are you dreaming about?"

"Nothing, Granddad."

"Bring your stool over here and I'll show you my stamp collection."

The stamp collection, Granddad's only passion; he spent most of his days sitting in the big leather armchair, with a card table in front of him, on which lay a large album and packets full of stamps sent from all over the world. They were from old friends of the 40 years he had spent in charge of the foreign mail division of the Liverpool post office. Granddad turned a page and handed me a large magnifying glass.

"Oh well, what do you think of this one?"

I looked around but could see nothing but hazy lights swirling up at me from the glass.

"Turn the thing around, child." "Haven't you ever used a magnifying glass?"

"No, Granddad."

I wanted to leave. Just get away from the prickly mustache, from below which the mouth always seemed to spurt words which hurt me if only he would do or say something to make me feel like I was his only grandchild.

Pat her on the head, hug her, like she had seen other grownups do. Instead of saying things like "Don't touch that vase, you'll break it! – Keep your feet still! – Go sit in the kitchen and talk to Mrs. Ball!"

Still, Granddad was being nicer to her today. Longing to please, she did as the old man asked and in a few minutes, she could focus the glass and see the stamps in detail. Silly old stamps. He droned on with facts of history and geography. How one stamp was quite valuable because of a printing error. This seemed strange to me since the error had planted a large wart on the end of General Kitchener's nose.

Granddad turned another page. Staring up at her on the page was a colorful 1915 tuppenny stamp, with a tin-hatted soldier, his rifle with a fixed bayonet.

I grew sleepy looking through the glass. His stamps took on another dimension.

Was it the small closed room I was in with its coal fire burning hot and red, or did I feel the hot, dry air of Egypt on my glowing cheeks?

The smell of camphor – did it emit from the old man's crumpled black suit, or was it the scent of a Chinese junk sailing across a sea of strange squiggles?

My reverie was broken by a tug on the album beneath my elbow.

Granddad tried to turn the page, but my eyes alighted once more on the tuppenny stamp with a soldier on it.

"Grandad! This stamp looks just like Uncle Harry."

"Nonsense."

"But it does, Granddad."

I searched the marble mantelpiece with its clutter of photographs and bric-a-brac until I found it, a smiling boy in an army uniform. The photo was incased in an ornate three-part frame, with a bronze and silver medal pinned to each of the outer frames.

"See, Granddad." I pointed to the photograph. The old man looked, saying nothing. His eyes glistened.

"What was he like Grandad? What was he like?"

"A boy, a fun loving, tender hearted boy. When he was your age he was forever bringing scraps of life into the house. Once a sparrow with a broken leg, that he splintered and bound and placed in an old biscuit box lined with a piece of blanket. That was the time he decided he wanted to become a doctor. A few years later, when I took him to see the launching of a great passenger liner, all he could talk of for weeks was being the captain of a great ship and sailing all around the world."

"All dreams. Life is all dreams. No substance. Don't believe in anything too strongly, child. It will just burst in your face."

The old man blew his nose loudly. I felt the void again, but I didn't want Granddad to stop talking.

"Granddad, what was the First World War like?"

"Ask your father, he was there."

"But he never wants to talk about it. He says it's best forgotten."

"And, so it is, child."

"Granddad, are there going to be bombs dropped on us now there's a new war? Will we be like 'Shell-Shock' Jones and never stop shaking?"

"Nonsense, child. The Hun will never dare, after the lesson we gave him the last time."

"But Granddad, everyone in school says there's going to be big bombs dropped and all the houses will be blown up."

The old man suddenly closed his stamp album and painfully pulled himself up out of the armchair.

"I'm hungry. Let's see what Mrs. Ball has left us to eat."

Soon the smell of sausage and eggs frying filled the air. The old man had cut chunks of bread and had made strong, dark tea sweetened with condensed milk. The tea had made me feel grown up. Granddad was treating her like she was big and didn't dilute the tea with lots of milk, like her mother would have done.

There was a sudden knock at the front door.

"I'll go, Granddad."

My mother stood on the doorstep.

"Thank goodness, Gladys you're here. I've looked everywhere."

Then, as if an afterthought, she stepped into the hallway.

"You wicked child!" She shook me by the arm.

"Don't you ever wander off by yourself again. Scaring me half to death!"

"But Mum, you weren't home. I thought I would surprise you."

"Never mind surprise. You've got no right wandering about."

They walked into the kitchen.

"Hello, Dad," said Mum, going over and kissing the old man on the cheek.

"I hope Gladys hasn't made a nuisance of herself. I'm sorry I couldn't get over to see you this afternoon."

"Oh, she's been just fine, Annie. Don't be so hard on the lass."

My mother sat and drank tea and talked for about ten minutes before standing up.

"Gladys, get your coat on. It's late and we have a long walk ahead of us."

I came back into the room, buttoning my coat.

"Say goodbye to Granddad, now."

I crossed the room to where the old man was sitting and put my arm around his neck, pressing my face to his cheek. I didn't even feel the awesome mustache as I softly said, "Bye, bye Granddad. I'll come and see you again soon."

We walked home through the frosty night. The sky was cloudless and full of stars.

Suddenly we heard a sound.

"Mum, what's that noise?"

We both stopped and listened. There was a faint wail that grew louder and then receded, and then grew in volume again.

"Hurry, it's the air raid siren."

A Child's Life in Wartime Britain

I learned to read when I was about seven years old and loved fairy stories. I haunted the shelves of our public library. My preference was for stories of emerald and crystal castles, not too many ogres, but nice, colorful, happy ending stories.

Our city library was well used. The children's books were always a little greasy and dog-eared, but they were still readable. Coming out of the library one afternoon, I bumped into my Dad, on his way home from police duty.

"What have you got there, Gladee? Another fairy story book?"

"Yes, Dad," I answered.

"Come on then, let's go and see what Dot's shop has in stock for Christmas."

We walked together across the street. Dot's shop was quite old. I looked up to its high, worn wood counters and shelves on the wall. Some of the candy jars were already half-empty. Dad bought me some jelly beans. Rationing for sweets would soon start.

"Dot, do you have any Christmas tree decorations?" asked Dad.

"Not much left, Jack," Dot said. "Production is closing down until the war's over. Have to make more essential things," they said.

"Rubbish," said Dad.

"Nothing more essential than the twinkle of Christmas lights." Dot reached up to a shelf behind her and lifted down a dusty, cardboard box.

"I've had these for years. Forgot all about them."

She lifted the lid of the box, pursed her lips, and gave a mighty blow. A dust cloud rose and swirled up in the air revealing bright, glittery, multi-colored, hand-blown glass tree ornaments. There were Santas, elves, princesses, angels, and many more. It was magical I thought.

"Oh, Dad. Can we buy them for our tree?" I said.

"They are from Czechoslovakia. We will not see them again for a while. The poor Czech people are probably on that blighter Hitler's list," Dot said. Dad bought six of them and they decorated our little tree for many Christmases.

The Queen Victoria Statue remains today, but look how much of the Castle Street / North John Street area was destroyed in the Blitz.

The Blitz Continues

During the Blitz in May 1941, 681 German planes dropped 870 tons of high explosive and more than 112,000 firebombs on Liverpool. Merseyside and Liverpool were bombed every night of the first week of May 1941 with over 1,750 people being killed. The worst single night was the 3rd/4th when an estimated 850 people were killed. The ammunition ship Malakand, being loaded with 1,000 tons of munitions caught the flames from nearby burning warehouses. Desperate attempts were made to control the fire but she blew up hours after the 'All Clear' was sounded on the 4th, killing four fire fighters. The fire continued for another 72 hours.

The public elementary school I attended was only about 50 feet from my home. Shortly after the war started, an anti-aircraft gun and crew were placed in the girl's playground which forced us girls into the boy's playground.

In those days, boys and girls play areas were kept segregated. The gun emplacement also had a very large silver balloon overhead with two large protrusions that looked like elephant ears. Everyone called the balloons "Dumbos".

The balloons were designed to stop German planes from dive bombing. By 1940 all the parents of young children were approached about letting their children be evacuated to the countryside, hopefully out of danger of the expected German bombing.

I was seven years and two months away from my eighth birthday. My Mum wouldn't let me go which I was mighty relieved about.

Our school classes were getting smaller in size and many of our teachers were missing, likely called up for war service or duty. Those teachers who were left bravely carried on with their duties.

Many of the children who were evacuated from the city limits of Liverpool were sent to North Wales, to family farms, where they had to help with the farm chores. Most had a happy time, living in the countryside, but there were a few negative stories.

We were also issued gas masks around this time. A few weeks later our masks were tested in our classroom. By that time, we carried our lunches in cardboard boxes, so we had to shake out the bread and cookie crumbs.

Holding our breath was pretty hard, while the man in charge of gas masks blocked the air holes, just to see if we could breathe.

The British government had been afraid that the Germans would use poison gas in the war, as they had done in the First World War. Thankfully, that didn't happen. Our first air raids in Liverpool and in Merseyside were in August 1940. Thirty-seven people were killed.

During the first eight days of May 1941, Merseyside was bombed almost every night. 1,900 people were killed, 1,450 seriously wounded and 70,000 made homeless. In Bootle, 8,000 out of 17,000 houses were destroyed or damaged. St. Luke's Church, one of many of the city's churches that were destroyed, was kept as a ruin as a permanent memorial of the May Blitz.

A total of 120,000 houses in the city of Liverpool were damaged. The number of people rendered homeless was very large. Liverpool alone dealt with 51,000. The military brought in field kitchens and tents plus 7,000 workmen to help clear debris and repair factories and homes. During the May blitz, many fires were fought.

The Germans dropped hundreds of incendiary bombs. Parts of the city of Liverpool burnt down because the water supply ran out. People said later that the whole city looked like it was on fire.

Iron pipes were placed along the curbs after the air raids. They were quite a hazard. Going to the cinema at night with my mother, she would grip my arm tight and we would take tiny steps, with Mum asking repeatedly are we there yet.

"Where's the curb?"

And nine-year-old me guiding Mum over the iron pipe with my young eyes. The iron pipe stuck up about 8 inches above the curb.

We had a total blackout during the war. At night, all the windows were covered with blackout material or even painted black. No lights were allowed outdoors.

You could have a flashlight, but it could only have a small pin prick allowing light from the center of the glass.

Air raid wardens, mostly older and disabled men, were very strict and always banging on people's front doors or shelters yelling "Put out that bloody light!" They must have been chosen for their loud voices.

During March 1941 the Morrison shelter, named after the Home Secretary, was introduced. This was an indoor alternative to the Anderson Shelter, the corrugated iron construction that was half buried in people's gardens.

When the bombing raids started we had already been given or allocated our shelter. The order was that every other house had an Anderson garden shelter and the others got an indoor Morrison shelter. We got the Morrison one.

A cozy example of a typical Morrison air raid shelter. - *Imperial War Museum photo.*

The Morrison shelter was like an animal cage, rectangular shape, about eight feet long and four feet wide. The shelter had iron mesh sides which you bolted into place after you got in and had a solid iron top. We all hated it. It was like being in a coffin. We never used it. Mum threw an old tapestry cloth over it and we kept a vase on top of it. During an air raid, we, that is Mum and I, sheltered under the stairs seated on two chairs.

Dad, when he wasn't doing double shifts in the Liverpool Police guarding the power station docks, went to bed and my sister was away on war work, or at a dance. We finally got to share our next-door neighbors garden shelter.

The nearby Smith family were much more fun. All their men folk were away fighting the war, so it was me and Mum. Elderly Mrs. Smith, her married daughter Cora, and her two young children, one who was just a baby.

We fixed the shelter up with lots of cushions, some chairs and a rug. Mrs. Smith had a chair to sit on due to her arthritis. Trying to sleep in the shelter was still pretty difficult. We mostly just dozed until the all-clear siren sounded.

One time I got nervous when I heard the sound of loud, nearby explosions. I started to cry.

"Stop that, you are too old to cry!" yelled Cora.

I stopped crying and never forgot.

The Anderson shelter was in a two to three-foot-deep pit. Corrugated steel sheets covered the sides and top which in turn were covered in several inches of soil and sandbags.

The top corrugated steel sheets were curved. I guess from the air, the shelter looked like a simple mound of earth, or so we all hoped. One night during an air raid, we must have opened the door and shown a light. We had an old oil lamp inside. An air raid warden was quickly on the scene, yelling when there was a nearby explosion and he fell in on top of Cora. He then huffed and puffed his way outside again. One time my Mum got up in the morning and lit the coal fire in the living room as she always did when there was a loud knock on the front door.

The sergeant from the anti-aircraft gun in the school yard stood there.

"Missus," he yelled, "put that damn fire out. Our balloon's broke loose and it's on your roof and your chimney's spitting out smoke and embers. It will blow up our barrage balloon!"

My Mum just looked at him and said "I wondered what that scraping noise was on the roof."

Thankfully, though, we didn't destroy the balloon.

German planes had come over every night since May to drop their bombs. It was quite a long time since we had spent a whole night in our beds instead of sleeping on lumpy mattresses and cushions in the shelter, the damp, moldy smell of earth all around us.

Tonight, the air raid siren sounded the all clear signal earlier than usual and we hurried back to our beds. I got up the next morning and threw on my clothes. I looked out the window as I always did. Hoping for something wonderful to happen.

This time I wasn't disappointed as I pressed my young face to the cold window pane. I couldn't believe my eyes.

No, it couldn't be. It couldn't be, could it? I thought excitedly.

I ran down the stairs shouting "Mum, Mum, quick come look! It snowed. There is snow all over the trees!" Mum and Vi were seated at the kitchen table drinking tea.

"Get your coats on and let's go look," said Mum.

We walked down the avenue looking in wonder at the white covered trees.

"How pretty it looks," said Vi.

"I wonder what on earth it is," said Mum.

Suddenly a man rushed toward us waving his arms in the air and shouting.

"Get way from here quickly. An ammunition train took a direct hit last night and more shells could explode!"

But Mum wouldn't budge until she had asked her question.

"Do you know what the white stuff in the trees is?"

"It's cotton packing from the shells," said the man.

But I knew better. It was Christmas in July.

One of the churches that was destroyed was St. Nicholas near the pier head. It was the oldest and also the parish church of Liverpool. At times, it was called the Seaman's Church. In the 1950s, we office workers used to take our bag lunches to eat in the garden of the church ruins.

There were many churches in Liverpool due to its diverse population. The largest portion of the local population was from Ireland whose migration to the city started when the potato famine occurred in the 1840s. Two and a half million Irish fled starvation to Liverpool and some chose to settle there. Many others chose to emigrate to America.

The Irish group were mostly Catholic, but some from Northern Ireland followed the Protestant faith. They were the Orange men. Growing up in Liverpool I witnessed parades every summer. Catholics and Protestants had their own parades – with flags flying, and playing drums and fifes or penny whistles. Marching through the town to catch the electric train to resorts along the coast to picnic in Southport or New Brighton. Boys would sit on top of the wall of the Protestant high school and throw bits of bricks and shout insults as the Catholics paraded past.

The very same thing would go on at the local Catholic high school. I don't remember hearing of any deaths or injuries. My Catholic grandparents had a card on the wall that said "Waiting for the True Religion to Return."

They had lived in England all of their lives.

Several times during the war I heard tanks rumbling down the street, late at night. They were waiting to be loaded on trains getting ready for the Normandy invasion.

Life was hard for housewives in the 1930s and 1940s. Mum had to shop every day. We didn't have a refrigerator, just a stone larder. We didn't have a washing machine or dryer. We used a clothes line across the back garden. What we had for washing clothes was something called a copper boiler built into the kitchen.

It would fill with water and soon be at boiling point. You stirred in a muslin bag called a bluing bag and waited while the clothes boiled or nearly I think. There was also an iron mangle or wringer to get our clothes semi-dry. All or nearly all of the housewives were house proud.

Mum, every morning would polish the front door's big brass knocker with Brasso and also whiten the doorstep. She would frequently wash the lace curtains on the front of the house windows.

In 1943 when my sister Vera was about 19 or 20 years old, she was drafted by the British government to perform war work. She was sent to the Rolls-Royce engine factory near Crewe in the Midlands. She would get one weekend off a month to come home for a visit.

My sister had really wanted to serve in the Women's Land Army and work on a farm.

There were American soldiers stationed nearby and dances were held frequently. The local girls were invited and my sister became quite good as both a jitter-bug and jive dancer. British girls were accustomed only to ballroom dancing.

During the Blitz an Irish nurse at a Liverpool hospital was caught signaling to German planes to guide them over the docks area, their main target.

Some people in neutral southern Ireland hated the British and even sabotaged British ships when they came into port.

In World War I, there was even talk that they had helped German submarines sink the SS Lusitania in 1915 with the loss of 1,198 passengers and crew. There were many Americans who were traveling on the ship.

Germany offered $1,000 in compensation to the U.S. government for each American killed on the Lusitania. The United States refused the offer.

But there were many Irish that did help Britain during World War I by serving in the armed forces and working in their factories.

An interesting fact that a friend in Liverpool once told me. He had attended a Catholic Church in the south of Liverpool and was looking through the church records one day. The name Hitler showed up. Further investigation revealed that Hitler's half-brother married a Liverpool Irish girl and their son had been baptized in the church. Also, Hitler had visited them for five months in 1912 when he was 23 years old. He had traveled under a false passport to escape being drafted into the Austrian Army.

This photo shows heavy damage on the corner of Strand Street and James Street which was bombed on 3 and 4 May 1941. In the centre of the picture an ARP warden can be seen inspecting a fire in a destroyed building while people look on. There were 1.4 million ARP wardens in Britain, most of who were part-time volunteers who had full-time day jobs. They patrolled the streets and supervised people getting safely into air raid shelters. © *Merseyside Police.*

A view of the devastation around the Victoria Monument in Derby Square after the first few nights of the May Blitz. The monument itself remained miraculously unscathed in the bombing which obliterated much of this area. © *Merseyside Police.*

Lewis's was a much-loved department store on Renshaw Street. My father played Father Christmas one year for the children there. On Saturday 3 May 1941 the store was hit by a small bomb which damaged the sprinkler system. The bombs that continued to hit caused a massive fire which resulted in three-fifths of the store being destroyed. On Monday 5 May Lewis's Bank opened in temporary accommodation at the Bon Marché on Church Street and by the end of the month the surviving two-fifths of the store was transformed into an emergency shop. The store was eventually redesigned in 1947 but it would take another ten years to make up for the damage done on one night's air raid when the building was finally finished in 1957. © *Merseyside Police.*

Just looking for shrapnel

I loved to collect stuff. When the Blitz had been going about a year, I started looking for pieces of shrapnel. Dad gave me an old leather case to keep it in. Soon, I couldn't lift the case and it fell apart.

My sister Vera loved to go dancing and one night walking home after an air raid found an intact incendiary bomb. I guess the interior flammable liquid had already leaked out. She got home safely and gave the bomb to Dad.

The next day my Dad swapped the bomb for candy bars with an American G.I. who was guarding the American supply warehouse across the dock road from where he was on duty guarding the power station for northwest England and Wales.

The American GIs loved souvenirs. I saved all the colorful candy wrappers. I remember that Baby Ruth bars were my favourites. I also had an old belt with regimental badges pinned on it. My mother's four brothers were all in the service.

Uncle Alex was a Royal Marine commando and gave me a green beret with a Scottish thistle brooch pinned on the side. I wore it all through the war.

By the third Christmas, at the end of 1941, I was nine years old. There was very little to buy in the shops for kids. The only thing in my stocking on Christmas morning was a small wooden plaque and painted on it were these words – *"All That Glitters Is Not Gold."*

That plaque hung on the wall of our family home for many years.

I didn't care.

During those difficult war years, we kids played out in the street for hours and made up our own games.

We didn't mind.

In the summer it stayed light until 10 p.m. Two of the old-time games we played were "conkers" where you tied a chestnut at the end of a piece of string and then swung it at your opponent to try to break his chestnut or conker.

We built a "Comet" in the winter. A "Comet" was a tin can with a long wire handle, put kindling inside and swung the can by the wire around our heads until it ignited. Toys didn't matter to most of us.

My mother kept all of our toys in a cupboard beside the fireplace. One day she let me take some out to share with Brenda from next door. I wouldn't let Brenda look at the one that I had never seen before and was trying to play with. My mother was very angry at me for not sharing and gathered up all of the toys and put them back in the cupboard and pushed the sofa up hard against the cupboard. I never could move that sofa. Before the Blitz got going we had a neighbor who used to make toffee apples. They were delicious. She would open her kitchen window and put them along the window ledge to cool. She only charged us 2 pence each.

Another childhood memory was the rag and bone man. He came a couple of times a month with his horse and cart. He moved slowly down the cobblestone street musically shouting out.

"Any rags, bottles and bones?"

I never took him any rags or bones. We made our clothes last a very long time.

Occasionally, my Mum would give me a glass jam jar and with that, the man would hand me a windmill on a stick.

"All is not lost. Don't give up hope."

Mrs. Smith's youngest son Benny who before the war had been training as an optician, joined the British Army when the war started and was sent to Singapore. His Mum received a telegram soon after the Japanese invaded Singapore saying he was missing in action.

One day when I was walking home from school I spotting something colorful at the foot of a tree. It was a Sunday School tract, with an uplifting message printed on it.

"All is not lost. Don't give up hope."

I thought it was a message from God for Mrs. Smith and the next day I went with my Mum on a visit to the Smiths and I gave Mrs. Smith the tract. She just smiled at eight-year-old me.

After one of the heavy May 1941 air raids, Mum and I went to visit her friend a few streets away. When we got there the whole street was gone. Just piles of debris everywhere we looked.

My Dad survived the war even though he was on duty at the main power station which served the whole of northwest England and parts of North Wales. It was right in the docks area which the Germans had tried so hard to destroy. He had spent five years in World War I as a soldier in France and in Gallipoli in Turkey. He was also wounded by poison gas. It was a horrible war he once said and never talked about his wartime experiences.

Life during wartime

During the Second World War (I was about 8 or 9 years old), my good friend Peter Williams who lived across the street and I decided to put on a puppet show in the backyard. I had one hand puppet, a monkey, and a couple of dolls. We rigged up a board across the rose arbour and hung some drapes in front. We pinned a notice on the back door and it was showtime! We charged one penny to come in and had two benches for the little kids to sit on. They were mostly under fives. Peter did a great job with different voices telling a story. My Mum peeked out of the kitchen windows and said the little kids were wide-eyed as they listened. She provided lemonade and biscuits for the refreshments.

My contribution to the war effort was making shell brooches and selling them to the neighbors. I collected small clam shells. Dad put a hole in the top for a ribbon with a small safety pin. I painted a "V" for Victory sign on the shells. I also raffled off a satin pajama case in the shape of a doll. All the money we made went to the Merchant Navy Charity Fund. So many Liverpool men had the ships they were on torpedoed and sunk.

Some of the younger boys that hadn't been evacuated ran wild, mostly because their fathers were away at the war.

One day my friend from next door came over and said her older sister had a friend, Molly who would teach us to tap dance, for one shilling a lesson.

We all loved Shirley Temple and her tap dancing, so we begged our mothers for the money. Molly had the use of an old brick building, used by the Boy Scouts.

It was down in the sports field by the railroad track.

We learned how to shuffle one foot, and the other foot, three shuffles in all, while singing "I'm a Yankee Doodle Dandy."

That's as far as we got.

As bricks came flying through the broken window at the back of the building, we all ran outside.

We saw little boys laughing as they ran off. Molly cancelled any further classes. I used to make up my own tap dancing routines on the tiled kitchen floor to the radio.

After the war started, I remember there was a lot of talk about a Hollywood musical called *The Wizard of Oz* with little Judy Garland. It was playing at our local cinema The Ritz. A few of us wandered down there after school and bumped into Frankie, an older boy. He was standing by a side door of the cinema.

"Quick, come look," he shouted and pointed to a small round hole in the door. I got there first and watched the movie totally enthralled until someone pulled me away. It was Nancy.

"Hey, you've been there long enough. It's my turn."

I reluctantly gave up my spot. I was still lost in the music and colour of the movie. When I got home I told Mum about this wonderful movie and she said "We will go see it tonight."

I was in seventh heaven. Movies and the radio were our main source of entertainment. We all loved the cinema and on Saturday, children's matinees weren't to be missed as long as our parents provided the necessary cash, probably 6 pence, for a ticket and two ounces of sweets.

Boys bought oranges that was before rationing started and spent the whole time throwing pieces of peel all over the theatre. We girls were disgusted, as we wanted to follow the plot of the movie. You got quite a show. There was a main feature, generally a cowboy western, a cartoon; a short comedy; and a serial, possibly, Batman.

The Cabbage Hall Cinema was a few streets away. Occasionally we went there. The doorman was a huge, older ex-army man who was kind of scary. He wore a ritzy doorman's outfit. Overcoat, cap and a lot of brass buttons. The scary part was that he carried a long, bamboo cane.

He used to make us sit on benches, three of them up front, very close to the screen. He would poke us with his stick and yell for us to move along now and make room for the others. Of course, we had paid a penny less to get in.

My sweet tooth. I loved sweets and now with rationing, they were hard to come by. I had a great idea. I found a bottle of peppermint essence in the kitchen. I decided to make peppermint balls. We had no sugar, just some saccharine tablets. But America, God Bless them. They were sending us powdered milk so with these three ingredients, I made peppermint balls. Pretty gross. But they had a remote taste of sweets. Another one of my less successful tries

I was in the pharmacy and spotted what I thought looked like licorice sticks in a jar. I asked the pharmacist if I could buy one.

No problem, he said.

I ate the whole stick and spent hours in the bathroom. He forgot to tell me it was a laxative.

We were allowed to keep chickens during the war, but had to give up our ration of one egg each a week. Dad built a hen house in the back garden with a chicken run. I think we were given grain to feed them.

All in all, I don't remember eating too many eggs. Mum, however, did kill and cook one of the non-layers. I loved her chicken stew.

We were so hungry for meat. My mum had to kill the chicken by stretching its neck over the door jam and then slamming the door.

It was the best of times and the worst of times. We ran out of tea. Our meager rations didn't stretch far enough and you can only reuse tea leaves twice. No teabags in those days until it tastes like dishwashing water.

Cigarettes were also in short supply. Most were sent to the troops abroad where a wounded or dying soldier would have a cigarette pushed in between his lips.

"Here you are mate, take a suck on this ciggy, it'll make you feel better."

The poor, dying man maybe thought he was suckling on his mother's breast.

At home people saved their cigarette stubs and put what was left into a bowl and rolled a cigarette with a paper and rolling machine. I watched my Dad and sister Vera do that, as they were both smokers.

Coal was also in very short supply. In one extremely cold winter during the war, we piled old coats on our beds and burned old shoes in the fireplace. People started to collect coal and coke from along the railway tracks which had fallen from the coal tenders.

A Delectable Chocolate Machine

As a small child how I loved these machines and still have pleasant dreams of them. The chocolate machine in question was made of solid iron and stood in most British railroad platforms, bus terminals and the ferry boat landing stages.

One of my favorite chocolate machines while waiting to cross the Mersey River on a day's outing to New Brighton holiday resort. If I could plead successfully for a penny from my Mum I would slide the large copper coin in the slot and wait a second or two and then pull out a small, stiff iron drawer where lay my prize, a flat bar of Swiss milk chocolate wrapped in silver paper and a red paper outer wrapper. Heaven! All of this came to an end with the start of World War II and the iron chocolate machines stood empty for many years.

There were no electronics to go wrong and nothing to break down. They probably are still in use today. Good solid Victorian workmanship and iron that never seemed to rust. At least to my small child's eyes.

I vaguely remember one Christmas getting a small cardboard replica of one of these machines with a supply of miniature chocolate bars and a coin to put in the slot which you could retrieve quite easily. The tiny bars didn't last long. I still have a voracious appetite for chocolate 80 years later, but for some reason, chocolate now doesn't taste as good as the penny chocolate bar of 80 years ago.

The Great Groundnut Scheme

When I was about 12 or 13 years old I decided one afternoon after school to go see my Dad in town. He was still on duty down at the Gladstone Power Station. I took the bus into town and then walked about two miles along the dock road.

I noticed after about one mile that there were piles of peanuts in shells laying all over the road. I got to the dock gates where my Dad was. He wasn't angry with me and just gave me a big smile. He said later "Don't do that again on your own. It's dangerous."

"Gladee, would you like a ride in the engine?"

He helped me up onto a real locomotive engine which carried coal to the power station all day. Afterwards, we sat in the police hut for a while and Dad gave me a big mug of hot cocoa. He also gave me the fare to pay for a ticket on the overhead electric train back to where I could catch the bus home. That evening I asked him about all the peanuts lying on the road. He said that's the daft plan the Ministry of Food had to produce more oil for cooking.

In 1946, Frank Samuel, head of the United Africa Co., a subsidiary of Unilever who made soaps and margarine fats came up with the idea to cultivate groundnuts in the British colonies for the production of vegetable oil. Britain was still on rationing and there was a shortage of cooking oil. After a three-month study, the Ministry of Food authorized 25 million pounds Sterling to cultivate 150,000 acres of scrubland in designated areas of Kenya and Rhodesia. It was assumed that somebody knew how to do the job, when in fact, no one knew. The proper equipment and techniques had not yet been invented and the operation was enormously underestimated.

They began to recruit for the "Groundnut Army" and 100,000 ex-soldiers volunteered. The area selected for cultivation was in Tongwa, in central Tanganyika, where the locals had already cultivated groundnuts. Major General Desmond Harrison was placed in charge of operations in Tanganyika.

The first problem was a lack of heavy equipment to clear the land for cultivation. A manager found some suitable tractors and bulldozers from Canada and bought U.S. Army surplus tractors from the Philippines, but they proved to light weight for the job. Equipment had to be transported from the port of Dar es Salaam on a single-track railway with a locomotive. Unfortunately, a sudden flood of the Kinyansugave River wiped out the rail tracks leaving a dirt road as the only means of transport. Local large baobab trees proved to be too hard to move. One was the local tribal jail, another was a site for worship and many had bees' nests. The fact that it was far from water sources caused more problems. The water had to be ferried in and poured into a concrete-lined pool. Locals used it for swimming, despite protests from European workers. Eventually, managers decided to train local workers. Enthusiastic, but inexperienced drivers wrecked many of the tractors. Two men from London were sent to help the locals form their own trade union who then decided to go on strike in support of the dock workers in Dar es Salaam and demanded more food. By the end of 1947, two-thirds of the imported tractors were out of use. At this stage, Major General Harrison retreated, burying himself in piles of paperwork and later succumbed to advanced anemia and a nervous breakdown. He was ordered back home on sick leave.

The original target of 150,000 acres was gradually reduced to 50,000 acres. After two years, only 2,000 tons of groundnuts were harvested (some of which I had found on the Liverpool dock road). The British government cancelled the project in 1951. The 49 million pound expenditure was virtually a total loss.

Early school days.
(Thaxton collection)

A precocious toddler on my Dad's lap in a photo taken at my grandfather's home - 1933.
(Thaxton collection)

With my Mum Lillian in our front garden in Liverpool - 1939.

(Thaxton collection)

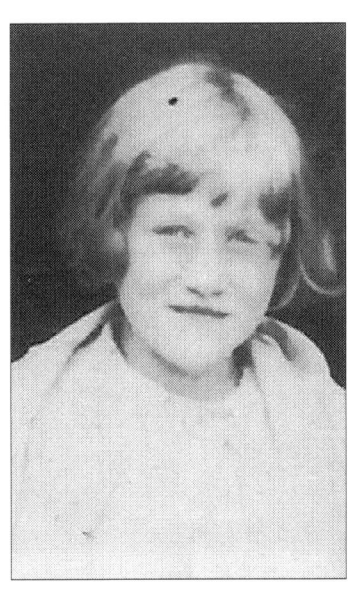 

My older sister Vera as a little girl, and as young adult. She married George Buchanan in Liverpool in 1947. They had two children, Ian and Pauline. My sister died quite unexpectedly as a young woman, prompting me to consider my postwar future in Liverpool and my plans to emigrate to the United States.

(Thaxton collection)

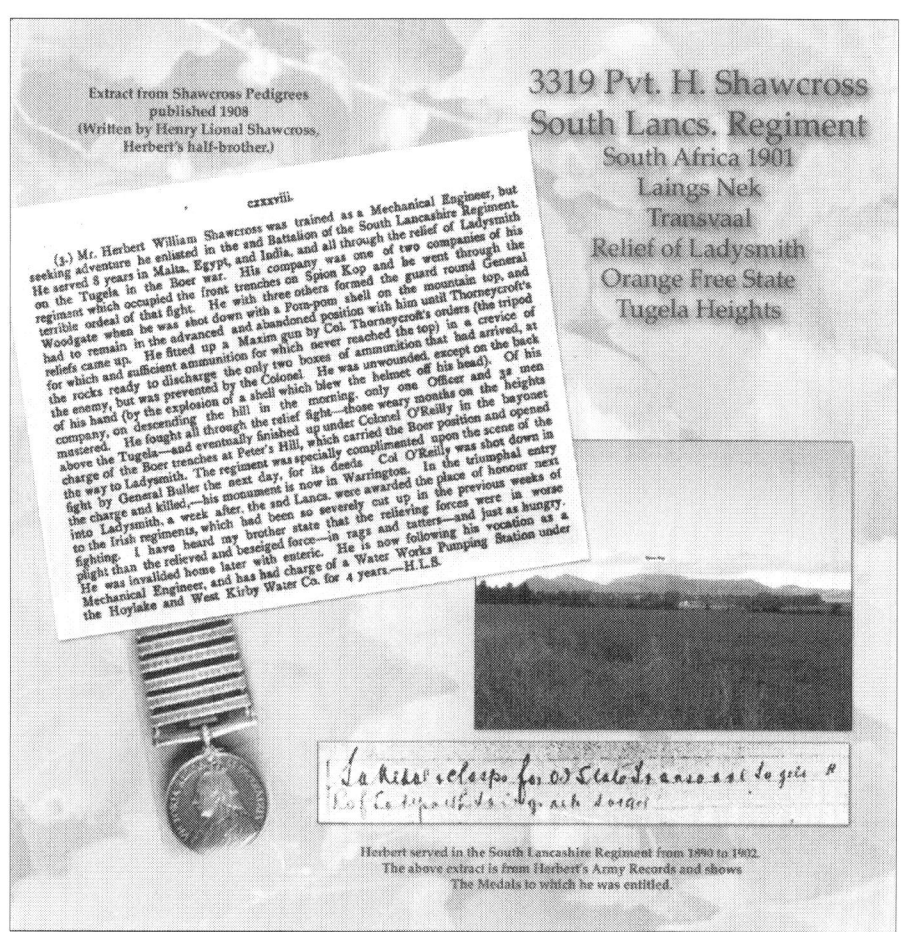

A TRADITION OF MILITARY AND PUBLIC SERVICE - My paternal grandfather, Herbert William Shawcross served with distinction in the South Lancashire Regiment from 1890 to 1902. He returned to active duty service during the First World War in the British Army serving with the Ordnance Corps from 1915 to 1917. *(Thaxton collection)*

A portrait of my grandfather, Armourer Sergeamt Herbert William Shawcross, and medals received while assigned to the Army Ordnance Corps during his World War I service in the British Army. *(Thaxton collection)*

My father, John Shawcross served in the Royal Engineers during World War I. He served in Egypt, Gallipoli and France. *(Thaxton collection)*

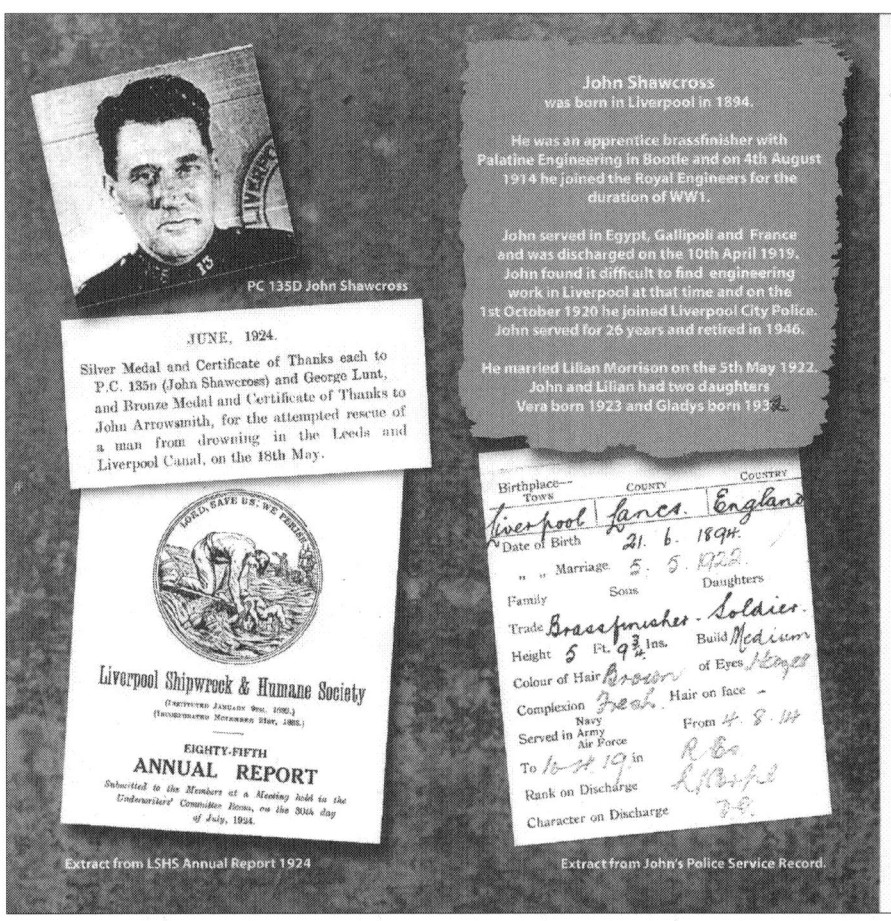

My father, John Shawcross was born in Liverpool in 1894. He was an apprentice brashfinisher with Palatine Engineering in Bootle and on August 4, 1914 joined the Royal Engineers for the duration of World War I.

In October 1920 he joined the Liverpool City Police and served for 26 years before he retired in 1946. He and fellow officer George Lunt earned the Bronze Medal and a Certificate of Thanks for the attempted rescue of a man drowning in the Leeds and Liverpool Canal. *(Thaxton collection)*

A favorite portrait of my mother Lillian Morrison in traditional Scottish highland wear. She looks confident in a tartan kilted skirt with tassels, boots and a long, draping shawl as she dressed for a Scottish festival in the 1920s.
(Thaxton collection)

Aunty Gladys, elegant in pearls and a wide brimmed hat, and her maid companion on a promenade stroll. She had an exceptional sense of fashion for the times. *(Thaxton collection)*

A motor carriage befitting a princess. A photo of Aunty Gladys shared by my niece, Pauline taken sometime in France in the 1920s. *(Thaxton collection)*

I'm named for my Aunty Gladys, a colorful woman, (right), a world traveler, who married well, and traveled extensively through the world as a young adult. I inherited my love for travel and adventure from her. Her first husband was a wealthy Egyptian banker. *(Thaxton collection)*

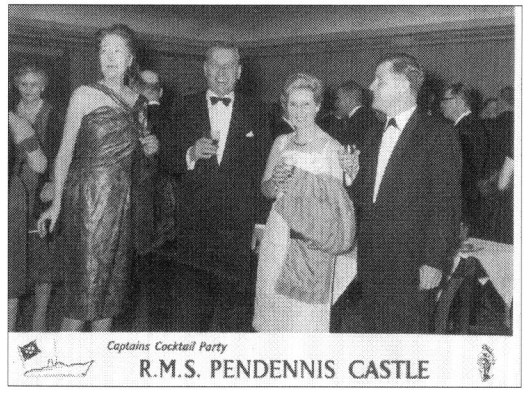

Aunty Gladys, left, attending the Captains Cocktail Party onboard RMS Pendennis Castle while enjoying one of her many cruises. The RMS Pendennis Castle was a Royal Mail Ship, passenger and cargo liner operated by the Union-Castle Line and served from 1959 to 1976 on a regular route between the United Kingdom and South Africa. *(Thaxton collection)*

Aunty Gladys, left, with her maid/companion in the south of France – 1920s. Second photo, her second husband, Sir William Garthwaite, Baronet. *(Thaxton collection)*

Going back to France from the Bahamas – 1946-47. Lord Bollingham, 21; my cousin Michael's tutor; Aunty Gladys; her husband, Lord Garthwaite; my cousin Michael, age 10. *(Thaxton collection)*

My mother's four brothers in 1942. Left to right: Uncle Alek, Uncle Charlie, Uncle Fred and her youngest brother Uncle Leslie. Charlie and Fred were veterans of the First World War. *(Thaxton collection)*

A cold, crisp day in Liverpool with my mother, Lillian, right.
(Thaxton collection)

My Dad's parents out for a stroll in New Brighton in the 1930s. On the back of the photo is a handwritten wartime recipe for peanut butter fudge.
(Thaxton family photo)

Holly and Tinsel

When I was a little girl and lived in England, my mother would scrape together a few shillings and take me for a few days holiday to Blackpool. I loved it – everything, the noise, the smells, the laughter, the colour, the sands and the rides on a tram along the promenade. But that was in summer.

Having spent most of my adult life in America, I've thought often about those days and when my daughter and I planned a November holiday in England, I happened to see in a British newspaper an advertisement for accommodations in Lancashire for the Blackpool Holly and Tinsel festive weekend. The price included all meals, five course dinners, four course lunches and entertainment every night. Two nights, just 60 pounds sterling.

I fantasized Oh! To experience again an old fashioned Christmas and to see the places of my childhood. Good times and the price was so reasonable. Plus the hotel is on the front. We used to wander the back streets, Mum and I, looking for a deal on a bed and breakfast. Seven and sixpence or ten shillings a night, tops. That was in the late 1940s.

Now it was 1998. My daughter wasn't too pleased about going, but to please me, she went along on the weekend trip. We arrived at our hotel about 1 p.m. Friday and were told we would have to wait for our room until 3 p.m. We left our suitcases and took a short walk as it was very cold. When we finally got in our room, it was colder inside than outside. It seemed the landlord didn't believe in turning on the heat until all the guests had arrived. We kept our coats on. My daughter tried out her bed. It had a big hole in the mattress, so we asked if it could be changed. I could tell by his expression the landlord didn't want to do it, but we insisted. At 6 p.m. we sat down to the evening meal. There were about twenty other guests. We all waited expectantly for the sumptuous meal, and suddenly a very elderly man and woman hobbled out of a back room, carrying large trays and moving surprisingly well. The first course was a half cup of canned fruit cocktail, followed by watery chicken soup, followed by canned tuna on toast. The two amazing waiters seemed to be moving faster after every course and whipped our dishes away as we put the last spoonful in our mouths. I was fascinated watching them as they avoided crashing into each other. In the narrow room they each moved like dancers. The main course was roast chicken, peas and chips, ending with apple pie and custard. Not too awful. We were all encouraged to adjourn to the bar and entertainment room. Later we were told, in the hall there would be coffee and tea and a big bowl of potato chips, which was soon empty, for some reason we were all still hungry. There was a middle-aged man who conducted a bingo game. After that he told jokes and sang songs, reminding the guests that the bar was open.

  The next day was a repeat of the first day. It was too cold to go for a walk on the beach. So we spent the day at the famous Blackpool Tower. I told my daughter it was just like the Eiffel Tower in Paris, to cheer her up. Feeling suicidal, she did the leap of faith.

We took the elevator to the top of the tower, where there is a glass floor through which you can see right down to the bottom 300 or some feet below. She was given a certificate to prove she had done it, leaping over the glass floor. We watched the dancers in the ballroom and went to see the crown jewels, replicas that is. As we left the tower, a Salvation Army band was playing Christmas carols. Things hadn't changed that much, I thought nostalgically. We took the street car back along the promenade. On the last night, the same entertainer, doing his best, and knowing by then we were from San Francisco, started to sing *"I Left My Heart in San Francisco."*

My daughter's large blue eyes filled up with tears. He seemed surprised. I think the cold was too much for my daughter, or maybe it was that mattress. Sunday morning, when all the other guests had left, off went the central heating once again. We waited for my nephew to arrive to pick us up.

The Yanks Have Arrived

My older sister Vera, left and I on a trip to Yorkshire before the war broke out. My Dad had to put our family car in storage. There was no petrol available to the public for driving for the duration of the war.

(Thaxton family photo)

Early in the Blitz when the bombing was intense. Though a few of them were duds which didn't explode. Mum and I went to see an exhibition of some of the duds across the river Mersey to Birkenhead.

The bombs were all lined up in order of size: incendiary bombs first, then 500-pound explosives to the biggest one seen at that time, a 1,000-pound explosive. We also went to see a bomb crater. Not far from our street that a 1,000-pound bomb had made and was also a dud. The bomb squad had disarmed it.

Crossing the Mersey, I remember seeing floating mines with spikes sticking out which our ferry boat had to weave in and out of to avoid hitting them. Sometimes shells from the anti-aircraft guns would fall short and land on houses. Some of them didn't explode.

Then there was one shell that landed in our neighbor's front garden. The Smiths had to be moved to another house down the street. I sorely missed them and the way they would tell stories and make us all laugh. One night I returned to my bed after an air raid and found that my bedroom window had been blown out by the blast. We were lucky that the broken window was the only damage our house received.

By 1943, there were a lot of American soldiers stationed in and around Liverpool. Liverpool was still the main English port receiving troops and supplies.

In time these GIs would get ready for the Normandy invasion. My friend Nancy and I hatched a plot. Her parents had invited a young American soldier to dinner, but they had no older daughters, so crafty Nancy and I said we would introduce him to my sister Vera, who was 20. He was a friendly, fresh-faced 20-year-old soldier far from home and we were brain-soaked by Hollywood romantic movies, and loved anything American.

On his second visit, Dad was eating dinner and had put his dentures under the tablecloth and the soldier put his hand on the lump when my Dad invited him to sit down and have a glass of beer. My sister was very embarrassed. In the early Spring Mum had saved up a few shillings and said come on Gladys, let's go for a few days to Blackpool. The town was full of GIs soon to join the D-Day invasion and hoping to have a good time in the resort town.

In May 1945, the war in Europe finally ended. Soon residents of our street organized a celebration party as did all the streets in Britain. Tables and chairs were carried out of the houses and placed down the middle of the street.

Flags were pinned up everywhere. All of the mothers baked and made sandwiches, all from their meager rations. There were things like jelly desserts, custards, a cake, scones with raisins, all stuff they had saved for a special occasion, and this certainly was a special occasion for all time. There was tea with milk to drink, beer for the men and lemonade for all us kids. After the feast, men wheeled out a piano from a house, and we sang and danced until it got dark. The popular song "Knees Up Mother Brown" was popular with us kids. The war in Europe was over.

In August 1945 the war in the Far East ended and we had another street party. Just before Christmas in 1946, I celebrated my 14th birthday and left school. This was the last year that children had to leave school at the age of 14, that is if they hadn't passed the scholarship examination to go on to a high school.

I wasn't given the opportunity because of the war to take the exam.

So, at the tender age of 14, I soon began my hunt for my first job in the adult world.

Jobs Carousel

On lunch break, right, in Liverpool - 1950s

(Thaxton family photo)

I was just 14 years old and I had left school the previous month, December 1946. I was a kid just about to start my first job which was in Littlewood's Football Pools main office in Liverpool where my older sister Vera worked.

All my clothes were shabby, so Vera bought me two outfits consisting of a skirt with a bib top and a blouse. One outfit was grey and the other was dark green. I still wore flat shoes and ankle socks. My hair which my Mum had always cut into a straight bob bothered me, so I tried putting curlers in which was a waste of time as my hair immediately resumed its natural straight condition when the curlers were removed. Later I became adept at getting permanent waves.

My job was mail clerk, sorting and splitting open the envelopes and then distributing them to my section. I managed not to destroy any of the money order enclosed with a coupon.

Everyone was dreaming of winning a better future with their few shillings or less money order. Wages were low then. My first job paid seven shillings and six pence a week for 40 hours. People did win, but mostly small amounts. Not like today's lotteries where probably one in a million wins a large amount and the rest win nothing. At least Dad won a 100-pound prize in the 1950s with which he bought our first television set.

Littlewood's and Vernon's pools, both in Liverpool were huge. A cavernous room with hundreds of desks where women sat one to a desk. Monday was the big day when the results from the previous Saturday's soccer matches (which were played all over the United Kingdom) came in and the results were then printed on cards which were passed out to the clerks. Things called permutations were popular. I never did understand them. They cost more but you could win more, so I was told. On Monday, all the doors were locked and nobody was allowed in or out of the building in case someone smuggled in a winning coupon. I stayed in that job for about nine months.

I then went to work in a wholesale/retail dress shop downtown. They specialized in women's hire purchase clothes. This was before credit cards. You bought a winter coat, and then made an installment payment until the coat was paid off. Most customers came into the store and paid cash every month. There were several of us young girls, we were called apprentices. One day we were sent up to the attic to straighten things up. We started doing handstands up against the wall. When I did it the others started laughing.

"What's wrong, I asked."

"You are wearing gym knickers and they are full of holes."

They were the only pair I owned. My other humiliation was when the boss told me that one of the salesmen had said that I needed to wear a bra. My Mum never prepared me for anything but she always bought fancy cakes and chocolate biscuits which were always on the table for company.

Another job I had in the late 1940s was at Sturla's Department store as an office clerk. An older clerk who had been there for many years told us younger girls that she had a house at the huge Anfield Cemetery nearby and her husband was the chief grave digger. We all looked shocked and said "aren't you scared" and "I wouldn't want to live in a cemetery" or some such remarks.

Mrs. D., I've since forgotten her name, told us the only time she was scared was when "Jack and I walked out in the morning after a German air raid and there were skeletal remains hanging in the trees. The blast from an aerial bomb that had fallen nearby."

A witty one in the group said to her, "tell your hubby to dig the graves deeper."

Delusions of grandeur

You could say that my mother Lillian suffered, from among other things, with delusions of grandeur. When she married my Dad, she found out that he came with a very old family pedigree going back to the Danes and with royal connections. She was always telling me that we were a cut above the rest, but I couldn't see it, not in my ragged underwear.

I asked my Dad once, if the story of our family history was true.

He told me that yes it was, but "there was no money in it."

"It's all gone."

We had a show and tell event one day at school and I took the very large book of our family pedigree and showed it to the class proudly telling them of all the royal connections down through the centuries. One in particular, the Black Prince, son of King Edward I in the 14th Century who fought in the 100 Years War with France.

After school that day a boy teased me saying "your uncle, the 'Black Prince,' is the coal man.

I never boasted again about pedigrees. There is nothing anywhere like snarky Liverpool humour.

Standing outside our family home on 78 Arkles Lane, Liverpool
(Thaxton family photo)

Enjoying a little post-work pub time as a young adult in Liverpool.
(Thaxton family photo)

Myself, second from the right, and just a few of the girls I worked with at Tavener Rutledge candy makers in the early 1950s. (Thaxton family photo)

The Austerity Years

I held a total of 11 jobs before I left England. One was at the Owen Owen Department Store where I met Marie, who was two years younger than me. We have been friends for over 60 years.

The office manager was a Miss Owen from Wales, a tiny woman, gray haired with an intimidating disposition. Even the male clerks were afraid of her. When she strode purposely into her office which was glass enclosed so she could watch us all in the main room, her eyes barely cleared the lower wooden part of the partition.

At 9:30 a.m. prompt, Mr. Shepherd, the company chief accountant would glide into the office. An elderly man, tall and very thin, and always wearing a homburg hat and an overcoat. He always carried a briefcase. He never spoke, but he would give us a slight nod of his head, and then go into his office and close the door. He would reappear at 4:30 p.m. and go home, we presumed. He did seem to be a friendly old soul.

Marie and I met when I worked in the export section preparing export documents for mostly household goods which were shipped to the British African colonies. In those days, 1949, I recall, the British Board of Trade had very strict requirements on goods and money leaving the country. The treasury would only let travelers to Europe spend 10 pounds.

The UK government was trying desperately to balance the books and pay off our debts from the war. These were known as the "austerity years". For five years after the Second World War ended there was still very little to buy in the shops and not much variety in food supplies. More union strikes were also occurring. One of our neighbors started hanging out a red sheet from her bedroom window.

The sad thing was because of the union strikes companies started moving their factories down south. Liverpool, a huge seaport and industrial city for over 100 years became a shell of its former self. Liverpool was a proud city where so many goods were made - from biscuits, toys, clocks, cars to ships, we did it all as well as transporting millions to the New World.

Now the city was filled with empty warehouses and factories, bombed out streets littered with debris. The Liverpool city council was unable to make up their minds for years on a plan for a new inner city center that had taken the brunt of the blitz damage. The one exception – was the downtown shopping district. That area was quickly repaired plus Queen Victoria was put back on her plinth and soon it was business as usual. Liverpool had always been a popular shopping venue. People came into shop from as far away as North Wales and it was not unusual to hear Welsh spoken.

My mother was fed up with austerity and with the coal shortages joined the Housewives League. On one occasion, all the women went up to London on a train to a big protest meeting in Central Hall Westminster. The red sheet was hanging out of our neighbor's window again!

Marie Finnegan and I on a work outing in Blackpool - 1950. We have remained best friends for many years after I emigrated to the United States. *(Thaxton family photo)*

Let's Go Traveling!

In the summer of 1949 when I was two months shy of turning 17, I and two girlfriends from work signed up for a working holiday on a farm harvesting potatoes in Lincolnshire. I would have liked to have gone further south but the government only gave us enough money for the train ticket to Lincoln city and we were so broke all the time and earning a few shillings a week. In Lincoln, we were driven in trucks to a nearby obsolete airbase from World War II which still had its Quonset huts which were our accommodations for one week. The next morning, early, at 6 a.m. we were awakened by a very loudspeaker and told to report to the dining room for breakfast. Then it was a short drive to a nearby farm. There were about six of us, three of us from Liverpool, and three from London. We watched as a tractor cut furrows up and down the field which revealed the potatoes. We were handed baskets and told to fill them!

It was stoop labor, but we did it, at least Brenda and I. Irene, our other friend, she wouldn't stoop but stood with one hand on her hip and elegantly reached down with her other hand to pick up a potato. The farm foreman didn't look too pleased. At noon we broke for lunch. We had all been provided with a packed lunch which we sat and ate, seated under a hedge and out of the hot sun. The midsummer weather was beautiful, in fact so hot, that the following evening in the multi-purpose room where a dance was being held for all the farm workers. I passed out from heat stroke. I probably should have worn a sun hat out in the field. We had worked for about four days when one of the male London workers decided the conditions were so bad that he called us out on strike. That was the end of our farming endeavor.

By 1950 more fashionable clothes for women became available. Marie and I had a great time buying pretty and reasonably priced dresses at C&A Modes downtown which we often wore to dances. We would sashay into the new Locarno Ballroom feeling like queens in our pretty new dresses. Nylons, high-heeled shoes, short curled hair and makeup trying to look aloof. I had a young man ask me to dance once and saying I would have asked you sooner but you looked so angry. I told him I was trying to look aloof.

The fashion style in the early 1950s was called the "New Look" and skirts and coat hems were down to mid-calf, with nipped waists. Pretty prints and lace were used, all very feminine. We stalked around even on cobblestones in those high-heels and pointed toe shoes, but years later lived to regret it when we developed bent toes and bunions.

At the age of 17 I already had the travel bug and never having been further than Blackpool, I decided to see London, only 130 miles away, but to us poor Liverpudlians, a land of mystery and excitement. A 12-hour bus ride through the night got me to Victoria Station. I walked for hours, seeing Buckingham Palace, Westminster Abbey, the park, Chelsea, all in my big, heavy long winter coat and high heels. At the end of the day I had blisters on my heels and chaffed upper thighs as I limped back to the bus station to catch the evening bus home. But I'd say it was worth it. I'd finally seen the "Big Kahuna."

I even got a kiss. I walked down a street in Chelsea gazing up at the buildings, when a young man who had been sitting on a doorstep with two other young men. He suddenly jumped up, probably on a dare, rushed over to me and kissed me quickly on the cheek. I blushed and just kept on walking.

My appetite for travel had been whetted and when I saw an advertisement in the local paper for a one-week trip to Ostend, Belgium for four pounds all inclusive (again it was 1953). I was off again on the overnight bus to London where I met up with my fellow travelers. Next, the train to Dover and the ferry boat to Ostend, and the hotel – yes a real hotel - (maybe a two-star?) Hard to believe that things were that inexpensive in those days. A small group of us took a trip to Holland for the day and later in the week we hired a 1930s Daimler touring car to drive us into Flanders in Northern France to see the World War I battlefields on our way to Bruges.

Bruges was a beautiful medieval city with canals running through it. We chatted with women sitting in doorways who were making the famous Bruges lace. We drove as far into Northern France as Lille, a very large industrial city.

We also went through villages where recent shell damage could still be seen. We saw Ypres and the area around the city where five major battles in world war one were fought. Chlorine gas was used in the second battle by the Germans and this was where my father was gassed.

We drove through a town where the Menin Gate Memorial to the Missing traversed the main road. The memorial is one of four British and Commonwealth memorials to the missing in the battlefield area of the Ypres Salient in Belgian Flanders. The memorial bears the names of 54,389 officers and men from United Kingdom and Commonwealth Forces (except New Zealand and Newfoundland) who fell in the Ypres Salient before 16th August 1917 and who have no known grave.

In the five major battles in Ypres, there were a total of 1.2 million casualties. The horrors of World War I and the suffering for five long years by the soldiers in the trenches would be impossible to describe if you hadn't been there.

My father never even talked about his experiences – his only reference was singing some of the old songs *"Pack Up Your Troubles in Your Old Kit Bag and Smile, Smile, Smile"* and *"Mademoiselle from Armentiers."*

He once claimed he had a girlfriend living there.

How could you smile with such insanity going on? The lace makers of Bruges seemed like they were from another planet. One evening back in Ostend we all went to a bar for a couple of drinks.

Needing the loo, I was pointed down some stairs to the basement. There were no doors on the cubicles and two were occupied by a man and a woman having a very animated conversation through the thin dividing wall. Viva Belgium!

Sixty plus years later, America is up in arms about the mixed sharing of toilets and not too long ago people were fined for using the opposite sexes bathroom.

The next year I found another good travel deal for a five-day bed and breakfast trip to Paris for just five pounds. It included two tours of the city and one to Versailles. I stayed at a small hotel on a side street in the Monmartre district which wasn't too bad. The line of prostitutes lining the opposite side of the street didn't bother me. But at 20 years old, I wasn't really sure why they were there, leaning up against the wall. I probably did make an educated guess. Parents in my day never told you about anything. It was all very hush-hush. So we grew up pretty darn ignorant. But I think we all have a vague memory from ages before. One evening when I was about 17, I remember walking through Williamson Square by the Playhouse Theater in downtown Liverpool and seeing young men standing in doorways. I thought it strange that I'd never seen them in the daytime, but then I knew. England up until recent times prosecuted homosexuals and put them in jail.

The tour of Paris was fun. We saw Napoleon's tomb. We looked down from above at a solitary sarcophagus in the middle of an empty floor. A tour of all the great buildings followed.

We even got to ride to the top of the Eiffel Tower. Again, I needed to use the loo. I was directed to a round, tin-looking structure similar to a miniature maze. A woman was waiting with her hand outstretched. I handed her some money and she pointed to a round hole in the floor. I wondered later where did it all go. To a tank or to the green lawn far, far, below?

Versailles was beautiful. We walked all over the extensive pathways. The gardens were very different from our English gardens. No riotous colour, but neatly laid out squares. The only room we could see in the place was the Hall of Mirrors. Gilt glittered all around the mirrors and chandeliers. The signing of the Treaty of Versailles took place in 1919 in this same hall. The signers wished to declare they were for a future peaceful world.

The last trip I made to the continent before I left Britain was with two of my workmates, Hilda and Margie. It was another very inexpensive holiday. A week in Innsbruck, Austria.

Bed and breakfast in an Austrian woman's apartment. We had a large bedroom with three single beds. Very Goldilocks and the Three Bears style with hearts cut into the plain pine wood. We were served a continental-style breakfast. A crusty bread roll, some butter and cherry jam. I loved the cherry jam, but my mouth got a little sore from the unfamiliar crusty bread. It was the very same breakfast they served us on the train. We had traveled by bus to Victoria Station in London and then got the boat train to Dover and a ferry boat to Calais where we got on a train which came right into the docks. We had a sleeper compartment. I ended up with the upper bunk. Hilda and Margie had the two seats facing each other which made up as bunks.

We traveled through France as it got dark and in the morning, we passed through Switzerland and saw Lake Geneva. For our stay we still had very little money and existed mostly on ham and eggs for our evening meal. We didn't speak German and the only thing we recognized on the menu was ham and eggs.

In those days we were very provincial in our tastes. On the last day we tried goulash. On a few evenings we went to a tavern called the Golden Adler, a very old inn in the Maria-Therese Strasse. They served food and wine. The wine was served in a glass container which fitted into an ornate iron holder. When you wanted a refill you just pushed your glass up against the bottom of the wine carafe and your glass would be filled. We sat at a large table with others, all Austrians, who sometimes linked arms and sang songs. One evening a 40-ish looking man asked us where we were from. I replied Liverpool,

England. He replied that he served in the German Luftwaffe and that he bombed Liverpool.

Another day we decided to take a short train ride up near the border. We arrived at an Alpine Village near the Brenner Pass. A double named village in two languages, Italian and Austrian. We had a light meal in a nearby café and got to talking and flirting as young people do with several young, Italian Alpine ski troops who were stationed nearby.

We said we had to leave to catch the train back to Innsbruck, so they accompanied us to the station. When we got there, we discovered that the last train had left. We were very worried and someone suggested we try to get a ride with one of the truckers passing through. It worked and the truck who stopped was enormous, a juggernaut as it was called in Europe. We three girls climbed into the cab with the driver. All I can remember is the multiple, tight curves of the Brenner Pass and being thrown up against the driver, repeatedly apologizing to him. He seemed very good natured about it and delivered us safely back to Innsbruck.

Doctors and Dating

In 1947 my beloved sister Vera married George, the brother of her best friend Joan. He had not been home long from the service in the British Navy in the Far East. He'd served on a motor torpedo boat. A pretty dangerous wartime job.

The following year, 1948, their daughter Pauline, right, was born on July 4th. Vera and George lived with us after the wedding. Housing was impossible to find, so much had been destroyed. So it was really close quarters until my mother managed to exchange our three-bedroom house for a much larger older house about a mile away. This was all done through the Liverpool City Council whom we rented from.

In November 1953, my sister Vera gave birth at home to a son, whom she named Ian. It was a very difficult birth and my sister nearly lost her life due to a hemorrhage that wouldn't stop.

A new special medical unit, the flying "Code Blue" ambulance was dispatched and they saved her life. My sister was very afraid of doctors and hospitals and would not go to them. It seemed that as a small child she had been treated for a throat complaint in a hospital and whatever they did so traumatized her she would not go near there.

My mother never went to a doctor and I was raised much the same way. The first time I saw a doctor was when I was about 13 or 14 years old and had anemia. The doctor gave me a prescription for an iron tonic as the food we had during the war had very little iron in it.

During the first year of the Second World War we had a very severe winter with lots of snow and ice. We children built an ice igloo. I thought it was lovely and sat inside it for at least an hour. That evening, I came down with a fever and couldn't stop shaking. My parents put me on the sofa near to the living room fireplace and piled blankets on me to keep me warm. I became delirious and started to turn blue until the chill abated. It was probably hypothermia, but no one ever called the doctor and I survived. There were no antibiotics in those days. I saw my neighborhood friend next door, taken away in a fever ambulance wrapped in a red blanket. Scarlet fever and diphtheria were quite common then. This was all before the start of the National Health System. What a wonderful plan this has been for all of Great Britain.

Pauline, my sister Vera's little girl and Santa - 1950s

When Pauline was about 2 years old, her mommy, my sister Vera worked in a local laundry to help out with finances. Her beautiful slender hands were red raw from hand-washing diapers and the laundry job. My mother babysat Pauline when Vera was at work.

One day, after the war, a stranger knocked on the door asking for Vera. Mum told him that Vera was married. He was an ex-British Navy sailor whom Vera had dated during the war and was still very fond of her. He had once taken her to meet his parents who lived in Northern Lancashire. They lost touch with one another. She never knew what happened to him. Had he been taken prisoner? Who knew? Strange things happen in wartime.

In the 1950's, my friend Marie and I went to dances. We met many seafarers, as Liverpool was still a busy port. We also met enlisted servicemen as the draft was still on and young men at the age of 18 had to serve two years in national service.

We had lots of dates going to places like movies or dancing. Boys then were more respectful of girls and though there was a lot of kissing and cuddling, no meant no, and we never had any trouble. Marie had three dates on the same day at one time. My best was two dates on the same day.

Around this time, 1953, I recall, I was working for a candy manufacturer, again in the export office. I became friends with a girl in the office named Helen. We went out a few times together.

On one occasion we met these two young men who were sailors off a small Dutch freighter and they asked us if we had a girlfriend for their friend – so we invited Margie from the office on our next date.

He was a Canadian named Peter Dollar, who was quite good looking and dressed in a long, naval officer's greatcoat which we thought was rather strange, as he was the ship's cook. We all had a great time. We said goodbye to the boys.

It was a few years later that I got a letter from my Dad with a newspaper clipping from the London Times of an account of a Canadian from Montreal on trial at the Old Bailey for impersonating a British or Canadian naval officer and wearing medals he wasn't entitled to. Dad had remembered me telling him about these three guys whom Helen, Margie and I dated.

Peter Dollar, who was from a well-off Canadian family was sentenced to one year in jail. I had visited Margie about a year later. She told me she was still very much in love with Peter and still hoped to marry him. On one of his visits to Liverpool he brought her a gift from Holland, a clock set in the top of a Dutch clog. Over the years, I lost touch with Margie.

The "Sweet Singers" of Taverner-Rutledge. I'm the third from the right.
(Thaxton family photo)

While working at Taverner Rutledge, a candy manufacturer from 1953 to 1955, I joined a singing group called the "Sweet Singers." There were about 12 of us in the group, which was made up from two different candy companies. I loved to sing, just like my Mum. We mostly performed at rest homes for older residents. We even entered a talent contest for north west England which was held at the Tower Ballroom in New Brighton. My parents came to see the show. They told me that I looked like "death warmed over" as I hadn't put on enough stage makeup. We sang "Happy Wanderers" and did a kind of stiff-legged dance at the same time. One of the girls took too many steps backwards and put her foot through a drum that had been left there. Our choir director quit shortly after and I moved on to a new job.

I also worked for a short time for a steamship company in the famous Liver Building down by the pier head.

It's Time to Move On

Sometime after a dance or a date we would go to the Temple Bar downtown and live precariously. It was the only place in the '50s where you could get a drink or something to eat after 10 p.m. Pie and chips, generally, and we would order Copenhagen Lager beer with a topper of lime juice. Supposedly ladies didn't like the taste of beer? The Temple Bar was around the corner from The Cavern Club. I was still a member of the Merseyside Jazz Club as it was known then. The Beatles hadn't yet existed at that time. My memories of the "Cavern" was of a strong smell of cheese as you came down the stone steps into the cellar where the bands played. The cobblestone street and buildings were very old and were probably used at one time as warehouses.

One evening after work, walking down by the river to catch my bus home I witnessed something that has always stayed fresh and clear in my mind. The police were pulling and tugging at something. It was the body of a young man. It seemed that the river was unwilling to give him up. His black hair flowed across his face which was bloated and very white. My glance was less than a second before I quickly averted my eyes. It was my first look at death, but it wouldn't be my last.

Helen, my friend from the candy company, had been dating an American seaman named George from South Carolina. They decided to marry. It was a wonderful church wedding and I served as her Maid of Honour.

A year later, she gave birth to a baby girl JoAnn and about the time of her daughter's first birthday, she moved with her husband and family to Charleston, South Carolina. She knew about my wanderlust and asked why didn't I emigrate to the United States and come to Charleston.

At that time, I had no desire to emigrate anywhere.

At 17, I had applied to emigrate to Australia under their scheme of a free passage if you agreed to stay two years, otherwise you would have to pay them back for what they spent on your passage. That didn't worry me.

It was the fact that because of my young age they stipulated I could only come if I agreed to be a student nurse for two years and live in nurse's quarters. I had wanted to go to Kalgoolie, a gold mining town. That put the cabash on it. I hated the sight of blood. Thousands of people and families emigrated out of Britain in the 1950s.

The class system was still active in post-war Britain. I was afraid to speak up in class and later talk to bosses I worked for, because of our Liverpool or Northern accents, Londoners made fun of us and thought we were uncouth, even stupid. That soon changed when The Beatles came along. Londoners sounded stupid trying to talk like The Beatles.

I was very shy as a child, even to the point of stuttering. Eventually, I would overcome it. My parents were always fighting about money. Mother was a world-class nagger and her nagging went on and on, until people would snap.

Once, I simply had enough.

I yelled out. "Stop it!" "Why don't you stab each other to death?"

I don't know where that came from. At least it was directed at both of them. They both stopped and looked over at the little shadow creature sitting in the corner. Generally, when my Mum was in one of her tirades, I would run upstairs and lock myself in the bathroom.

The second time I spoke up in public was on a crowded tram coming home from work. The conductor was hurling insults at an elderly man who was blocking his way into the inside of the tram.

I yelled out. "Don't talk to people like that. Have some respect for them!"

Dad had given me two books when I was in school. One was Jane Austen's "Pride and Prejudice" and the other was Cervantes "Don Quixote." Each of these two books taught me something of the nature of the world. Don Quixote and his tilting at windmills, a hundred years too late – trying to make the world a better place had rubbed off on me.

Liverpool was a rough, tough city at times, especially on a Saturday night. The pubs closed at 10 p.m. That went on for years. Men would drink too fast and too much. You would see fights break out as soon as they tottered outside into the street at closing time. I once saw two men on a bus trying to punch each other, while holding the end of one another's neckties. Men, all dressed in suits and ties in those days even while digging ditches. Though the suits were generally wrinkled and stained, no one could afford dry cleaning, that was for the toffs. The age of wrinkle-free, washable polyester had not yet arrived.

In 1951, the British government held a festival on the south bank of the Thames river to celebrate the end of austerity measures after World War II. Mum and I took the bus up to London and had a nice day out looking at all the attractions at the festival.

In 1952, King George VI died. He was my King, a good man, who cared about his people. In 1938, as a five-year-old, I had witnessed his coronation procession to Westminster Abbey. My Dad lifted me up onto a bank window ledge so I could see. Later in 1952 I went to London again with my Mum to witness the coronation of Queen Elizabeth II.

We were standing by a small movie theatre as the procession passed by and we were able to get into the theater to see a closed-circuit television broadcast of the ceremony then going on inside the Abbey.

How lucky could we get! Our lucky streak ran out later though. Mum spotted what she thought was a café or tearoom and started to push open the swinging door. A uniformed man pounced out and stopped her.

"Madame, this is a gentlemen's club. No women are allowed inside." We were I believe on Pall Mall. My mother said "I thought we could get a cup of tea."

It was nearly impossible to get a room. Hundreds of thousands had come to London from all over the world to see the coronation. We finally found one in South London, in Brixton. We had to sleep in a room with a piano and every time I turned over, my feet hit the keys of the piano, but then we were lucky to find a room in the first place, when they were in such short supply on this occasion.

Autographs by the stage door

My parents loved going to the theatre. At that time in the 1950s, there were three variety theaters and two playhouses in downtown Liverpool. We always went to the pantomime at Christmastime. Dad would buy us a big box of chocolates to take with us.

I think Dad would have loved to have been an actor. When he was a boy, he got a walk-on job at the old Hippodrome Theatre which put on operas and needed lots of people on stage. I also loved the theatre, and in my teens went every week. The Empire Theatre was Liverpool's largest variety music hall. I saw all of the big entertainers there. Quite a lot of Americans, such as Danny Kaye and Donald O'Connor, singing and dancing. Sometimes all of the seats were sold out and I'd buy a standing room only ticket.

At the Royal Court Theatre, I saw Sir. Lawrence Olivier and his wife Vivian Leigh in *Anthony and Cleopatra* by William Shakespeare followed in the next week by *Caesar and Cleopatra*.

I waited at the stage door after the performance to get their autographs. I did that frequently and had quite an autograph collection. One special autograph was from Noel Coward. He had a musical comedy at the Royal Court Theatre called *Ace of Spades* in the '50s which never became as popular as his earlier plays. When he walked out of the stage door, he turned to a young woman behind him and said, "put that in your Bible, dearie."

Another autograph I remember at the Royal Court was that of American actor Sam Wanamaker in *Winter Journey* by Clifford Odett. Wanamaker produced and directed the play. Again, I got his autograph and several others from actors in the play including Sir Michael Redgrave, American Arthur Hill and George Withers. Sam Wanamaker later sent me a very nice letter and an autograph. This was in 1952. Stall seats ran from 7 shillings up to 8 shillings and 6 pence.

Mr. Wanamaker worked and dreamed for many years, at least 30, to get a replica built of Shakespeare's Globe Theatre on London's South Bank. His dream came true sadly after he had passed away.

My daughter Susan and I were able to visit the famed Globe Theatre in the 1990s shortly after it was finished. We sat on the front bench while snow fell all around us.

An amazing event was at the Empire Theatre in 1951. Bernard Delfant and Paul Gregory presented Don Juan in Hell by George Bernard Shaw. It was called the first drama quartette and the four actors were Charles Boyer as Don Juan; (who would have guessed) and Charles Laughton as the Devil. A good choice, I must say. Sir Cedric Hardwicke (the father) and Agnes Moorhead (Donna Ana) who was wooed by Don Juan. All great movie actors. I believe it was done as a reading with the actors seated. Stall seating started at 7/6 pence and went up to 21 shillings.

I mentioned my Dad's love of the theatre. When he retired from the Liverpool police force after 26 years because of ill health, he still tried to keep working. One Christmas he took a job at Lewis's Department Store as Father Christmas. Lewis's was the biggest store in Liverpool, and they needed two Santas. The other was drunk all the time and he was fired. One day a manager came up to my Dad and told him they all thought he was the best Santa they'd ever had and asked if he would be willing to go to their flagship store on Oxford Street and take over as "chief Santa." My Dad refused. It would have been too much for him. He was wonderful with children and wrote me a fairy story when I was in school. I was about 7 or 8 years old and had homework to write a story and I couldn't think of what to write. The teacher's comments the next day read: "A very good story, but not your own work."

I still love the theatre and go as often as I can, but Broadway musicals cost $100 dollars for a stall seat now and are not always that good. The 7/6 days were better. But we do have a lot of small theatre groups now in the San Francisco area. My husband Bill acted in our local theatre in the 1970s.

Before the advent of our first television, Dad and I would listen to the boxing matches on the radio. Dad had boxed in the British Army and in the Liverpool Police Athletic Club.

After the broadcast was over, he'd stand up and demonstrate to me what they did wrong. I learned quite a lot about boxing from him! Dad was also a good swimmer. He had been awarded a life-saving medal for diving into the Leeds-Liverpool shipping canal to save a drowning man. He dove into the filthy, murky waters several times as he searched for him, but was unable to find the man in time.

The Great Smog

In the winter of 1952, the Great Smog hit. The worst of it was in London. Thousands of people died. The culprit was coal. It was used to warm most homes and in the factories. The smoke was so thick that little daylight shone through. I saw a bus conductor walk in front of the bus I was on with a lantern to guide the driver. This was at 8 a.m. and I was on my way to work!

After this catastrophe, strict laws were passed about burning coal.

We now have a President who wants to bring back coal mining. Go figure.

My sister Vera, my father and I in a photo taken on June 26th, 1955 the day before Vera died unexpectedly. *(Thaxton family photo)*

Death, your sting is still with me

In late 1954, my sister Vera and her husband George managed to buy a small house nearby. It cost just 50 pounds. Hard to believe now.

George hadn't been getting along with my parents. My father thought George could do better for my sister. George insisted on holding on to the job he had before the war, that of a junior clerk. The owners had told George that when they retired George would get the business.

And yes, he sure did.

Years later they closed the business down and poor George got nothing for his effort. The owners claimed the export business wasn't there anymore in Liverpool. It was a sad lesson not to rely on promises. You had to get that promise in writing.

One beautiful sunny, Sunday morning in June my sister came over to our house to invite us to go with her and George and their children to the beach at Freshfield, a small village outside of the resort town of Southport. The beach had glorious white sands and dunes that we children loved to slide down. My mother stayed home. We took the electric train from downtown about a 30 or 40-minute train ride and then walked through a pine tree-lined pathway to the beach.

It was such a beautiful day that we even had time to have our picture taken by a local beach photographer. (Dad, Vera and me.) We got back from the beach in the early evening and Vera asked me to go for a drink with her at the local pub, something we had never done before while George watched the children. We had one drink and then said good night. See you soon.

It was never to happen. I came home from work Monday evening and walked into the kitchen where my Mum stood.

"I've got some bad news for you. Vera is dead."

"No, no, it's not true," I protested. My loving sister, who had never spoken a mean word about anyone couldn't be dead. She was the bright light of this mixed-up family. She loved to dance, and had even taught me ballroom dancing. She loved to laugh. Now she was dead at just 32 years old. She had died from a malignant goiter on her thyroid gland. Her six-year-old daughter Pauline came home at lunchtime from school and found her Mommy slumped down in a chair by the fireplace, her baby brother Ian, just 10 months old, playing on the rug. There was no telephone in the house so Pauline picked up

Ian and wrapped him and herself in a long woolen scarf and walked several blocks to the doctor's office. She would be seven years old just one week later.

What courage and resourcefulness for a child so young!

She has stayed that way all her life.

If only Vera had gone to a doctor. George took the children and moved in with his parents. One year later he remarried, a woman who also worked as a clerk at his office and moved into a district about 20 miles away.

I couldn't accept that my sister was gone. I would see her in my mind all the time. A few days after her death I woke up in bed and felt something pull my arm upward. I knew it was Vera's spirit. She didn't want to leave. I think the old adage is true. "Only the good die young" and Very was a very sweet and good person.

Just a few years later I was on holiday with two girlfriends in Austria and leaving the bed and breakfast we were staying at, preparing that evening to go to dinner. My friends were standing at the bottom of the stairs looking up at me, telling me to get a move on. They swore they saw someone or something behind me. I wondered if it was Vera.

While George lived in his parents' house, he refused to let my parents see his children. It really upset them, especially, my father. He found out what school Pauline attended and went to the schoolyard during playtime and looked through the fence to catch a glimpse of Pauline.

Vera had been the apple of my Dad's eye. She was a beautiful person inside and out. I was the wild one. I think it came from the Irish side of the family, especially the woman I'm named after – Aunty Gladys. She was as poor as poor could be, but she ended up hooking a millionaire for her first husband and a rich Lord for her second. In between her two husbands, she dated the ex-King of Greece, Prince Philip's father when he lived in the south of France. Mum and I continued to see the children for a short time before George remarried. Life went on, but I didn't.

Workmates from Ellerman Lines, the last job I held before I left Liverpool. Walking by the Queen Victoria statue downtown.

(Thaxton family photo)

My good friend Helen Grimes before she left for the United States in the early 1950s. Once situated in the United States, she and her husband sponsored me to travel to America.

(Thaxton family photo)

S.S. Manchester Progress

Time to Say Goodbye to Liverpool

I didn't care much about anything. All I knew was that I didn't want to settle down for the rest of my life in Liverpool.

My friend Helen wrote and said she and her husband would be happy to sponsor me should I decide to emigrate to America. I decided to emigrate and went to the American consulate in Liverpool and got the necessary paperwork.

I first had to save my passage money. At that time I only earned 6 pounds a week. I had to look for a second job. The ship's passage would cost 70 pounds. I tried working as an usherette at a downtown cinema. I hated it.

Next, I got a job in the evening at a local pub as a bar maid at the Cabbage Hall Hotel. It was a fairly new building with a big carpark in the front. I made about 4 pounds a week. I liked the job and the clientele. Percy was the manager and had been a pub manager for years. His feet were so bad from constant standing that he walked like a ballet dancer between the many rooms. I worked in the saloon that had the biggest bar.

After several months, Percy allowed me to pull pints, which is quite an art, to get the foam at just the right depth on top of the pint of beer. British men are quite fussy about this. When I wasn't behind the bar, I waited on tables and cleared the empties.

Two old dears were there every evening at the same table, nursing a half-pint of Brown ale all night. Just before 10 o'clock closing time, they would stop me and ask for "two packets of potato crisps, dear."

It took me nearly a year to save enough for my passage and 25 pounds extra to land with. I had to have a medical and a chest x-ray, which I carried over with me, and to this day I still have. I also needed fingerprints taken at the local police station which were required and a smallpox vaccination shot. The vaccination was my first ever.

My British passport, visa and letter of sponsorship needed to all be in order. These were the dark days in the United States of McCarthyism and fear of Communist influence.

I purchased my ticket for the *S.S. Manchester Progress* which was sailing from Manchester on December 6, 1957. In August, I asked my parents if they would go with me and my friend for a few days to Brighton in Sussex. The weather in Brighton was windy and a little cold, but the skies were bright and blue. We all enjoyed seeing the sights and Dad even managed to go to the Brighton races one afternoon, which he loved.

I still felt in a kind of dream. That I was driven to do what I was going to do. I found an old suitcase that had belonged to my grandfather. It still had wooden bands around it and bought a cheap case. A friend painted my initials on the top. The days were going by so fast. My parents knew what I was planning to do, but they didn't discuss it. Soon it was my last week of work and on the final day I met Marie in town and we had a last meal together. We said our goodbyes tearfully. We promised to keep in touch with one another which we always have – even after so many years. I said goodbye to the office staff where I worked and even the taciturn manager wished me well.

My two workmates, Grace and Sheila gave me a very pretty nightgown as a Bon Voyage gift and a card signed by everyone in the office. A lot of people thought I was crazy, doing this on my own.

In 1970, Grace and her cousin Nan emigrated to Canada. I thing every English family had someone or knew of someone who had emigrated to "the Colonies: - Canada, Australia or New Zealand. America was predominantly for the post-war GI brides in the late 1940s and the 1950s. Most of us wanted more and better opportunities for ourselves, and all had a sense of adventure. The number one consideration was the bloody weather. We wanted sunshine.

A few days later I was packed and ready. I had said my goodbyes – Dad offered to come to the train station with me. Mum stood by the front door and the only thing she said was, "So, you're leaving us."

I said "I'll be back, Mum."

We weren't a family for long speeches.

Dad got a taxi and we arrived quickly at Central Station. He saw me on the train for Manchester. It was a sad farewell. He said the usual things a parent says to a daughter.

"Be careful, Gladee. Don't take any risks. Write soon. You're an intelligent girl. I don't blame you for getting out of this country. I wanted to do the same in the '20s."

My father said he wanted to emigrate to Australia after the hell of World War I that he went through. He liked the Australian soldiers he met at Gallipoli and probably would have done well in Australia, but my mother wouldn't go.

Dad stayed. There were no jobs after the war. He had served an apprenticeship as a maritime tool maker, but couldn't find work. He joined the Liverpool police force in the 1920s but there was a depression on and there was a threat of a general strike. The government brought in a Royal Navy destroyer with orders to fire on the city if the general strike happened. What a great reward for all the suffering the people of Liverpool had gone through. People with power and wealth gutted Merseyside in the 1950s again!

When the train arrived in Manchester I got a taxi to Salford Docks. It was dark when I arrived and the cobblestones were shiny and black from the rain. The ship looked like a grey specter. There were few lights visible along the dock. I could read the name of the ship in large white letters. It was the S.S. Manchester Progress. It was strange, but I only felt a modicum of fear. I stood waiting on the dock for someone to com help me with my luggage. It was as if some other power controlled me. Soon I heard a cheery voice.

"Hello, luv, already to board?"

It was a youngish-man in an officers' uniform.

He introduced himself as Rush Worthington, the ship's second officer. He was a wonderful, kind-hearted man.

I slowly climbed the steep gang plank and Rush showed me to my cabin.

"We only have eight passengers on this trip, so you don't have to share your cabin with anyone."

The cabin was quite roomy. The metal walls were painted with white enamel. There were two portholes with curtains, a sink, a shower room and a toilet down the hall. My cabin also had a closet and a small desk. The bunk was comfortable with a raised wood side to prevent you from falling out. I noticed raised door jambs at every door on the ship.

We were scheduled to sail that night. I ate a light meal with the other passengers in the dining room which doubled as a recreation room. The ship's captain introduced himself and the other officers and passengers who were already onboard when I arrived. There were two sisters from Yorkshire going on a holiday to Florida to visit their sister who was married to an American.

In the cabin next to me were a middle-aged American couple who were returning from a tour of England. A married couple from Blackpool were also doing a round trip. Lastly, there was a young man, very quiet who kept to himself. He had his MG sports car in the ship's hold and planned to do a motor tour of America.

I went to bed early and could hear the ships engines roar as we pulled away from the dock. I awoke early and looked out the porthole. We were in the Manchester ship canal and approaching a lock. I'm not sure which one, as there are many. Suddenly, we stopped.

I went to breakfast. The captain stood, coughing loudly as he cleared his throat.

"Well, it looks like we may be here for a while. The canal workers have gone on strike."

We all tut-tutted. The American man said it will only be a few hour's delay, I bet.

He didn't know British union workers in the 1950s.

It took seven days before we sailed past Liverpool, right past the shipping office I had worked for. We were not allowed off the ship, so I couldn't telephone anyone or send a telegram.

Off we went again across the Irish Sea to Waterford, Ireland. It was a Friday when we reached Waterford. Unfortunately, it was also the 13th. We were told that Irish dock workers never worked on Friday the 13th, plus they didn't work weekends. Our ship was a passenger-freighter, so we would make quite few stops loading and unloading on our voyage. On Saturday, a local priest came aboard and invited us to a Saturday night dance and pot luck supper. We had a great time and sang a lot of traditional Irish songs I had grown up with.

By Monday evening, we were off again and soon heading out into the Atlantic Ocean. All of the officers, especially the younger ones we shared a table with at dinner, were very pleasant to us. There was only one incident I recall.

One evening when I was in my cabin I saw someone peering through one of the portholes of my cabin when I went to pull the drapes closer together. He quickly disappeared. I never found out who he was. I told Rush, the 2nd officer about it at dinner that night and he gave me two big safety pins to hold the drapes together.

After a few days, our captain reported that the ship would not be stopping at its first scheduled port, Boston, Massachusetts. The weather had turned nasty with high seas and we would instead go to Philadelphia, Pennsylvania. The seas were indeed getting rougher and ropes to hold onto had been placed all around the docks.

We spent the evenings playing the board game Scrabble, a game I'd just learnt, and generally chatting with each other. The meals were delicious, not too fancy, but tasty and fresh.

As the weather grew worse, the American wife didn't appear at meal times and also one of the Yorkshire sisters. My cabin was right next door to the American couple. The wife was suffering terribly from seasickness and I could hear her moaning and saying, "Let me die!"

Seasickness can be an awful thing and I soon felt sorry for her. Soon we approached Philadelphia and the sea calmed down. I could hear American radio stations playing music, mostly singer Frank Sinatra singing, "Chicago, Chicago" and "When Somebody Loves You" which are still two of my favorites.

Setting sail across the Atlantic Ocean on a new adventure. Standing with Rush Worthington, second officer of the S.S. Manchester Progress. - 1957. *(Thaxton family collection)*

Ship's officers of the S.S. Manchester Progress enjoy a topside break. - 1957.
(Thaxton family collection)

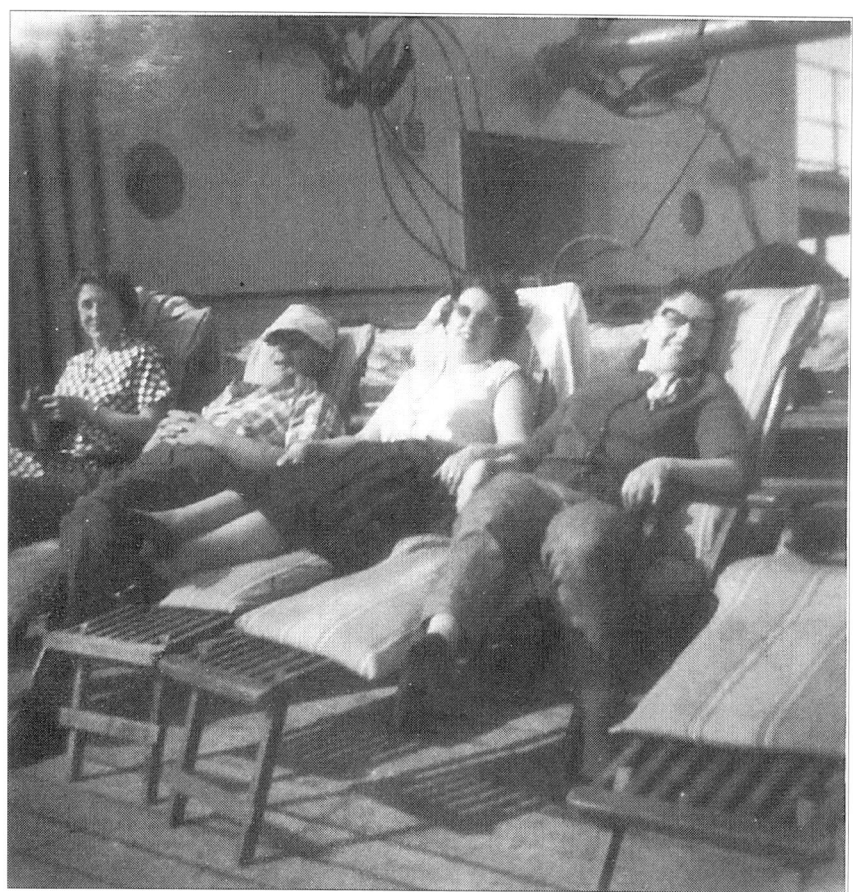

Fellow passengers onboard the S.S. Manchester Progress enjoy the sunshine. *(Thaxton family collection)*

Independence Hall - Philadelphia - 1957

Christmas Day in Philadelphia

My first sighting of America was slightly disappointing. It reminded me of the river Mersey. I don't know what I really expected to see in my romantic mind perhaps the shiny white marble towers of Kubla Khan. It was all industry as we sailed into Delaware Bay and then up the Delaware River to the Philadelphia docks. The sounds of shunting trains and huge cranes unloading and loading ships. This was the real America of industrious, far-seeing people. Later when I looked at a map of the United States, I read that famed general, and future president, George Washington had crossed the Delaware River on Christmas Day escaping the British Army during the American Revolution. Today was Christmas Eve.

The young English boys' sports car was unloaded and we waved him goodbye. We felt a little sad, that we had never really got to know much about him.

The captain said we were free to go ashore. I went on my own. The girls had gone off in search of a telephone to call their sister. I came upon a small shopping district just a short walk from the ship and it was brightly lit with lots of colorful Christmas decorations. I saw many people scurrying to do their last-minute shopping. On one street corner stood an office supply store which sold greeting cards. I suddenly felt very homesick. I went into the store and bought two Christmas cards to send back home. I asked the man behind the counter if he sold postage stamps for overseas air mail. He said yes, and handed me two stamps. I paid him for the small purchases. He smiled at me and wished me a Merry Christmas as he handed me a small object. It was a small measuring tape in an oval metal holder about one inch long. On one side was an embroidery of a flower. I kept it for many, many years. This was the America I had hoped for where they gave gifts to strangers. I felt much happier as I walked back to the ship.

      The dinner onboard ship was festive and the captain even provided two bottles of wine. He told us we would be sailing the next day, Christmas Day, on the afternoon tide and if we again went ashore that we had to be back onboard one hour before our scheduled sailing at 4 p.m.

      I hurried ashore on Christmas Day determined to see the Liberty Bell and Independence Hall. I'd picked up a small tourist leaflet the day before, showing me where it was located in the old part of the city not far to walk from where our ship was docked.

      I reached Independence Hall, a beautiful old building where the Founding Fathers had signed two ground breaking documents: The Declaration of Independence and the U.S. Constitution. I next went to see the Liberty Bell. It was no longer in the tower but on the ground floor. The tower, years before had been declared too fragile to hold the Liberty Bell. The Liberty Bell has been a treasured item for centuries. There were quite a few people visiting that day. The cost of the Liberty Bell which was made in an East End of London foundry was £150 pounds, 13 shillings and 8 pence. This included shipping and insurance in 1752. The recasting cost slightly more than £36 pounds in 1753. An impressive looking object, 12 feet in circumference, weighing 2,080 pounds with a clapper weighing 44 pounds. Inscribed around the top is a Biblical verse.

"Proclaim liberty throughout all the land unto all the inhabitants there of."

The Bell has had three homes. Firstly, Independence Hall from 1753 to 1976; the Liberty Bell Pavilion from 1976 to 2003; and the Liberty Bell Center, 2003 to the present.

The bell cracked in 1835 and was rung for the last time on February 23, 1846 in honour of George Washington's Birthday. It is no longer open for viewing on Christmas Day.

I realized it was getting late and hurried back to the ship. A frantic ship's second officer stood on deck.

"Where have you been? Ten more minutes and we would have sailed without you!"

I smiled not believing him.

"No, it's true," he said. "The captain would not have waited. He has to catch the tide. You would have been here on your own."

A thoroughly chastised me went to dinner that evening.

Baltimore and Jacksonville

Our next port stop was in Blaltimore, Maryland, another industrial city and seaport.

I had one day there and then spent two days at sea until we reached Jacksonville, Florida. The weather was getting warmer. We went ashore in the evening in Jacksonville for a couple of hours as the ship was due to sail the next day. There were about six of us, three girls and three of the officers. I was late getting ready and came down the gang plank to see the others walking off in the distance. I started to follow when I heard a siren coming up behind me. A police car pulled up in front of me. A big burly policeman in a khaki uniform leaned out of the open window of his car.

"Where do you think that you're going?"

I explained I was a passenger on the nearby docked ship and a group of us were going out for a drink at a nearby tavern.

"They should have waited for you," the officer continued. "This is a dangerous place for a woman on her own. Get in the cruiser and we'll catch up with your friends," he said.

He did so in less than two minutes. I thanked him and soon we were all together at the tavern. Music was blaring out from the jukebox as we entered. What struck me as strange were the women. They all seemed to have their hair in curlers with scarves tied turban-style around the curlers. Their bodies were not confined by the bras and girdles we British women still wore. They wore sleeveless cotton blouses, Capri-style slacks, Bobby sock and flat shoes. They were totally relaxed and comfortable. We didn't stay long, just one drink and we took a cab back to the ship.

The next day we were on our way to Savannah, Georgia. It was New Year's Eve. At dinner, I suggested we all go to bed early and get up at 11 p.m. to celebrate the New Year. Big mistake. None of us woke up in time.

Savannah, Georgia - A genteel old city

Dinner and Dancing - A great way to celebrate New Year's Day

We arrived in Savannah, Georgia on New Year's Day. It was a genteel old city. The ship glided slowly to the dock past a tree-lined riverbank where large, old mansions stood.

In the evening, we young folk decided to celebrate the New Year at a nightclub. It was a very well built night club with a small dance floor, but no band. We were the only ones there. All the Savannah folk were resting up after the wild parties the night before. We ordered dinner like the one we had in Philadelphia which was delicious. I've kept a menu from the Philadelphia dinner and here are some of the prices for 1957. Hard to believe now.

The name of the place is *"Club Internationale."*

Beluga Caviar Europe - $3.00 dollars; **Snapper Soup** – 40 cents; **Roast Duckling de Orange** - $4.00; **Prime Rib of Beef** - $4.50; **Broiled Lobster Tails** - $3.50; **Roast Suckling Pig for four** - $21.00. All dinners came with potato of your choice; vegetable and salad. The cost of a half-bottle of French Bordeaux Clavet - $3.00; Crepe Suzette - $1.75; Greek Coffee – 40 cents; and a pot of coffee – 35 cents. We slowly waddled back onboard the ship which sailed the next day to Charleston.

The Yorkshire sisters got off the ship in Savannah, along with the American couple who were on their way home to California. Only the couple from Blackpool and I were left onboard. I was filled with a mixture of fear of the unknown and excitement as I wondered whether Helen and George would be there to meet me.

They were both there!

I clutched a bag carrying a small gift for them. I heard Rush, the second ship's officer's voice as he ushered them into my cabin.

He had a little advice for me the evening before we arrived.

"If you don't like it here, Gladys, we will be back in a few months and you can come home on the ship!"

A friend sent me the letter below many years later which she thought I might like to have. The letter was sent when the ship reached Jacksonville, Florida. I'd kept it, and searched high and low in boxes of papers and notes until I was lucky enough to find it. What a difference the voice of youth makes. So much I had forgotten.

My original 1950s British passport photo. Full of confidence and ready for a bright new adventure in the United States. (*Thaxton family collection*)

At Sea

SS Manchester Progress
Monday, 30 December 1957

Dear Sheila and Grace,

I've finally managed to reach America. It seems a life time ago since I was in Liverpool. I never thought I would be so long in getting here when I went on board in Manchester.

We were held up in the ship canal, with one thing and another, for five days and did not sail past Liverpool until the following Thursday. I think if we had been delayed one more day I would have come home. I felt that homesick, but after the first week I got used to life onboard a ship and really the time passes very quickly.

I hope you have had a good Xmas. How did the boys in the office behave themselves? It is going to be awfully hard settling down to work again, when I reach Charleston after living a life of leisure these past three weeks.

The service and food is "first class" and I have a very well-equipped cabin to myself – with lots of room. Altogether we have five meals a day and lunch and dinner are five-course affairs.

I'm afraid I'll have to go on a diet when I get to Charleston. There are only 8 passengers including myself on this trip so the stewards wait on us hand and foot. Two of the passengers are American. They have been touring Europe by car for 18 months and are now on their way home to California. Then there is a married couple from Blackpool who are doing the round-trip and two sisters from Yorkshire who are going on a three-month visit to see their married sister in Florida. They are really good fun and have a dialect you could cut with a knife. The last passenger was a fellow from London, very tall and handsome who is emigrating to San Francisco. He got off at Philadelphia, and is motoring across the States.

After we left Liverpool we spent two days in Waterford, Ireland. I had two really good evenings ashore there with some of the passengers and some of the ship's officers.

On the last evening, I went to a dance with the ship's Third Mate and rock and rolled for three solid hours (my feet haven't been the same since). We should have only stayed there a day but they couldn't sail on the Friday as it was the 13th.

The Atlantic crossing was very good considering the time of year and the fact that we aren't carrying much cargo. The majority of the passengers were seasick, but somehow, I managed to escape it and still got plenty of sleep. I've been nicknamed the horizontal champ on board the ship.

The deck and engine room officers are all young and a real nice crowd – nearly every night somebody is throwing a party for us. I sit next to the chief officer at meal times. He is really nice. He has one of these tape recorders and we are always having little recording sessions. It is really funny hearing it played back.

The three apprentices have rigged up a skiffle group and we sing calypso, and rock and roll. In fact every song there is, I don't think I have sung and danced so much in all my life.

The first week onboard we all used to sit in the passenger's lounge and read or played different card games but I don't think anyone has been near the lounge these past two weeks. We don't see much of the Captain. He keeps to himself a lot, but occasionally he pushes the boat out and sends us over a liquor after dinner. The older passengers sit as his table. I've managed to get on deck every day and some time we play deck quoits or sit and sunbathe. The weather is really hot here in Florida, even in the North Atlantic it was sunny and I'm beginning to get quite suntanned (or weather beaten).

We did not call at Canada, our first port over here was Philadelphia – which we reached on Xmas Eve. We had four days there and had plenty of time to sightsee. It is quite near New York. If I had the cash I would have liked to have paid a visit to New York. Philadelphia is the third largest city in America – It is very big and easy to get around in.

In fact, the first day there I nearly missed the boat. There is plenty of night life there and our first night ashore we went to a place called the "Club International" which was like something out of a Chicago gangster film.

I don't think I would like to live there though – it's too big and fast. I'll say one thing for America, they are certainly very modern. I've never seen so much up to date equipment and all kinds of gadgets, even in the poorer districts.

Everything is very well maintained and everyone seems to own a car. And the cars are all huge compared to ours. Even the stevedores unloading the ship all have cars and park them right on the dock. I was chatting with one and he said he earns an average of $170.00 dollars a week!

Christmas onboard was also quite good. Even though the dinner got ruined. The cook got drunk and blamed the baker who hit him. Everything was overcooked and the plum pudding had so much rum and brandy in it, the first mouthful took my breath away.

But we made up for it with three Christmas parties that day in Philadelphia. There is one street there which is known as the "block" and is full of nothing but night clubs and Burlesque shows. Everybody was disappointed that we didn't have an evening in Baltimore, as all the boys had been talking about it for weeks and had promised to take us ashore and show us around the 408 Club, the Oasis and another place where a girl called "Battleship Annie" performs.

It seems this is the first time they've ever had three young girls on a voyage. The passengers are usually retired people – so every time we get into port we have dozens of offers for dates. We have been at sea for two days now. The pilot has just come onboard to take us into Jacksonville. We should dock about 9'oclock tonight. We expect to get away tomorrow night, which means New Year's Eve at sea (another disappointment). We will be in Savannah on New Year's Day and leave there the following day and all being well in reach of Charleston on Friday. It has certainly been an education this voyage and I have enjoyed every minute of it.

I'm afraid my knitting has been sadly neglected. I've only done about two rows – though I don't think I will ever need to wear it, it's so warm here. Tell Trevor I will knit it, into a pair of winter combs for him.

How is your romance progressing Grace? Is David still driving you wild, Sheila? I will close for now, but I will write and give you all the news when I get settled in Charleston. With best regards to the "3 Great Lovers" and everybody else at E.P. I hope you all have a very Happy New Year.

Yours sincerely, Gladys

P.S. My address in Charleston is at the moment:
149 Spring Street, Charleston, S.C., U.S.A.

My very first job in the United States was as a front desk manager at the Yeaman Hall Club, a private golf club for the winter season.

Charleston, South Carolina

George and Helen had a car waiting as I took one last sad look back at the ship and saw Rush waving to me from the upper deck. We put my two suitcases in the trunk and piled into the car. We were soon on our way. Their apartment wasn't too far from the old town of Charleston. George pointed out some of the famous historical buildings of which there were many. A port city steeped in history had hardly changed since its founding in 1670. A gracious, genteel city, much like Savannah.

We soon reached their apartment. They had made a bedroom for me out of an alcove with a curtain for privacy. It was quite cozy. Their little two-year-old daughter Karen ran towards me throwing her arms around me. Her hug felt very comforting. She was blonde like her father. A very sweet little girl. Helen and I stayed up late into the night talking about old times. I asked her about getting a job in Charleston. She said there didn't seem to be a lot of office work there.

"But don't worry about that now, just enjoy your stay with us."

I started to feel unsure again. I took a walk early my first Sunday morning in Charleston on a quiet street of old wood-framed houses.

Suddenly a front door swung open and out tumbled a laughing, squealing group. A black family of women and girls in pretty pastel colored cotton dresses, white gloved hands, flower bedecked hats looking like bouquets of spring flowers.

Men and boys, black suited, white shirts and ties, hair oiled down, mirror polished shoes. Off they hurried, joyfully down the street, behinds swinging and into the church on the corner whose bells were ringing more urgently. The street grew quiet again, with only the smell of dust and cockroaches from the old houses. The joy had left and I hurriedly walked back to Helen's apartment.

Later that Sunday morning at breakfast Helen had told me that I could register at an employment office for clerical work. It seemed to be the way things were done there.

After the weekend, I did just that and then went back to the apartment to await a telephone call. For five days, there was no call, and I started to worry. I'd arrived in Charleston with 25 dollars. How stupid of me not waiting until I saved up more money. But it would have taken forever. I had only earned £6 pounds a week. Then on Friday, I got the call.

Mr. and Mrs. O'Brien, who were the managers of Yeaman Hall Club wanted to meet with me. They asked if I could I get down to her office right away. They had read my resume and were interested in meeting me. I practically flew down. It was only a few blocks away.

The O'Briens were a couple in their 50s and very friendly to me. This was very unlike any interview for a job I had ever had in England, where during some, you felt like you were assessed by a hanging judge. They went on to describe the job to me.

Yeaman Hall Club was originally a plantation and now it was a private golf club and hotel for the very rich and old established money of New York and New England families who nearly all had what they called their winter cottages. They were huge bordering on being called mansions anywhere else. The small hotel was just for guests of members.

Like many Southern plantations, Yeamans Hall went into decline after the War Between the States, and the house was lost in a fire precipitated by the earthquake of 1886.

In 1915, seeking to reuse the land, in 1915, North Charleston developer E. W. Durant invited the renowned landscape architect Frederick Law Olmsted, Jr., to survey the land and assess its suitability as a golf resort. Olmsted came away impressed with its natural beauty, extended golfing season, proximity to Charleston, and its accessibility by rail, as did several other experienced resort developers. Olmsted's design firm was commissioned to generate a "general plan" for the proposed Yeamans Hall Club, and Rogers designed its clubhouse, which opened in 1928 and still functions in its original capacity.

The winter season ran from December through April. They explained that they needed me to fill the job of one of the hotel desk clerks, a woman who after one month had quit and complained of being homesick. The other clerk, a male had been doing the job for years. They listed my duties. I had to answer guest's questions. Sell cigars from a small humidor and also sell postcards.

"Do you think you could handle this, Gladys?"

"Oh, also you will work the switchboard and teletype machine."

"Oh, I can do that," I said. I had one job in the past where I had worked a switchboard for a few weeks.

It was a 7 day a week job. I shared the hours with Pierre, the other clerk. He was a French-Canadian and spoke very little. Some days I had a split shift, working 9 to 1 p. m. and then coming back at 6 p. m. until closing at 10 p.m. on those evenings.

I was always ravenous and would stop by at the hotel kitchen to say goodnight to the German chef and his wife. He also did all of the baking which he was superb at. And he always offered me a delicious bran muffin and got me to love the taste of molasses on it. Of course, my weight started to climb again.

I slept in staff quarters with all of the other hotel staff who were mostly from New York and were white. I lucked out and got a room to myself. We had all our meals in the staff dining room. The food was pretty much what the club members received, which was gourmet!

Segregation was still very much a fact of life in the South. All of the grounds staff were black. In the late afternoon, I'd see the men walking slowly, tiredly up the long tree-lined avenue that led to the main entrance gate to go home.

My pay was $150 a month and included room and board. I'll save every penny, I thought. I was getting scared of what lay ahead.

"Would you like the job," Mrs. O'Brien asked.

"Yes, I think I would," I replied.

"Good," said Mrs. O'Brien. "We need you right away. Can you pack up and be ready for us to pick you up tomorrow morning?"

"Yes," I replied and gave them Helen's address.

So this was it then, my first job in America. I had been at Helen's exactly one week. I rushed home to tell her the news and to pack.

The grounds of the Yeaman's Hall Club were beautiful with lots of oak trees with Spanish moss hanging from most of the trees. Lush, green grass covered the 18-hole golf course. Through the trees, I could see large houses. Later I was to learn that a lot of the wealthy members from up North had built their own houses that they called their winter cottages. Most of these cottages were the size of mansions. There was a large creek named Goose Creek and a warning sign about the dangers of alligators.

"Beware of Alligators," the sign said. I don't recall seeing any at that time. This part of South Carolina is called the low country for good reason and has lots of waterways and rivers. We weren't very far from the Cooper River on which my ship, the SS Manchester Progress had docked.

When I did get homesick, I used to gaze up Goose Creek in the same direction, dreaming it was sailing right up the creek to take me home.

All of the staff were considerably older than me and were very helpful and friendly. At 11 p.m. at night we would all go to the lounge and watch the Tonight Show with Jack Paar on NBC television. It was always very funny and a treat to me. We still only had shows on the telly until 9 p.m. in the evening in England.

Our staff dormitory was just a few minutes walking distance from the hotel and at night in the dark, it could be a little scary with the mysterious Spanish moss moving with the late evening breeze. The moss looked like long fingers, just ready to grab you. I always walked very fast at night. Equally scary were possums which hung from the branches of the trees. I never knew if one would climb down from the tree to frighten me.

There was a golf shop which was run by the golf pro and his assistant, who after a few weeks asked me if I'd like to learn the game and gave me some free lessons which included the loan of equipment. I had only ever played "pitch and putt" or miniature golf in England with my Dad. I loved the game, and on my afternoons off, would practice when none of the guests were around.

I talked to my friend Helen on the telephone a couple of times a week. After two weeks of work at Yeamans, I called Helen one afternoon and she told me that her husband George had left her. I was shocked. Theirs seemed to be such a happy marriage. She never told me the reason for their breakup.

I wondered if it was over the job she had recently started. Helen told me she started a part-time job as a cocktail waitress at a roadside tavern on the outskirts of Charleston owned by a man named Harold who was maybe 15 to 20 years older than her.

After her divorce, she married him and later they operated a tavern in Arizona. They had one daughter together. When Helen's little girl was about five years old, and after a couple of years in Arizona, they moved back to Charleston.

Once in a while, Harold would drive over, and on my evening off, would take me to the tavern for a few hours, and then give me a ride back to Yeamans.

The place wasn't very big, just a few booths along a wall and three or four tables with chairs. It had a very old, long wooden bar along the opposite wall with a jukebox in the corner. A large hot plate sat on the bar featuring Harold's specialty, a large, hot pot of chili con carne. He and Helen prepared it before the customers came in. Cans of beans and tomatoes, chunks of steak, fresh and powdered chili, onions, garlic and probably Harold's own secret seasoning. It was always delicious, and of course, very popular with the patrons of the bar. He had to replenish the ingredients on most busy nights.

On one evening, I started talking to a young man who had just been discharged from the U.S. Army. He had spent most of his military service in Germany. He was a very polite young man named Paul, and finding out where I was living, offered to give me a lift back to the hotel. We drove a short distance and then he asked me if I would like to drive his car.

"Love to," I answered.

I had never driven anything before, but after a couple of highballs, I had no fear. I knew how to steer and he told me where the brake and the accelerator were. I had the car going 100 miles per hour and didn't even know it. After about a mile Paul very calmly shouted at me to slow down, and take my foot off the gas. We glided to a stop and he took over the car.

"I thought you could drive," he said.

"Who told you that," I answered.

Poor guy. He had just bought the car. We were very lucky that no police saw us speeding by.

I did learn how to drive a car many years later.

Another morning, a tall, somber-looking couple came into the lobby. The wife wanted to buy a postcard. She picked one from our small selection. The man paid me with a one dollar bill. I thanked him and handed him the change. They started to walk out, and then the man turned back, holding his hand with the change out to me.

"You have short-changed me a nickel," he said.

I grew red-faced.

"I'm not used to American money yet. I only arrived in America two weeks ago," I said.

He was silent as I handed him a nickel. I later learned that he was millionaire John D. Rockefeller, the third scion of one of America's wealthiest families.

It was a lesson I never forgot. The rich hang on to every penny. That's how they got rich in the first place.

The original John D. Rockefeller used to give out dimes to those down on their luck. But that was when a dime would actually buy something.

Charleston was a Confederate state, where the first shot of the American Civil War was fired on April 12, 1861 on Fort Sumter, a Union fort in the middle of Charleston Bay. It was the start of three years of carnage. One of the bloodiest wars in history. It was many years later that I learned of Liverpool's part in helping the Confederacy. Liverpool had become rich on shipping from the southern U.S. States cotton crops to the Lancashire Cotton Mills. They, the South, had their own consulate down near the docks.

At the start of the war a Confederate agent commander James Bulloch arranged to have John Laird & Sons, shipbuilders across the Mersey River from Liverpool build the CSS Alabama, a screw sloop of war.

Under prevailing British neutrality laws it was possible to build a ship designed as an armed vessel, provided that it wasn't actually armed until after it sailed into international waters. In light of this loophole the CSS Alabama was built with reinforced decks for cannon emplacement and ammunition magazines. The sloop left Liverpool on August 13, 1862 to be outfitted with cannon on Teressa Island in the Azores. The ship's captain was Raphael Seminoes. The ship was launched as the "Enrica" in May 1862. Following her commissioning as a commerce raider for the Confederate States of America her motto was "God helps those who help themselves."

Eighty-three men, many of them from Liverpool signed on to fight on the CSS Alabama. She burned 65 Union ships and boarded nearly 450 vessels and captured 2,000 prisoners.

CSS Alabama was sunk in June 1864 at the battle of Cherbourg, France by the USS Kersarge whose captain challenged Captain Seminoes of the CSS Alabama to a ship's duel the next morning. The superior training of the gunners on the USS Kearsarge won the day and the Alabama sank.

A second ship, the CSS Shenandoah, also did a lot of damage to the Union navy. It also went up to Alaska near the end of the war and sank some Yankee whalers.

The last act of the American Civil War was in Liverpool where the captain of the CSS Shenandoah surrendered his ship and crew at the Liverpool town hall where the Confederate flag was lowered on his ship for the last time.

Sad to say that the city of Liverpool also had a hand to play in the Slave Trade. The triangular slave trade here was described in one slaver's sea experience.

"Sailed from Liverpool to West Africa. The ship then purchased or captured as many as it could carry. Then took the middle passage across the Atlantic Ocean to the West Indies. The slaves who survived the gruesome passage were sold for sugar, rum, tobacco and raw cotton which were then brought back to England for profit.

For many years on the dock road, you could see iron rings set into the walls which were used to secure slaves, or so it has been told.

In 1776, any slaves remaining in the United Kingdom were considered free men and in 1830, slavery was banned in Britain.

"One Ringy Dingy, Two Ringy Dingys"

I soon got the hang of the telephone switchboard and teletype machine at the Yeamans Hall Club. Neither was heavily used.

Long distance calls had to be routed through the Charleston main telephone company switchboard. I would write down the guest's request and then call the Charleston switchboard with the phone number, and they would call me back. I would then connect the call to the guest's phone. It was a three-way job, not like today, with smart phones and instant, high speed connection.

One guest with a very deep voice made a lot of calls.

"Yes, sir. No sir," until I found he was a she.

Georgia accents were kind of deep-throated. She was a sweet, older woman though, and gave me a nice tip at the end of the season.

I once asked the Charleston switchboard operator if she could understand my British accent.

"Oh, yes! You are clear talking," she replied. "It's those darn Yankees from up North we have trouble with."

Mrs. Douglas was another guest. She was the wife of U.S. Supreme Court Justice William O. Douglas. She asked me what I planned on doing when the season ended. I said I planned on travelling across the United States to San Francisco.

"Don't go there," she said. "There's nothing there."

"Go to New York City, and see the English-speaking Union office. Give them my name and they will help you."

I often wonder what my live would have been like if I'd followed her advice, but . I guess I was on a different mission.

Whenever I thought of New York City and its gangsters, they scared me. I'd seen far too many Hollywood movies towards the end of the hotel season. Miss Russell, a member whose home was in

Charleston, invited all the staff, white of course, to dinner. Her home was a large, old mansion filled with Victorian furniture. We sat at a very large dining table. There were about 15 of us. Two maids brought in all of the main dishes. Turkey, ham, sweet yams, and lots more. It was like a Thanksgiving dinner. I learned that Miss Russell did this every season. Old Southern hospitality was not dead.

Congresswoman Claire Boothe Luce was another celebrity guest at Yeaman's. American author; politician; U.S. ambassador and notable public conservative figure. She was the first American woman appointed to a major ambassadorial post abroad. A versatile author, Boothe Luce is best known for her hit play, "The Women." (What a woman.) She was the wife of Henry Luce, publisher of *Time, Life, Fortune* and *Sports Illustrated* magazines. She sent several telegrams to her husband when she was a guest at Yeamans. Knowing what I know now, I wish I would have taken time to speak with her, if only briefly. We were ships that passed in the night. I had no real knowledge of any of these illustrious members. Boothe Luce died in 1987 at the age of 84. Her husband, Henry passed away 20 years earlier.

On one of my afternoons off, Helen and Harold took me to see one of the older North Charleston plantations, which was turned into a popular tourist attraction.

Now known as Cypress Gardens, it featured paths and water trails where paddle boats could travel through a 165-acre black water swamp in the wonderland of Cypress Forest.

Bright colors of azaleas; camellias; and spring bulbs, delighted us on our way as our rented rowboat glided slowly through the dark water. We wanted to touch the hanging blossoms. It was truly a magical place.

Towards the end of the hotel season, I started having an awful toothache. I guess it was the consequence of too many sweets. My face swelled up and Mrs. O'Brien took me to see a dentist in the city. It was one of my wisdom teeth and what a relief I felt when the tooth was pulled. The club paid the bill. It was the beginning of April and soon the club would close. I had been there three months and soon I would have to pack.

I returned to Yeamans Hall Club, in South Carolina, the site of my first job in the United States and the front desk and switchboard looked much the same. *(Thaxton family collection)*

Moving On from Charleston

The last week before the Yeaman closed for the season, several members handed me little envelopes with ten or twenty dollars tucked inside. With my saved salary and the tips that I'd earned, I had about 400 dollars. I'd been worrying about how I would make it to San Francisco, this might just do it.

I'd seen an advertisement in the local Charleston newspaper. The Greyhound bus company was offering a fare of $99, unlimited time and travel to anywhere in the country. I bought one. Helen and Harold picked me up from the Yeaman with my luggage the first week of April and I spent a few days in Helen's old apartment which she still rented. I told her of my plans. She wasn't too surprised at my news.

"Well, you might as well give it a try. There doesn't seem to be much work here that would pay you a living wage."

She went on. "Once my divorce is final, I think Harold and I might move to Arizona."

So, it was settled. A few days later they put me on the evening bus to Jacksonville, Florida. An older man sat next to me on the bus and I told him of my plans.

When the bus reached Jacksonville, the next morning, the gentleman said, "Look, I live with my sister in town and seeing your bus to New Orleans doesn't leave until 6 p.m. tonight, why don't you come home with me? My sister would love to meet you. You can rest up and have a nice meal with us."

Can you imagine any young woman today agreeing with that offer? But this was the 1950s and people then were much more trusting.

I accepted and his sister, quite elderly, was as sweet and nice as he was. They even let me take a nap in their guest room for a couple of hours, then we all sat down to a delicious meal. They had an old, red bicycle in the front garden and I took a short ride on it around their neighborhood.

A wonderful Jacksonville, Florida couple who treated me to a delicious home cooked meal on my way to New Orleans. *(Thaxton family collection)*

They drove me back to the Greyhound station to catch my bus and wished me good luck and with a promise to write to them when I got to San Francisco. Such amazing hospitality. True Southern hospitality to a complete stranger!

I reached New Orleans the next morning. Much of our journey was done at night. The Greyhound bus company, generally had a hotel right next to the bus terminal at their major city stops.

The fabled city of New Orleans

They were called "Post Houses" and were quite comfortable, "two stars", maybe, but always very clean. Downstairs would typically be a café. I don't think "Post Houses" even exist anymore. I was booked in for two nights. I was excited about seeing the fabled city of New Orleans. After checking in, and a couple of hours of sleep, I went to see the sights.

My first destination was the famed French Quarter where I quickly found the nearby Café Du Monde for breakfast and their world-famous beignets, sugar-coated, deep-fried doughnuts which are oh, so delicious! The market area was fun with lots of food and fresh produce, arts and crafts and souvenirs available for sale.

I took a long walk around the French Quarter to work off my heavy breakfast. I stopped by the St. Louis Cathedral, one of the city's most famous landmarks. I thoroughly enjoyed my visit to the Louisiana State Museum. In time, I headed slowly back to my hotel.

On my walk there, I heard a wonderful brass band playing Dixieland jazz on a narrow city street.

I at an early dinner in a small café near Bourbon Street of delicious shrimp gumbo and rice. Bourbon Street was charming with its old iron filigreed balconies. After a full day, I headed off to bed.

I awoke early the next morning ready for more sightseeing. I went back to the French Market and took a walk along the Mississippi riverfront to see where the riverboats dock. I decided to take an inexpensive, short ride on an old paddle steamer. In the afternoon, I rode in an old iron streetcar on St. Charles Avenue to the Garden district and Lafayette cemetery. So much history there! What a wonderful city with so much to see and do. I still had to keep moving on before my money ran out.

I promised myself I would return to New Orleans one day.

So this is Texas!

After two nights in New Orleans, Houston, Texas was the next stop. I arrived after a few hours' ride in the early morning, but there would only be two or three hours' layover, before continuing on to San Antonio.

I took a short walk down a main street. There was a rather large sign of a cowboy boot hanging in the front of a bar. So, this is Texas!

I was on the Greyhound bus once again in the early evening, but trying to sleep was impossible with three young men in the back of the bus singing raucous songs like "The Eyes of Texas Are Upon You." The next stop was San Antonio. Arriving in the morning, I decided to try doing two nights' travel on the bus. A very wrong choice, as it turned out, but I was young.

San Antonio is a pretty town with a river running through its downtown. The river is lined on both sides with cafes and shops. On the Paseo del Rio river walk you can stroll along through a garden edged area of the river or drift along the river in a boat.

I took a walk downtown and came across a large crowd in front of an old adobe building. It was the Alamo, where the freedom of the Republic of Texas was defended.

San Jacinto Day at the Alamo in San Antonio, Texas – May 1958

On that day, a special remembrance ceremony was held. I stood and watched as a U.S. Army Band played rousing marches and several dignitaries gave speeches. I went inside the museum where there was much to see and learn about the history of the Alamo.

Spanish settlers built the Mission de Valero, named for St. Anthony of Padua in 1718 on the banks of the San Antonio River.

In the early 1800s, it became a Mexican army garrison called The Alamo. In December 1835, in the early stages of Texas' War for Independence from Mexico a group of Texas volunteers overwhelmed the Mexican garrison at the Alamo and took it over. The following year in February 1836, a Mexican force numbering in the thousands, began a siege of the fort. Led by General Santa Anna, the Alamo's 200 defenders, commanded by James Bowie and William Travis, included famed frontiersman Davy Crockett, held out courageously for 13 days before the Mexican army finally overpowered them. Santa Ana ordered his men to take no prisoners and only a small handful of the Texans were spared. For the Texans, the battle of the Alamo became an enduring symbol of their heroic resistance to oppression and their struggle for independence which they won later that year.

Ten years after Texas won its independence from Mexico and shortly after it was annexed by the United States in 1845, U.S. soldiers revived the "Remember the Alamo" battle cry while fighting against Mexican forces in the Mexican-American War of 1846-48.

I had an early dinner before catching the next leg of my bus journey to the city of El Paso. It was a very long and tiring journey. The weather was also getting much warmer and the view out the window of the bus was rather boring with long stretches of highway with nothing but scrub and desert to see.

When the Greyhound bus finally reached the city of El Paso the next morning, I staggered over to the nearby Post House and paid for a room for the night.

I just about managed to reach my room and fell onto the bed, actually in it, fully clothed and immediately fell asleep.

When I awoke, it was in the evening. I'd slept for nine hours. I was very lucky getting to check-in so early. These days, check-in seems to be around noon. Like I said before, two nights on a bus, is one too many.

I went down to the coffee shop and got something to eat. I went back to the bus ticket office to check on the scheduled times of buses leaving for Arizona. I'd decided I'd take a side trip to see the Grand Canyon.

Tomorrow I wanted to see something of El Paso and take a look at Juarez, Mexico. There wasn't much to see in El Paso, which was a very hot, dusty, town. I soon found myself walking across the bridge, over the Rio Grande River connecting the United States and Mexico.

Mariachi music spilled out of the main street. Bars and the squeals of women and deep-throated laughter of men. They seemed to all be having a good time. There were a lot of gift shops and taco stands.

I stopped at one café to have lunch. My first taste of Mexican food was unusual to me, but quite tasty. I looked at all the souvenirs and picked out a small pair of framed pictures. They were nicely carved wood frames and in each was a picture of tropical birds which were made from real feathers which I mailed home to my parents in England.

Soon, it was time to head back to the hotel, collect my luggage and catch the bus to Flagstaff, Arizona where the tour to the Grand Canyon would leave the next morning. After a very long drive, we pulled into Flagstaff and I found a room for the night.

Enjoying a day at the Grand Canyon in Arizona, May 1958

I booked a seat for the next morning to the South Rim of the canyon. The drive was pleasant and took less than two hours, driving through a green pine forest.

Soon we were at the canyon village where we were led down a pathway to the south rim of the canyon. I walked gingerly to the viewing spot. Afraid to look down, instead I looked across to the far side.

The colors were stratified and amazing – stripes of gold, yellow, pink, orange and gray-violet. And all around the canyon walls. A natural wonder of the world!

Finally, I looked downward until my eyes reached the bottom to a minute black ribbon of water below which was the Colorado River. Gripping the metal railing, I stood for a few more minutes and then walked away. That's all you need. The impact of your first sight of the Grand Canyon is everything and will stay with you forever.

After lunch in the village, the local Hopi Indian tribe, who live nearby, put on a display of dances and chanting dressed in their beautifully decorated clothing.

I had thought of staying another night so I could go see the Meteor Crater the next day. I decided not to.

The Golden State of California was calling me.

Welcome to the Golden State

We reached the downtown Los Angeles bus terminal late in the evening. I decided to try the YWCA for a bed. It was nearby. I booked two nights. It was dormitory style with about four beds to a room. I slept soundly and didn't awake until after 9 a.m., drowsily rubbing my eyes as I saw a figure moving past my bed towards the door. A very large figure, I thought, over six feet tall. Dressed in a flowery print dress, a deep voice spoke.

"Bye. Have a nice visit to L.A."

Who the hell was that, I thought? The other two young women in the room were laughing.

"Was that a man?" I asked them.

They nodded yes, and started giggling again.

Welcome to California.

I saw a poster in the Greyhound ticket office advertising "Knott's Berry Farm." A smaller, older version of Disneyland which had just opened.

Knott's Berry Farm was easier to get to and much cheaper. It was a lot of fun, the type of entertainment which we didn't have in the U.K. at that time. Such a large, park-like setting with lots of Western-style cowboy ranch themed features and costumed workers. Plenty of carnival rides, places to eat, and souvenir shops. The Knott's Berry Farm company started as a jam manufacturer and still sells their jams today, which are delicious and the best in the United States.

The next morning, I left for San Francisco which would be a 12-hour bus ride beginning in the huge metropolis of Los Angeles and leading to the northern coastal highway.

We traveled along the California coast for a while. Beautiful scenic areas of the central California coast gave way to the inland farmland of the Salinas Valley and its rich crops of fresh fruits and vegetables which are shipped and sold all over America. Twelve hours later we were crossing the Bay Bridge and into the city of San Francisco. The famed Golden Gate Bridge would have to wait.

"Way out West" Wearing a colorful Native American headdress with one of the cast members at Knotts Berry Farm in Los Angeles, California. *(Thaxton family collection)*

Hello, San Francisco!

I hailed a taxi outside the downtown bus station and asked him to take me to the YWCA. I asked the driver if the "Y" was in a good area.

"Yes", he replied. "It's north of Market, up on Sutter Street."

"Don't go to 3rd Street, south of Market, it's full of winos, or the Tenderloin, a block or two up from Market that's not too safe either."

I thanked him for his sound advice.

"Welcome to Frisco!" were his parting words to me as I paid him.

I got a two-bed room at the "Y" this time. One bed was already occupied by a young woman named Connie, age 31. We chatted for a while.

She told me she had been living abroad for the last 10 years. After she got her three degrees from Syracuse University in New York. She was one of those brilliant students that go to "Uni" when they are 16 years old. She had received a teaching credential and had decided she wanted to travel.

She taught in Naples, Italy, where she had relatives, and Istanbul, Turkey. We are still good friends. She has traveled all over the world, often for several months at a time each year, well into her 80s.

I honestly don't believe there is a spot on this earth where she hasn't been to.

I registered for work with a downtown employment office. I was fortunate to find a job in just two days, working as an administrative clerk for a large steamship line in the City's financial district.

Connie told me she was soon moving into a guest rooming house on Stockton Street. I decided to join her. The downtown YWCA only allowed their guests short stays of a few days.

The new guest house on Stockton Street was delightful. The rental price was reasonable and the management provided their residents breakfast and dinner meals. The quality and quantity of food they offered was quite good.

Everyone staying at the Stockton Street guest house tended to be from another nearby town or foreign country. Most were young people, all working in the city. All were very friendly.

One evening, Connie serve a small group of us Turkish coffee in her room. I read an advertisement in the local newspaper seeking a young woman to serve dinner in the evening in exchange for room and board.

I called and the woman who answered the telephone asked me if I could come right then to their residence to interview. Their home turned out to be a penthouse apartment on Nob Hill, right behind the famed Mark Hopkins Hotel.

I got the job.

I was still worried about saving money and whether or not I could keep my day job, and try to save on my overall living costs.

My employer, a Mrs. O'Neill, said my specific duties would be only to serve her and Mr. O'Neill their dinner. Her husband, Mr. O'Neill owned a large real estate company downtown. The couple employed a Chinese cook.

"Oh! And, every once in a while we hold a cocktail party," said Mrs. O'Neill.

I would have to wear a maid's black dress, with a cap and a white lace apron. No problem, I thought.

When I arrived dressed for dinner service, the cook would have the food on plates ready for me to carry them in.

Everything went well, but I did experience just one small glitch when I served them dinner. I never could get the frozen pats of butter onto Mr. and Mrs. O'Neill's bread and butter plates without at least one of the pats flying off and landing on their dining table.

"Serve from the left, take away from the right," was my guiding mantra.

At home in Liverpool, our family moved the dishes away when we were done with our meal any way we felt liked.

I thought the first two weeks of my employment with the O'Neills had gone rather well.

Mrs. O'Neill reminded me she would be holding a small cocktail party in two days. I hurried to her home from my other employer.

There were two hostesses and a bartender at work for this occasion. There were ample bottles of wine and liquor and platters of hors d'oeuvres on every counter in the kitchen.

Mrs. O'Neill told me I was to answer the doorbell and to usher the guests in, take their coats and put them in the cloakroom. I was then to carry platters of hors d'oeuvres around their crowded lounge.

After about an hour, I noticed the waiter seemed to be listing more to the portside as he proffered glasses of wine to the guests and was spending more and more time in the kitchen fixing drinks.

The situation got so bad the three of us who were tending to their guests had to move more sharply out of the bartender's way.

I could see Mr. O'Neill glaring at him. Mrs. O'Neill focused her stern gaze directly at me.

I continued to politely greet each guest by saying, "Would you care for an hors d'oeurve, Sir or Madam?"

Mrs. O'Neill fired me the next evening.

Her words to me were, "Gladys, I don't think you are cut out to be a maid. You talked to my guests too much. You can leave at the end of the week."

It wasn't long before I needed to move from the guest house on Sutter Street and find a new place to live. A co-worker at the steamship line suggested Mrs. Tanner's Boarding House on Leavenworth where she lived.

"She's got a couple of rooms to rent and is a real nice lady."

My new landlord was a big, jolly motherly type, and was married to a much-smaller Swiss gentleman, who once a week would vacuum the hallways and clean the bathrooms. Tenants were asked to take care of their own rooms.

Mrs. Tanner showed me to a small room on the second floor across from the bathroom. It was adequate for my needs and only cost six dollars a week, a bargain. The next day I went to the nearby Five and Dime store on Market Street and bought a hot plate, saucepan, a few bits of china and cutlery.

Oh! And one egg cup!

There was a Mom and Pop-style grocery store on the corner and I would buy two or three eggs at a time to fix myself breakfast which consisted of a soft-boiled egg and a rye crisp biscuit and a cup of tea with powdered milk. I had no refrigerator.

For lunch, I took two rye crisps with American cheese and an apple. I had never eaten so healthy before in my life.

In the evening, I would walk down several blocks to Polk Street where for just 89 cents, I could get a four-course Chinese or American-style meal including soup or salad; a main dish; small dessert and coffee. Unbelievable today!

Their boarding house was not far from the corner of California Street on which the famous San Francisco cable cars run. It's a very steep hill. I tried walking up California Street a few times, but mostly caught the buses that ran on Sacramento and Clay Street to the office and back home at night. You needed the agility of a mountain goat to walk this hill.

There are seven large hills in San Francisco – just like in Rome. A block away was the famous Nob Hill named after the Central Pacific Railroad's "Big Four" – called the Nobs – who built mansions there. On one side of the Square is the Grace Cathedral, the largest Gothic structure in the West. It's Episcopalian, and one of its many splendors is its cast, gilded bronze doors created by Lorenzo Ghiberti for the Baptistry in Florence, Italy. These are the 15th century portals which Michelangelo deemed fit to be the gates of heaven.

There are several luxury hotels on the square. The Fairmont, the Huntington, the Stanford, and the last one, the Mark Hopkins. Military servicemen flocked to the Mark Hopkins during World War II on their way to the war. The famed "Top of the Mark" became a symbol of the good life back home.

The Huntington, though is smaller, with just 140 rooms and suites which have secluded a succession of royals. Princesses Margaret and Grace and Prince Charles have stayed there.

What a strange few weeks it had been. The YWCA, to the Navarre Guest House, then on to a Nob Hill penthouse and now Mrs. Tanner's Boarding House. I hope I'm not sliding down the hill of life.

Newlyweds on our Las Vegas honeymoon – 1958 – The Arabian Show Room, Dunes Casino.

(Thaxton family collection)

A familiar accent

How did I eventually meet my husband?

I have to thank two young women from Liverpool I met in the ladies' powder room in a seafood restaurant in San Francisco's famed Fishermen's Wharf for setting those lucky stars in motion.

I settled in to my new life in the United States and continued to work as an office clerk for the General Steamship Line in their downtown office.

I hadn't found lasting love yet, but my luck would soon change.

One weekend I went to visit Fisherman's Wharf, a popular tourist attraction. After dinner in one of the popular seafood restaurants, I stopped in the Ladies powder room and overheard two young women talking in what I could readily tell were very pronounced Liverpool accents.

I asked them if they were from Liverpool just to make sure.

"How did you guess," one said.

I replied that I was also from Liverpool and left for the United States after the war.

We struck up a conversation and introduced ourselves. They were lovely young ladies, April and Emily who I looked forward to getting to know.

We exchanged telephone numbers and a short time later, I was invited to dinner at April's house in the city.

The other young woman, named Emily, lived in San Bruno, a small town on the San Mateo peninsula, about a 30-minute drive south of San Francisco. A week later I got a telephone call from Emily asking me if I would like to go on a blind date with her neighbor's son Bill, who had just got out of the U.S. Army the year before.

Bill's mother said he didn't know any young women his age who were living in the city of San Bruno.

Bill was lonely and by then, so was I. So it was agreed through Emily, that we would go out together.

My husband Bill in his U.S. Army uniform.

Myself, happy, smiling and in love after meeting "My Bill."

(Thaxton family collection)

"He's just my Bill"

We arranged to meet on the corner of my street. We were both shy on our first blind date. Bill had just bought his first car, a brand-new Chevrolet Bel Air, a cream and tan colored sedan. He asked me if I would like to go for dinner to Fisherman's Wharf. He helped me into the car which he had parked across the street, and off we went, that is for a few feet.

Bill wasn't used to driving on hills and put his foot on the brake pedals too hard when he thought he was moving too fast. I shot forward and hit my head on the dashboard. No seatbelts were required in the 1950s. He apologized profusely and I was fine. I told him I didn't hit my head too hard. We had a real great evening and started going out every week.

Bill didn't have film star looks – except to me. I always thought that he looked a lot like the movie star Spencer Tracy. He was well-built with broad shoulders. But the most important thing to me was his wonderful sense of humor. He would have me in stitches doing accents and impersonations of people. He had a quick wit and was very intelligent. Over the years which we spent together, he taught me much. To many, he seemed shy, until you got to know him. He was a sweet and generous man.

Within three months of our first meeting, we were married.

All ready for the parade. This was taken in the garden of our first San Francisco apartment. *(Thaxton family collection)*

Bill and I lived in a small apartment built on the side of a house by Mario and Vicky, his wife. Mario drove a Yellow Cab and Vicky plucked chickens in a factory downtown. They were both Italian-Americans.

After a little over a year, I became pregnant. Bill was working for Xerox Office Machine Company at the time and I was selling Avon cosmetics.

Neither of us made much money. Bill's mom gave us $5,000 as a deposit on a new house and three weeks before the birth when we learned I was having twins, we moved into a little house in the woodsy area on the coast south of San Francisco, called Pacifica where I still live.

My sweetheart Bill passed away in 2003. We had twins, a boy John, and a girl, Susan. Bill went back to college to study electronic engineering on the GI Bill when the twins were three years old. I got a part-time job as a checker in a small, local super market.

The customers were all very nice, as were the owners, Mr. and Mrs. Root. Mr. Root allowed some to get groceries just by signing the cash register receipt which I filed in a small box, kept under the counter. The customers always seemed to clear their debts, when they got paid.

Pacifica is a beautiful scenic small town with beaches and tree covered hills. It was quiet as was nearby San Francisco in the late 1950s and early 1960s. San Francisco, then, only had two buildings that could be classified as skyscrapers. Today there are many, many, more. Things started to change with the advent of the Vietnam War. Bill's 19-year-old nephew joined the U.S. Army and was sent to Vietnam to serve as a helicopter mechanic. It was early in the 1960s, thank god. The real slaughter hadn't started yet. Things started to change in the '60s, though, more crime, drugs, and of course rock and roll.

The little local market where I worked was held up in 1967 by a gun wielding robber and my boss, the owner, was marched out of the store until the thief let him go and jumped into his waiting car. I knew what was going on, but instinctively knew not to panic. My boss kept calm too. As soon as the two men walked towards the door, I ran to the telephone and called the police. I was shaking so much I had to dial the phone number twice. When I ran to the phone I had the awful feeling I was going to feel a bullet hit me between my shoulder blades. The store had two check stands. I was on one and my boss was on the other. I had happened to look up, and saw the robber leaning over my bosses' counter with a gun in his hand. All of the customers had been coming through my check stand, not one ever guessed what was happening. I kept mouthing words, "Get the police, robbery", but not one seemed to read my lips.

One of the robbers, who as the getaway driver, went to Texas where he had tried to rob a store. Unfortunately for him, the guy behind the counter was an off-duty Texas police officer who carried a gun and immediately shot the thief dead.

The other robber plead guilty so when my boss and I went to court it was all over in about 30 minutes. He wasn't a very successful robber either. He had been hiding out in San Francisco for a couple of weeks when the police recognized him from the description Mr. Root and I had given them. It was the first armed robbery in a store in Pacifica.

Earlier in the 1960s, I had decided to learn keypunch card work. It was the start of commercial computer use and I enrolled in a six-week course in San Francisco. I did well in the course and we "graduates" were taken to a very large insurance office across the street to see their keypunch room. It was in the basement. About 50 young women placed cards in their machines which generated a lot of noise. It all looked very Dickensian. I took one look and decided this wasn't the place or the type of work for me. Keypunch card use didn't last very long.

I will never forget that course. Not the work, but my last day there. Someone came into the office and said President John F. Kennedy had been shot. It was November 22nd, 1963. He was our bright light and he gave so much to us, a promise of a better future. Now he was gone. People were in shock for a very long time.

The year before, in October 1962, the Cuban Missile Crisis occurred. The Russians had built missile bases on the island of Cuba. My husband, Bill, was a civilian worker with the California National Guard. He also served in the National Guard. When the crisis started, he came home one day and told me, "Honey, I'm going to be away for a few days," as he packed a small bag. "It's this Cuban Crisis. But I don't want you to worry. Everything will be OK.

My husband was one of the radar operators at the local Nike missile defense base. We didn't get too much news in those days. After about a week we heard that President Kennedy and the Russian premier, Nikita Khrushchev had agreed to end the crisis and that missile bases in Cuba were being dismantled.

Bill also said, "I'm only going to let the telephone ring once. When you hear it, get out of the house right away." What he meant was that we were in the danger zone of nuclear attack.

Days later Bill told me that if the Russians had fired their intercontinental ballistic missiles, they were ready to shoot them down – and that when they couldn't do any more, they had been told to take arms from the armory and go home and defend their families.

I see a correlation between Britain in World War II and America during the Cuban Missile Crisis of the Cold War. In Britain, if the Germans had invaded (they were only 20 miles away in France) the Brits would have fought them with everything they had including pitchforks.

Cuba is but 90 miles away from the United States coastline, but had the nation been struck by nuclear missiles, Americans would have fought the Russian bullies with everything they had.

Will we humans ever be really civilized?

1960 – A baby shower held at my sister-in-law Eleanor's home in San Bruno, California. *(Thaxton family collection)*

1961 – Holding our twins, Susan and John Thaxton, six months old.
(Thaxton family collection)

You Can't Go Home Again

The throb of the engine propellers blocked out all of the passenger noise on the Icelandic flight to England – but not quite. My two little 23-month-old bundles of joy were having a great old time jumping up and down in their seats and yelling. At this point they had been awake for 20 hours. How did I find myself in this predicament, you may ask?

A few weeks prior I had received a letter from my mother at home in Liverpool that my father had another heart attack. I was worried and had a brilliant idea to spend Christmas with my parents. They had never seen the twins who had been born in San Francisco on Dec. 21, 1960. I had emigrated to the U.S. in 1957.

My husband Bill and I had very little money, but came up with enough to get me a ticket on the Trans World Airlines (TWA) 11 p.m. "red eye" flight from San Francisco to New York which then connected to an Icelandic Airlines flight to Prestwick, Scotland. I would then have to take a short bus ride from Prestwick to Glasgow and then take a train down with my children to Liverpool.

I should mention that in those days that children under the age of two years flew for free. We caught the 11 p.m. TWA flight from San Francisco with no problem. I had no idea that this flight would hop city to city across the U.S. making about six stops before landing in New York.

When we arrived in late morning in New York, the twins still hadn't slept. I fortunately had brought their twin stroller which I managed to get from the forwarding baggage department. We weren't scheduled to leave until evening, some six hours later. I pushed them around for a few hours in the airport and then had to return the stroller. I spotted a child-minding room for TWA but when I asked if I could leave the children there for a while, the woman in charge said "No, they were too old to put in the play pens."

I should have complained, but being young and foolish, I didn't. I fortunately did bring along what were known in those days called reins, 1 for each child, like a body harness with a long rein for Mommy to hold onto so they wouldn't keep running off. All was fine for a few minutes until they each decided to toddle off in opposite directions and managed to bind me up quite neatly with the reins. A kindly passerby helped me unravel myself. Later I was desperate for the twins to sleep so the Icelandic stewardess suggested giving them a spoonful of brandy in their bottles. Oh, sweet sleep, all of two minutes. I heard and noise and my son John was crawling up the aisle towards the emergency exit door. His sister Susan was right behind him. We eventually arrived in Reykjavik, Iceland after flying through lightning and thunder for several hours which hardly disturbed me. I was so exhausted. We were put on a bus and driven into town where we had some refreshments. I remember it was daylight and there was lots of snow and ice everywhere. If Santa Claus had flown by on his sleigh, with his eight reindeer, I wouldn't have been surprised.

Our plane took off for Prestwick, Scotland airport and after a short flight we again had to take a bus into Glasgow where we caught a train down to Liverpool.

I felt like a zombie by this time. The twins were still wide awake and played happily on the floor of the train compartment. Being 1962, it was a steam train so they looked three shades darker due to the coal dust.

By the time we got to my parent's home, we had been traveling for 30 hours. My mother didn't look too thrilled to see us. She hadn't made any provision for us to sleep there. Maybe she though we would go to a hotel? I had written to her and explained that perhaps she could rent a bed and cots for the children, but it was too much for her to handle and my money was not enough for a hotel and there was no car available.

The children slept that night in my mother's room which had a very large bed. My father had his own room. I woke up to a loud crash a few hours later.

My son John had crawled from the bed and onto the dressing table knocking everything off.

The next morning Mum was very upset. She said she'd slept in an armchair all night and had had very little sleep. Later I had to wash some nappies for the twins, (there were no disposable diapers in 1962) and I was hanging up their clothes on the line in the back garden. When a woman popped up by the fence saying "Hello, Luv, how are you doing" I looked at her and burst out crying from exhaustion. I told her there was nowhere for us to sleep and I would have to go home, right away. She said come on over to my house with the kids which I did. She was very kind to us and gave us tea. She told me she had been worried about how my Mum would handle things, on account of my Dad being so ill. She offered to let us stay with her while I arranged to fly home.

We had our own room, plus a bed for me and one for the kids. I accepted her offer right away. She and her husband were in their 60s like my Mum, or maybe a few years older. The had one child, a daughter who lived in her own house and was married with two children. May Nichols was a wonderful, practical, kind hearted person. She watched the twins while I went into the city and made arrangements to fly home with BOAC Airlines from Manchester to New York and then on to San Francisco.

I had phoned my husband Bill, the second day and told him what had happened and that there was no way I could stay. He got some money from his mother to pay for the BOAC airline ticket for the difference in the return fares. Icelandic Airlines had been cheaper, but not by much and the return journey was much quicker. We didn't use credit cards in the 1960s. If we had, things would have been a lot simpler. We stayed with Mrs. Nichols for six days. The weather was very cold and damp so by 3'o'clock in the afternoon the light was beginning to fade. I went to the bank and exchanged some U.S. dollars I had into British pounds sterling to buy a few things. I also went grocery shopping for Mrs. Nichols. I took the twins over to my parent's house to visit a few times before we left. We talked very little.

The flight to New York was smooth and uneventful. Going through U.S. Customs in New York the customs official asked me why I was returning so soon. I mumbled I didn't get along with my mother. He just nodded and passed us through. I didn't care what anyone thought. I had a terrible cold and took a swallow from a bottle of cough syrup I had in my purse. The children had caught colds too. When Bill picked us up at the San Francisco Airport, we must have looked like a sorry threesome.

In February of the following year I had a miscarriage and was told I should not get pregnant again as my blood type was not compatible with my husband Bill's. I was O negative and Bill was O positive.

My father died in August 1963 and my husband Bill's mother passed away a short while before. 1962 and 1963 were not good years for us.

In 1964 Bill used his federal G.I. Bill to further his education in engineering. In May 1964, I got a part-time job at the local super market to help out our finances. I worked mostly evenings so I could take care of the twins in the daytime and bill would take over in the evening when he came home. I was there five years and worked 24 hours over a six-day week. Bill also worked part-time jobs while going to school and with the aid of the G.I. Bill, we managed. In those days, we used to go on camping trips for a vacation up and down California, staying in state parks. On our first such trip, the twins were only 18 months old and they loved it.

In later years, we started to travel further afield to Oregon and Washington states. We saw wonderful scenery. One trip to Gold Beach in southern Oregon was exciting. We took a jet boat ride on the Rogue River and saw bald eagles and golden eagles and all manner of wildlife until we landed for lunch at Singing Spring Lodge, a 64 mile round trip. The first time I saw a bear was one evening at our campsite. It came by our tent and I told my husband Bill a big dog had just walked through our site.

He said "That's not a dog, it's a bear!"

One morning I got up and found animals had got into our food locker. Probably raccoons. They scattered the breakfast corn flakes cereal all around. Another time up in Wyoming, a wolf ran right through our campsite. We slept in a cabin that night.

After a while we started camping in Mexico on the Baja Peninsula at a campground called Rosarita Beach, south of the town of Ensenada which was 80 miles from the border. We set up our tent right on the sand like everywhere else. The first time we went there an older lady, close by, was having difficulties setting up her tent which seemed to have, what looked like a hundred pieces of small wood to connect together. It must have been quite old. Bill and several other men put it together. It was still standing when we left.

Another incident was when someone fired a skyrocket and it went right into someone's tent and set it on fire. It was very easy to purchase fireworks in Mexico.

We brought some of our own food with us but had to buy fresh produce and milk and bread from the little grocery store in the camp. Also bottled water. I say that reservedly. One day we witnessed the store clerk filling up bottles from a water spigot at the back of the store. We were lucky because "Montezuma's Revenge" or "Delhi Belly" never hit us. It did effect us many years later staying at hotel resorts in Mexico. Everyone in the compounds were friendly, including the local vendors. We tasted the best tamales sold by women who would walk along the beach, carrying enamel buckets filled with these delicious meat-filled (chicken, pork, beef) tamales to sell for a few pesos.

On our last camping trip to Mexico, we had arranged to visit Connie, my matron of honor at our wedding, on our way home. She was teaching school in

El Centro, a small town inland from San Diego and very near the border. We had to drive through the Anzo-Borrego desert.

Tent camping in Ensenada, Mexico. Susan standing on a chair, son John, middle, and Bill beside our Volkswagen bus – September 1966. *(Thaxton family collection)*

Our old Volkswagen van stalled just as we came to a gas station in the middle of nowhere. Called Coyote Wells, it also had a small bar attached where they served snacks. Bill couldn't get the van to start again, so he called a repair shop in El Centro who specialized in Volkswagens who said they would send a mechanic out to look at it. We settled down to wait and had something to eat and drink inside the bar. The temperature outside was 101 degrees.

The owner went into one of the rooms in back of the bar and then carried a woman out in his arms. We watched fascinated as he placed her gently on the counter behind the bar propping her up with pillows.

"This is my wife, she is very ill, but she still likes to say hello to the customers, don't you hon?"

She gave us a slight smile. She looked so very ill. Maybe she was about 40 years old. Living in the desert and in that heat and in a very lonely spot could kill anyone. We all felt very sorry for her.

After about one hour's wait the mechanic arrived to check on the VW and announced that its engine was kaput. He hitched up the van to the tow truck and we all piled in with the driver. He drove us to an El Centro motel. He told us he could probably have an engine delivered and installed in a couple of days which thankfully he did. Thank God. By that time we had a credit card to pay our expenses with. There was a swimming pool at the motel and we all went in to cool off.

I couldn't get the image of that poor woman in Coyote Wells off my mind. How lucky we had been. We called Connie and arranged to meet her the next day. She took us to see Calexico, Mexico, across the border from El Centro and then we had dinner, a barbecue. Her friend cooked. Connie just rented a very small apartment. She would soon be on the move again. She would eventually become a high school librarian in her hometown of Syracuse, New York.

The heat died down a little in the evening and we took a walk. I remember big fat bugs falling out of the trees and making a plunking sound as they hit the ground. Beautiful fire flies floating above me. I guess you can always find beauty of some kind anywhere.

Bill, John, Susan and I on a camping holiday in Mexico. We splurged one evening on a dinner in town at the Bahia Resort Hotel - 1966. *(Thaxton family collection)*

The Swinging 1960s

Just a few thoughts and memories from the Swinging 1960s as I remember them.

The late 1960s were an exciting time to be living in the San Francisco Bay area. We saw more and more hippies in town. The Haight-Ashbury district and Golden Gate Park was ground zero for the 1967 Summer of Love and the fashions, music and culture spread out to the coastal suburbs. Men and women grew their hair long and beards and mustaches were common. Fashion-conscious women wore peasant skirts and flowery blouses. By the end of that summer, it lost the "love" as thousands of young people poured into the Haight-Ashbury district thinking they would be taken care of. Instead many turned to drugs. Many overdosed and quite a few lost their young lives.

For many, the clean-shaven look of button-down shirts, stiff collars and ties of the 1950s was no longer in style. So too were crew-cut hair styles for men.

In 1964 Bill finished with school and went to work in the electronics industry in Palo Alto. He worked on the development of spacecraft power supplies.

Of course, we were delighted in July 1969, as we all watched on television as Apollo 11 astronauts Neil Armstrong and Buzz Aldrin made man's first landing on the moon. What excitement! Some people just wouldn't believe it was real.

We watched The Beatles first appearance on American television in February 1964 on the Ed Sullivan show. Proud to see four young men from Liverpool take America by storm.

I felt slightly embarrassed by The Beatles, having never seen them before and not being acquainted with rock and roll music. They were just babies when I was a young girl growing up in the wartime Blitz in Liverpool.

But over the years I grew to love them. The funny thing is I had been a member of the famed Cavern Club in Liverpool and used to go there for lunchtime concerts in the mid-1950s. Then it was called the Merseyside Jazz Club.

My friend Marie in Liverpool, her youngest son Stephen, played drums dressed as Ringo Starr, at the later Cavern Club. Her other son John and her three grandsons all played music in Liverpool. The music of The Beatles caused many bands to be created in Liverpool and here in America. My own son John is a musician.

The war in Vietnam by 1968 was brutal. So many young men dead or wounded with no end in sight. Civilians slaughtered and homes destroyed. During this time, there were a lot of protest marches in San Francisco and Oakland. The war ended in 1975 and nothing had been achieved from it.

In 1969 a new community college, now known as Skyline College, opened up near our Pacifica home and I signed up for classes. I enrolled in mostly English, literature, creative writing, philosophy and art. I earned a degree and loved every minute of my classes.

Two proud graduates – My daughter Susan and I in our red cap and gown received our Associate of Arts degrees together at Skyline College in San Bruno. *(Thaxton family collection)*

I remember in 1969 several members of our class walked out and held a protest against the Vietnam War. It was on the front lawn. We weren't shot by National Guardsmen as they were at Kent State University where four students were killed. All we got was grass stains on our slacks.

My husband Bill joined the local little theater group here in Pacifica. He had taken our daughter Susan to try out for a Christmas play. She didn't make it, but they asked Bill if he would like to join. He did and acted in several of their plays. My husband had a rich speaking voice and was a natural actor.

Susan is the dancer in the family and still dances in a show every year.

I'm proud to say that in 1968 I became an American citizen. My brother-in-law Bob and a family friend Bernie were my two witnesses. Lucille, our next-door neighbor, gave a little party in our back yard to celebrate. It was a proud, but humble day for me. They were all wonderful and kind-hearted people. The way I will always think about America and its people. The good will always outnumber the bad. Even in dark and scary times.

Lucille and Oren were our next door neighbors in our little house in the woods. The two of them had also just completed building their log cabin-style home but with all modern conveniences, I should add.

Lucille was raised in Iowa corn country, and Oran in Kansas. She helped me a great deal. I was so new to the country, marriage and motherhood. She showed me how to sew curtains to cover our front windows. Lucille gave birth to her first son three months after my twins were born. There were a lot of babies in our community at that time and Lucille started a co-op babysitting club. She was our first secretary and kept the records. We all babysat for one another so we were all able to go out in the evening with our husbands without it costing anything.

I also joined the Pacifica Teapot Club at that time which included between 20 or 30 British women then living in Pacifica. Most were "G.I." brides from World War II. We used to sell to each other baby and children's clothes which weren't needed anymore in a mock auction. We'd have a good chin-wag and a laugh, and of course lots of hot tea and delicious cake. We even had a brooch in the shape of a teapot to wear. Sadly, the club only lasted a few years as people began to move away to new jobs or bigger houses. I was sorry to see the Pacifica Teapot Club end.

We sold our old house in Pacifica and moved to a larger one during the summer of 1967. I carried on with my retail grocery job but had to take the local Greyhound bus to get to and from work. It meant I had to take a two-mile hike down the large valley we lived in to the coast road. The Greyhound Bus only drove Highway 1, the only main road in our community. I did this for one year. I then learned to drive and my husband and I bought our second car, a Rambler station wagon. I drove for about a year to work and then I had to take time off for hospitalization due to an unexpected heart condition.

Myself, second from the left, second row, seated with fellow members of the Pacifica Teapot Club, a group of between 20 and 30 British women living in Pacifica. Good friends, plenty of chin-wags and laughs. *(Thaxton family collection)*

Our next door neighbors in Vallemar. Wonderful pool parties – 1966.

My son John wears a German trench helmet his grandfather brought back as a souvenir from World War One. His sister Sue, center, and Frankie Simon, son of Mildred Owen. *(Thaxton family collection)*

My husband Bill in San Francisco standing in front of the Balclutha, an old sailing ship – 1960. *(Thaxton family collection)*

Bill, on duty in the California Army National Guard at a Nike missile base located here in Pacifica, California. *(Thaxton family collection)*

My husband, the actor

My late husband Bill enjoyed performing with the Pacifica Spindrift Players. He was a natural actor and had a great stage voice. In the top photo, stage right, he's taking a bow and wears a top hat. Center: he stands stage left; and bottom group cast photo: marked with an "X" in the back row, fifth from the right. *(Thaxton family collection)*

1970's - Visiting Liverpool

1970 - Our family trip to the UK at the Tower of London. A Beefeater guard stands between my son John, left and daughter Susan, right.
(Thaxton family collection)

In 1970 I visited my mother in Liverpool with the twins who were now 9 years old. We stayed about 10 days and this time there was no problem in sleeping arrangements. It was summer and the weather was good. We took Grandma to New Brighton and Blackpool on days out.

We also went with her to see a science fiction movie, "Close Encounters of the Third Kind," which she couldn't understand. Every morning while we were there, my son John, who had discovered a bakery around the corner and he would ask me for a shilling to buy two jelly donuts. Everyone in the store called him the "Little Yank."

My daughter Susan made friends with a nice little girl next door who was about her age and they played out in the street. We learned about one year later that Susan's friend had been killed by a car in the street.

1970 – To visit Grandma with good family friends, the Finnigans in Liverpool. *(Thaxton family collection)*

A family visit to Liverpool in 1976 with members of the Finnigan family. Our son John, back row, second from the left, my husband Bill, just under the lampshade and daughter Susan, foreground in pink pants. *(Thaxton family collection)*

Our son John is a talented musician and plays a variety of instruments. He started with the guitar as a teenager and also plays keyboards and ukelele. *(Thaxton family collection)*

My daughter Susan is a dancer and world traveler. *(Thaxton family collection)*

Mum suggested we might like to go and see Shallcross Manor, the one mentioned in Dad's family pedigree book. She had already visited and didn't want to go again. The kids and I traveled by train to Stockport, near Manchester and then caught a bus to the Peak District in Derbyshire. It was late when we got there so I decided to spend the night in the town of Buxton nearby, a very attractive town in the Peak District National park at The Old Hull Hotel the oldest hotel in England built in 1552 and with connections to Mary Queen of Scots. It was right in the center of Buxton near to where the ancient warm springs were discovered 3,000 years ago by the Celts and were during the Roman conquest. The Roman Baths were built which they called "Aqua Arnemetiae" named after the Celtic goddess of spring.

Buxton Aqua Arnemitiae was an important Roman settlement. It was at the intersection of two main military roads. It was also at the intersection of three main Celtic routes. The spring under the hotel was considered to be an important sacred shrine in pre-Roman times. Unfortunately, the ancient Roman baths are now gone.

We slept in a four-poster bed. The hallways had low, beamed ceilings and as I remember were quite spooky. We enjoyed a great big country breakfast the next morning and left to catch the bus to Taxal Village a few miles away and home of Shallcross Manor.

I had telephoned the home farm which was also named Shallcross Farm. The owner, a Mrs. Lomas said they would meet us at the bus stop.

I should explain that being a very ancient family name some descendants had chosen to use the name Shawcross and not Shallcross. My maiden name was Shawcross. One of the first spellings was Shackelcross.

When we were met by the Lomas family - they broke the news that the manor house was no more. What a disappointment! It had been demolished a few years prior to our arrival. It had been badly damaged and it was decided to tear it down and build a small estate of new houses on the land. It had stood empty after World War II and robbers had stripped all of the copper from the roof causing massive damage from rain. Though my mother claimed it was caused by the Duke of Devonshire's coal mine which went under the house and had caused the real damage.

My mother wrote a letter to the Duke complaining of this. He turned her letter over to the local council and they wrote a letter to my mother saying that they would look into the matter. She never heard anything further. The Duke of Devonshire is the owner of Chatsworth House in Derbyshire. He is one of the richest men in Britain and Chatsworth House is one of the greatest palaces.

My ancestors lost control of Shallcross Manor many years ago. The last time they had anything to do with it was when my great-grandfather leased it for a while on his return from India. He was a civil engineer and worked for the East India Company building the first Indian Railway from Calcutta and Delhi which was an amazing feat. It opened up the country enabling communications, economic prosperity, and of course an ease of moment for the military. Interestingly, in the 1870s at a time of famine the ETR built branch lines to enable food to reach some of the more remote villages. My great-grandfather also worked on the Belfast to Dublin and the Portsmouth to London lines. When he leased Shallcross Manor he and his wife had several children and had brought a "Nana" (nursery maid) back from India with them. At that time illumination at night was by candle light and when the maid was coming down the stairs with a candle in hand she set fire to some drapes and caused a small fire. After his return to India he died in Arras in 1881.

We didn't get to see the manor, but the kids did get to see a working dairy farm and we were given a wonderful farmhouse tea, everything baked fresh by Mrs Lomas and daughter Maureen who kept in touch with me for years.

While we were in England I decided to take the kids to Butlin's Holiday Camp. I had read about them but this was my first opportunity to go to one. The cost again was very reasonable for a one week stay in a chalet for three with breakfast and lots of entertainment!

The one I chose was in Minehead in Somerset. Mum didn't want to go, so we said goodbye with promises to return soon. Bill and I and the twins visited my mother again in 1976 and 1978.

It was a long train journey to Minehead but we enjoyed our stay there which had a lot of activities for children and swimming and concerts and dances in the evening. Susan entered the donkey derby race on a real donkey. The parents placed bets on the race. We also took coach tours, one to Devon and the other to Cheddar Cove and Glastonbury. My son John threw up on the bus. The sausages he had for breakfast didn't agree with him, but the bus driver was very kind and helped with the clean up.

We also spent a few days in London. The kids got to see all of the sights. At the Tower of London a Beefeater took them under his wing. No he wasn't a tower raven - but he explained the old prophesy that if there were no ravens left, the Tower would fall. He also showed us the Bloody Tower and the White Tower.

1970 and 1971 was a time of unrest in America. People were sick and depressed with the Vietnam War. The economy was in a recession. A lot of workers were laid off.

In 1970 the U.S. invaded Cambodia. Thousands of protesters clogged city streets. American troops did not leave the region until 1973.

In 1972 the Watergate break-in happened in the office of the Democratic National Committee. Police found that President Nixon himself was involved in the crime. He had demanded that the Federal Bureau of Investigation stop investigating the break-in and told his aides to cover up the scandal. Before Congress could impeach him, Nixon announced that he would resign. Because of all of the turmoil and unrest many left the United States to go to Canada and even Australia. Most moved out of the larger cities to the countryside or even remoter areas of America.

People were sick of the Vietnam War, sick of all the violent demonstrations, sick of unemployment and government dishonesty. (It sounds a lot like the Trump Administration.)

Bill and I looked into emigrating to New Zealand, but you had to have a job skill they could use. Bill continued to work in the aerospace industry. If we knew how to shear sheep, we would have been accepted.

But life went on and is still going on for me with all its ups and downs and challenges. To paraphrase the poet Dylan Thomas, "I will not go into this dark night quietly. But rage, rage against the dying of the light.

I desperately need a new pair of spectacles.

Printed in Great Britain
by Amazon

THE BULLDOG AND THE BURIED BODY

DOG DETECTIVE - A BULLDOG ON THE CASE

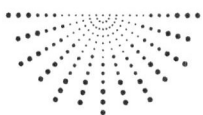

ROSIE SAMS

SWEETBOOKHUB.COM

INTRODUCTION

So many of my readers enjoyed meeting Lola Ramsay and Sassy the Lilac Frenchie that I knew I had to write more books with these wonderful characters.

If you missed them you can find the two books with Lola and the introduction to Sassy in my 20 book box set - The Bakers and Bulldogs Collection.

Sassy is modeled on Lila my Lilac French Bulldog. Lila had been returned to her breeder as she was unwanted. At the time, I was looking for an older, small, short-haired dog to rescue. Something I could cuddle, that would keep me company while I was writing. When I met Lila I fell in love with her and that as they say, was that.

INTRODUCTION

Can you believe that anyone would not want her? She is the sweetest little bundle of love you could ever meet. Well, someone's loss was my gain. She is a joy to live with, though she does like to pinch my socks. Nothing makes her happier than getting out of bed and pinching my socks. It has become such a joke that I put a pair on the bed just for her.

Below are a few of her poses.

Now, all I needed was a new name and so I asked you, my wonderful readers, to come up with a name. There were some great ideas but the one that suited the character the most was Sassy Pants by Sandra H. Thank you, Sandra, we love the name.

I'm so pleased that my wonderful cover designer has managed to bring photos of Lila/Sassy to life for the covers. Much of what Sassy does comes from Lila, you will have to decide if I can hear her talking. 😊 I hate to admit this, but I talk to her constantly.

Read on for my next book, where Sassy and Lola realize

INTRODUCTION

that the house they have bought may come with a lot of trouble. I hope you enjoy it.

Join my newsletter at SweetBookHub.com to grab a FREE copy of Smudge and the Stolen Puppies FREE here

We aim is to entertain you with sweet books that you will love to read and can share with all the family.

If you missed the first book you can grab it here

CHAPTER ONE

OH OH

*L*ola Ramsay relaxed in her seat. Tonight had been a good night and she felt as if everything was going right for once.

Don't jinx it! The thought came automatically, but she pushed it aside.

Even though the steering wheel was on the wrong side, Lola was enjoying the drive. It had been a good night. As they headed out of the historic town of Lincoln, stars shone in the black shy. There was no traffic on the road and she could relax, finally getting used to driving in this sleepy British town.

Next to her, almost dozing in the car, was her friend, Tanya Buchanan. Tanya's neat blonde hair was for the first time ever, a little messy. She leaned against the headrest, trying to catch a few minutes shut-eye. They had been to an exhibition that Tanya had organized at the Lincoln Arts Center.

Lola chuckled as she ran a hand over her own long black hair. How could she find such a simple style so difficult, when her friend was always immaculate? Even sleeping, her hair was neater than Lola's.

"Who cares, me likes you."

The words appeared in Lola's mind and she checked the rearview mirror to see her lilac French Bulldog strapped into the back seat. The small dog's greyish brown mixed coat looked even more lilac as they passed under the yellow glow of a street light.

"Thanks, Sassy," she said back. "I love you too."

A feeling of warmth filled Lola's mind and then Sassy curled up on the seat, her job done.

Lola glanced at Tanya, she hadn't heard anything. Luckily, she just thought Lola was eccentric. So far, Lola hadn't confided in her friend that she could hear animals talk. Well, you wouldn't, would you?

Lola was US ex-military, recently moved to the UK, to see if a change of scenery could help her PTSD. Living in a quaint village, South-Brooke, near to the historic city of Lincoln she had made a new start as a Private Investigator. So far, it was working and she loved her new life. An art exhibition wasn't really her scene, but this one had been special. As a PI, she often had to deal with divorce and cheating spouses, along with one missing cat; they were not the jobs she really wanted! Her last case, however, had been a mix-up. Lola chuckled, those were the words Conner, the son of the murdered man, had used. It must have been a mix-up murder, he had said, as *no one would want to kill my dad*. Ah, the innocence of youth.

During that case, Lola had met the man's PA. A lovely young woman called Louisa Meek. Louisa loved to paint and was very good at it. Life hadn't been kind to her though, and she had been taken advantage of by the rich, older man. Lola had introduced her to Tanya, an art teacher, and recently the new manager of the Lincoln Art Center. Louisa was now their star attraction, and they had just been to her first exhibition. It was an astounding success.

It was late now and driving back, Lola had to concentrate on which side of the road to drive on. Gradually, she was getting used to the differences, but it took time.

The traffic lights changed to red and she slowed to a stop.

"Are we back?" Sassy asked.

"No, a few more minutes."

"Ok."

The lights changed, Lola turned the car left down a narrower street into the village of South-Brooke. The road was on a hill, and in the daylight had a spectacular view out over the countryside. It was a small, quaint village famous for its yew hedges. Lola had recently bought a property there. It was an old garage come office and house. The workshop part was long gone, the rest was currently being renovated ready for Lola and Sassy to move in. As they drove past Lola spotted a light and slowed.

The work was coming on well, soon she would be able to live there but what was the light? Out of the corner of her eyes, she spotted a van and three men. Alarmed, she hit the brakes and stopped the car a little abruptly.

"What is it?" Tanya asked, sitting up.

"There are people there, what are they doing?"

Tanya looked up and peered out of the window. She lifted her phone and took a series of pictures. "It can't be good at this time of night." Tanya rang Wayne Foster, her Detective Sargent boyfriend.

Lola tucked the car into the curb, just past the garage, and opened the door as silently as she could.

"Wait," Tanya called and put her hand on Lola's arm. "Wayne is sending a car, it will be here any minute."

Lola sat back and heard Sassy growl behind her. "I know," she said. "I want to chase them off too."

Tanya laughed. "I swear you talk to that dog as if she understands you."

Lola shrugged, just as they heard the police sirens approaching. The sound of doors slamming was followed by the roar of an engine and a rusty white transit van screeched across the tarmac. As it came up to them, Lola noticed a snake transfer on the door. She could hear Tanya taking more pictures and then the van pulled out onto the roar and raced away.

Lola started the car.

"No, we should wait," Tanya said, panic evident in her voice.

Lola could see she was afraid. She nodded, even though she longed to chase after the van. Still, an American in the UK, tired, late at night on twisty roads she didn't know well... maybe Tanya had a point.

The police arrived and one car set off in pursuit but Lola doubted they would find anything. Where the van had gone there were no cameras and plenty of side roads for the perps to disappear down. Why was she assuming they were up to no good? They could have just been parked there. Then she remembered Alice Beecham, the lovely lady who sold her the garage, saying she had had four people interested in buying it. It seemed strange at the time, the place had been empty for a few years and no one had shown any interest. As soon as Lola wanted it, so did four others. Shaking her head, she clipped a lead onto Sassy's harness and stepped out of the car. Tanya followed, running a hand through her blonde bob. Lola's jaw dropped a little as her hair settled back into perfect form.

Lola and Tanya joined the officers on the large open driveway that used to be the garage forecourt. Wayne arrived just as they got there.

On the ground were a jackhammer and shovels. The men had dug up the tarmac and were starting to dig up the ground.

"What is this about?" one of the officers asked Wayne.

"I don't know lads but I guess we'd better see what they were after," Wayne Foster said and smiled at Tanya.

"Oh-oh," Sassy said. "I know what that smell was, from before."

Lola had an idea she knew what it was too. What had she gotten herself into?

Wayne, a Detective Sergeant, said a few more words to his men and crossed to them. In some ways, he reminded Lola of home. He was tall, maybe a little over 6 feet, with dirty blond hair that was deliberately unkempt. Tanned skin and a beach-ready body, he would look great on the set of Baywatch. He was also Tanya's boyfriend and had helped Lola on her last case.

"What happened?" he asked Tanya.

She took his hand and shook her head. "I have a few pictures but I was sleepy, so I didn't see much."

"Ok, love, send them to me."

"Me too," Lola said.

"Wayne gave Lola a look. "I'll get you taken home," he said to Tanya and waved at one of the men. Tanya was escorted home in her own car, the constable would no doubt make the short walk back.

Wayne turned to Lola. "Do you own this property, Miss?" he asked in a serious voice, before winking at her.

"Yes." Lola quickly explained how she had seen the 3 men bent over the tarmac. "There must have been another as the van drove off quickly."

"I'm sure it's nothing," Wayne said.

Lola felt a tap on her leg. "Body," Sassy said. "Was hard to sniff before, engine oil."

Lola remembered her little bulldog had taken a lot of interest in the ground where the hole was when they first visited the place. At that time, she couldn't work out the scent, as it was masked with engine oil. Now, she obviously could.

"Do you know any more?" Lola asked the bulldog.

"Not yet, hold your horses," Wayne said, chuckling. "I only just got here."

Lola turned back to him, she had, of course, been talking to Sassy.

The Frenchie gave a little grunt of amusement knowing Lola couldn't say more to her even though she wanted to. "Female, buried long years."

"Do you want to stay? It's probably nothing or contraband," Wayne said.

Lola shook her head. "I know this will sound weird, but Sassy was very interested in that spot when we first visited, she's even more so now. I think there might be a body down there."

Wayne's eyes opened wider.

Lola almost said, of a female, but she stopped herself because that would look really weird. "And yes, I want to stay."

Wayne nodded and turned back to his guys. "Ok, lads, we need to dig carefully, this is now a crime scene."

"Boss, it's late and really!" Leo, a young constable with wide eyes and a touch of acne stood with his hands on his hips.

"Do it," Wayne said.

The attitude of the officers changed and the scene was roped off while forensics was sent for. The guys stepped back to wait.

A call came through on the radio, they hadn't found the van and were calling off the search.

Wayne took Lola back to his car, a big blue, unmarked Volvo. "You may as well sit inside," he said, picking up Sassy and rubbing her ears. "We could be here a while."

"Thanks."

"Looks like you might have bought a whole load of trouble," Wayne said handing her Sassy.

Before Lola could reply he was called over to the excavation as more people arrived.

"I think he might be right, Sassy," Lola said.

"Tired now, need to sleep, birds to chase tomorrow." Sassy curled up on Lola's lap and was instantly snoring.

"Oh, if only I could sleep like that."

CHAPTER TWO

A PRINCESS AND A PORTIA

"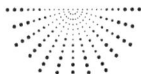eed wee-wees," Lola heard in her mind and she felt a warm breeze brush across her face. Batting it away, she grabbed the covers and rolled over. It was too early to get up, all she wanted to do was sleep.

The luxury of the bed tugged her down but the covers were pulled back again. With a sigh, she grabbed them and pulled them over her once more. Too sleepy to realize what was happening she snuggled down even deeper into that luxurious early morning snooze.

"Woof," Sassy barked in her face and then squealed her high-pitched squeal. The one that sounded like a baby pig being murdered.

Lola's eyes burst open.

"What is it, little monkey?" Lola asked.

"Need wee-wees." Sassy sat looking at her, her eyes wide and her bottom lip stuck out very slightly.

"Okay." Lola threw the sheets back and climbed out of bed. She was wearing dark blue pajamas with a dancing dog on the front. Quickly, she grabbed a dressing gown and tried to slip her arms into it. It was almost as if the sleeves had been sewn up, the more she tried the harder it was.

Stumbling, she sat back down on the bed and managed to get her right arm in.

"Desperate," Sassy said hopping about at the closed bedroom door.

With her dressing gown now on, Lola ran a hand through her hair and despaired. It would have to do. "Come on then, Monkey, let's let you out."

"Not a monkey." Sassy trotted off down the hallway and disappeared down the stairs as Lola followed as quickly as her muddled brain and sleepy body could.

Downstairs, Tanya sat at the table drinking coffee. She looked immaculate and Lola felt her confidence sink a little bit more. It didn't matter, she opened the door and let the little Frenchie run out into the garden.

Lola stumbled to the table and sat down to find a cup of coffee waiting for her. She smiled her appreciation at Tanya. "Is Wayne in?"

Tanya shook her head. "He left me a message, he didn't get back last night. I'm not sure when he will be back today. How are you doing? What does this do to your move?"

Lola let her eyes open wide. "First, she doesn't want me to go, now she's worried I won't be going!" she said, chuckling to let Tanya know she was joking.

Tanya punched her arm gently. "You know I don't mean that, you can stay here as long as you want... but how are you doing?"

"I'm not worried about the garage or the move," Lola said. "That will come when it comes. I'm kicking myself because Sassy was sniffing at that area before I bought the place. I should've known something was wrong."

"You can hardly call SOCO every time Sassy sniffs at something, now can you?"

Lola chuckled. "SOCO?"

"Scene of Crime Officer."

Lola was gradually getting used to the different terminology here in the UK. "You're right, I guess I'm just tired."

"You should get some more sleep," Tanya said just as the postman knocked at the door. Tanya opened it, accepted the letters and a small parcel from him, she thanked him, and came back to the table. "This one's for you," she said handing over the parcel.

A smile crossed Lola's face for she knew what it was. Sassy was going to be so happy but how could she describe it to her friend. After all, she had bought this for a French Bulldog!

"Are you going to open it?" Tanya asked.

"You will laugh," Lola said hanging onto the parcel.

"Now you have to open it, I'm intrigued."

Lola tore open the packaging just as Sassy came running through the door.

"Is it for me?" Sassy asked.

Wrapped in an abundance of tissue paper was a small, pretty pink tiara, a dog tiara.

Tanya laughed. "Only you could do this, come on, I have to see her wearing it."

Lola removed all the paper and told Sassy to sit. The little Frenchie was finding it hard to keep still. Her bottom kept almost touching the floor but was actually polishing it with the jiggly movements she made. Lola could see a bright smile on her face and her eyes were wide in her excitement to prove that she was a princess.

"If you don't sit still, I can't put it on," Lola said.

"There you go again, I swear that dog understands you," Tanya said.

Lola chuckled. "She better, if she wants to wear this." Lola held out the Tiara.

Sassy whined and managed to sit still, but her body was still shaking. Lola put on the tiara; it fit perfectly and she had to admit that the little Frenchie did look very regal. "What do you think?" Lola asked, turning to Tanya.

"It suits her, here let me take a picture," she said pulling her phone out of her purse and taking some quick snaps. "Now, I have to run. Why don't you get another couple of hours of sleep; you must've hardly gotten any sleep last night." With that Tanya was gone and Lola was left alone with her best friend.

Sassy was bouncing about on the floor moving her head from side to side and trying to be as regal as she could. "What look like?"

"Like a Princess," Lola said.

Sassy spun around in a circle, jumping up and barking, and then spinning around again.

"Careful, you'll shake it loose."

The little Frenchie slowed and walked gently to the door with her head high. Looking back over her shoulder and then at the door. "I have to show Princess Portia Ebony Blaze," Sassy said. "She can't deny I'm a princess now, every bit as good as a cat. She will have to call me Princess."

Lola opened the door and let her through it again. Sassy ran out into the garden, but the cat was nowhere in sight. It didn't deter the little bulldog; she went down to the favorite spot that Portia liked to sit and sat waiting for her. It had amused Lola so much that the next door's cat called herself Princess Portia Ebony Blaze and said that all dogs were stupid. She had come up with the idea of getting Sassy the tiara to put Portia in her place. It was going to be amusing to see the cat's reaction.

Lola heard her mobile beep and scrolled to find a new message. It was from Mia Simpson, a young local girl who was constantly losing her own cat. It appeared that Tiger had gone missing once more. Mia didn't want to go to school until he was found.

Lola knew she had to stop this, or Mia would have her searching for the cat every day. However, there was no point going back to bed and she had nothing else on so she decided she may as well have a walk and see what she could find. She sent a quick text back saying she was on the case.

Sassy sat in the garden, her head high, showing off her tiara. Lola glanced around, she could see that Portia was hiding. The black cat was on top of the fence, sat behind a tree, and was watching Sassy. Her black tail swished back and forth with agitation. The cat didn't know that Lola could hear her and so she snuck down to the garden. Pretending she couldn't see Portia she got close enough to listen.

"That mangy mutt," Portia said. "Pretending to be royal; it takes more than cheap jewelry to be a royal, you have to be born with it. I should maybe scratch her and chase her out of my garden."

Lola couldn't help but chuckle. It seemed that the rivalry between the two of them was heating up. Luckily, Sassy didn't really mind, she just hated it when the cat had called her a stupid dog.

"Is it really your garden, Portia?" Lola asked staring straight at the cat.

Portia leaped up into the air meowing and landed on the ground on their side of the fence. "Witch!" she said arching her back and hissing before running as if to cross the garden only to find Sassy blocking her way.

"Morning," Sassy said, waving her head to show off the tiara. "You have to call me Princess Sassy now."

Portia jumped into the air once more, reaching what looked to be about 5 feet off the ground, and landed back on her feet.

Sassy's eyes opened wide at such an amazing display. "Wow, that was really cool."

Portia sat and started to preen, by licking her feet. "Cats are cool," she said pretending as if she'd never jumped out of her skin.

Lola jumped as she heard her mobile ringing. It wasn't a real scare of a jump, not her PTSD kicking in, maybe she was too tired for that. Taking one last look at the two animals she walked back to the house to answer the phone.

The call had gone to voicemail; it was Alice, the lady who owned the garage before her. Lola listened to the message and knew she had to call her back straight away. Maybe she had a case, after all.

CHAPTER THREE

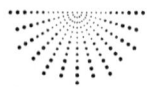

ONE CASE SOLVED

Alice Beecham was in her early forties. A little eccentric but someone that Lola had grown to love. The woman rode her pushbike everywhere and had an 82-year-old brother who was in a home with dementia. Lola had never asked about the age difference between Alice and her brother, but she knew her parents were deceased.

Finding Alice's number she called her back.

"Lola, oh it is so good to hear your voice," Alice said. "I don't know what to do, you know I don't like him but this... I can't believe this."

"Alice, it's all right, what is the problem?"

"It's Mick, he's to be arrested for murder. Did you hear..."

Lola tried to interrupt but Alice was babbling at such a pace that she couldn't get a word in and she knew it was best to let her speech run its course.

"There was a body found in the garage. The one my brother used to own. Oh, thank goodness he doesn't own it anymore, what would that do to him? Oh no, I'm so sorry I sold it to you, and now you have all the stress. Mick was a bad sort but I don't believe he could ever be involved in a murder. The problem is that he won't remember. Will you help me? I will pay your normal rates, just please say I haven't damned him by telling you he was a bad sort. I could never forgive myself if I had." Alice stopped and drew in a deep breath.

"Of course, I will help you and him," Lola said. "I was there when they discovered the body. Don't worry, I will see that justice is served."

Thank you, thank you so much," Alice said.

Lola found out a little more and soon realized it was not as bad as Alice first thought. The police were going to question Mick this afternoon; she would call Wayne and see if she could be there. She had been careful to not promise Alice she would get her brother off; if he was guilty, then he would pay the price.

Hanging up the phone she dialed Wayne, but he was not available so she left him a message. There was nothing she could do, for now, so she would take Sassy for a quick walk and find Tiger. Dropping the phone on the table she poured another coffee; 5 more minutes wouldn't hurt.

A ping on Lola's phone drew her eye. She picked it up from the table and saw that it was Mia, still worried about Tiger. Sending back a quick message, that she was on the case, she noticed the text from Tanya the previous evening. It had the pictures that Tanya had taken while they were outside the garage. Lola had looked at them the previous night, but the light was so bad that she hadn't been able to see anything. As Sassy was in the garden looking for a place to do her business, Lola decided to take another look.

Opening the first picture she couldn't see much. It was blurred and dark and all she could tell was that there were three people and a white van, but she couldn't see much else.

The next photo showed a tall slim person. It had to be a man; however, she couldn't be 100% sure. He was turning away from them and you could only see a touch of his profile.

More photos showed little else. On one, you could see that one of the men was shorter and broader and had grey hair. The third man she could never really get a good look at. Tanya had, however, got a picture of the van. It didn't show the registration plate but it did show the transfer on the driver's door of the snake. It was a cobra, small and worn and quite indistinct. However, anyone who knew the van would recognize it. This was the first clue.

Sassy came trotting in. "Portia's hiding," she said and sat in front of Lola with her back legs stuck out in front of her and her bottom lip protruding just a little.

"Don't you worry, you are my Princess."

Sassy jumped up and spun around in a circle. "Walkies!"

"Just on time," Lola said as she got the service harness down that the Frenchie wore. As a fully trained support dog, Sassy was allowed into all sorts of different places, as long as she was wearing her special jacket. Lola didn't expect to be going anywhere where they would need it, but she was sure that Mia would find it comforting if they couldn't find Tiger.

Lola attached the harness and took off the tiara.

"Oh, I want to be a princess!" Sassy's bottom lip was out again and she was giving a fair bit of side-eye.

"You can be later," Lola said as she attached the lead and they set off out the door.

Tiger was a big ginger tomcat who knew that Lola could hear him. The chances of him being anything but out on the prowl were rare, but she knew that wouldn't stop Mia from worrying.

As they stepped out of the house Lola bent down and whispered, "can you find Tiger?"

Sassy closed her eyes, raised her nose and sniffed into the air. It made her look as if she was trying to stop a sneeze. With her nose high she sniffed and sniffed turning left and right slowly. "Can't find."

"Never mind, keep sniffing and hopefully, we'll find him soon." Lola set off along the road planning to walk to the next street and then up the hill and then around in a circle. Tiger was probably at the park or in one of the big gardens. He liked to hunt birds and lady cats.

As they turned onto the hill, Sassy increased her pace. "Tilly?"

"Not just yet," Lola said. Sassy was asking if they were going to the shop, Tilly's Place, owned by one Tilly Trotter. The rather eccentric shop owner had become a firm friend and a great source of information. Tilly looked a little bit like a mole peering out through her round glasses and wrinkling her nose. However, she was sharp as a knife and had her finger on the pulse of everything that was happening. Once they found the errant tomcat, they may go and see her. Perhaps she would recognize the van?

"This way," Sassy said and led them down the street towards the churchyard.

"Can you smell him?"

"Not sure, think so, faint." Sassy continued trotting along sniffing the air and occasionally the ground. Then she stopped, her whole body stiffened and her eyes almost popped from her face. She was straining against the lead, leaning into her harness, desperate to escape.

"What is it?" Lola asked.

Sassy let out a squeal of such desperation. "Squirrel!"

Hopping along the wall of the churchyard, about 30 feet in front of them, was a grey squirrel. Sassy was convinced that the squirrels were working together and were planning something bad. It was her mission to stop it. Never once had she got close to catching a squirrel, but if off the lead, she would certainly try.

The furry tree rat hopped off the wall, into a beech tree, and was gone. The pressure on the lead released a little and Sassy sat down. "Lost it," she said in a despondent voice.

Lola tried not to chuckle and then she spotted Tiger walking across one of the yew hedges the village was famous for. When you looked at them they didn't look real, they were like something perfectly molded and yet they were living breathing trees first planted in the 1800s.

Walking along the top of one of the hedges, Tiger was stalking a blackbird. Crouching down, he moved along so slowly that the bird didn't see him. Just as he was about to pounce Sassy let out a yip of excitement. "Found him," Sassy said.

The blackbird took to the wing with a squawk of warning to all the other birds around. Tiger turned his eyes on Sassy.

Lola and the Frenchie made their way across to the hedge. The cat sat at about eye height and glared down at the bulldog.

"That was not very sporting," Tiger said. "I was looking forward to a bit of blackbird."

Sassy was so excited she was jumping up and spinning around in circles. "Have you seen Portia?" she asked. "I have something I need to show her... again. I saw her but don't think she noticed."

Tiger sat up straight and licked his right front paw, taking his time to answer the question. "Rather snooty that one. I tend to avoid her."

Lola knew she mustn't chuckle or the cat would not cooperate but she remembered Sassy telling her that Portia had scratched Tiger's face when he became rather amorous one evening.

"Hey, Tiger, how you doing?" Lola asked.

The cat slowly turned his eyes to Lola and blinked. He was actually quite a friendly cat, but he still liked to pretend that he viewed all humans with disdain. After another few licks, he put his paw down. "It's been a good morning," he said. "Well, until just now!" His eyes opened wide and he shook his head.

"Mia has been looking for you," Lola said. "Is there any chance I can take you home so she can go to school?"

Tiger sighed as if it was all too much trouble and then his eyes opened wide. "Do you have any of those shriveled fish?"

Lola remembered that he liked the dried sprats that she sometimes kept for Sassy. "Not on me, but I can certainly get you some."

"Well, in that case, as the dogs chased off all the birds, I may as well go home. I think you should carry me."

Lola bit back a chuckle and picked the big cat off the hedge stroking his head as she tucked him into the crook of her arm. It would only be a couple of minutes' walk home; however, he was quite a heavy little pussycat.

Lola knew that she couldn't keep searching for the cat every day. "Would you do me a favor?" she asked.

"I'm not sure about that," Tiger said.

"How about for five sprats?"

Lola could hear Tiger umming and ahhing in her mind as he tried to make a decision. "Okay, what is it?"

"Could you delay your daily walk until after Mia has gone to school?"

"I will do my best," he said as they arrived back at his home.

Mia came running out of the house, her long brown hair loose and flying around her like a mane. Her big brown eyes were red and tears smeared her face. "Oh, you found him!" she said running to grab Tiger from Lola's arms.

The cat leaned into her and purred for all he was worth. At least one case was solved successfully today but, how would she do on the murder investigation?

CHAPTER FOUR

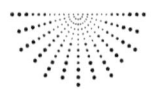

TILLY'S PLACE

*L*ola tried Wayne once more, but he still wasn't answering. It either meant he was busy, or he was avoiding her call. That was slightly worrying, but there was nothing she could do about it for now. As a local detective inspector on the Lincoln Police Force, she really could do with his help; however, she had to understand that his bosses may not like that.

What could she do to help Mick now? Then it came to her, a visit to the shop to talk with Tilly might give her lots of ideas. After all, if anyone was going to recognize that van it would be Tilly.

"Should we go see Tilly?"

Sassy spun in a circle and gave a quick bark, so her mind was made up. Lola stopped to check the road, but it was all clear. There was never much traffic in the village; the peace and quiet was one of the things she loved about it. Crossing the road they headed up the hill towards the shop that Tilly owned. At one time, some of the local youth would crowd around the entrance, but it seemed to have stopped now. One of the boys, Sam Smith, had become a good friend of Lola and Sassy. They often met him at night and walked together. The boy had once been trouble, but he had pulled himself around and was now even thinking of joining the police force. It was things like this that made Lola's work so rewarding.

As they walked along Lola began to wonder how useful Sassy's nose would be on this case. The dog was great at sniffing out the clues, but the body had been buried for a few years. She guessed there was only one way to find out. "Sassy, the lady buried at the garage, could you smell her?"

Sassy stopped and turned and sat and looked up at her, tilting her head from side to side. "Yes, of course."

"I understand. I mean would you be able to smell something of hers, now."

Sassy closed her eyes and sniffed the air. Lola had to stop herself from chuckling. "I don't mean here right now."

"Can't smell her," Sassy said.

"What I mean is... well... if there was something of hers that we found, would you be able to tell it was hers?"

Sassy scratched her ear, a sign that she was stressed.

"It doesn't matter, don't worry about it," Lola said.

"Sniffies are different on different things. Some hold sniffies a long time, others not long."

That made sense. If there was evidence remaining there for Sassy to find it, it would depend on what the evidence was. Lola shook her head. She didn't even have a suspect and so there was no evidence for Sassy to find.

"If I found her socks, would smell," Sassy said and grinned. "Socks are the best."

Lola nodded, however, she doubted that a murderer would have kept socks. Unless they were a murderous French Bulldog!

They arrived at Tilly's shop and the doorbell jangled as she opened it and walked through. Lola felt only the smallest twinge of panic, and Sassy bumped her leg and sent the feeling of love to her. Lola knew she was getting so much better. At one time the harsh jangling of the bell would have sent her into a panic. It would have transported her back to the heat and oppression of Afghanistan, back to the terrors of war.

Tilly was behind the counter, serving a customer. The elderly woman turned and nodded at Lola as she walked out.

"Oh, my," Tilly said as she came around the counter bending down to pick up Sassy. "It seems like forever since I last saw you, how are you both doing?"

"We are good, thank you," Lola said.

Sassy was lying on her back in Tilly's arms having her belly rubbed. She was certainly good.

"I was just about to stop for a cupper, would you like one?" Tilly asked, without waiting for an answer she turned to walk through the door in the back of the shop into her private quarters.

Lola followed and sat down at the table. The small back room was a little cluttered with bottles and jars everywhere, but the table was clear and Lola took a seat while Tilly put the kettle on the stove.

"I was wondering if you could look at some pictures for me," Lola asked. "You might be able to recognize the van, or possibly even the people in them."

Tilly turned and pushed her glasses up her nose. They seemed to make her eyes look huge but her smile was bright and excited. "Is this to do with the case?"

"It is; did you hear about the body at the garage?"

Tilly nodded. "That was really sad. Oh, and you own it now! Is that going to cause all sorts of problems?"

"It puts things on hold for a little while but I'm not worried about that," Lola said. "After all, I was probably in Afghanistan when the murder took place."

"It's definitely a murder then!" Tilly looked even sadder.

"I haven't had it confirmed but it would seem strange to bury someone in such a way if it wasn't."

"Of course, that was silly of me. I just hate to think of someone being murdered in our little village."

Lola nodded and felt a strange sense of belonging at the use of the term our village. She guessed she was accepted here.

As she spoke Tilly prepared the tea, putting a large green teapot on the table along with 2 cups. Sassy had been following her around the kitchen and Tilly suddenly realized she hadn't given her anything. With a little chuckle, she grabbed a gravy bone treat and passed it to the little dog. Sassy took it gently and then curled up in the corner to enjoy her prize.

Now sitting down, with the tea poured, and a piece of cake each, Lola pulled out her phone and scrolled to the pictures.

"Can you have a look through these, and see if you recognize anything?"

Once more, Tilly pushed her glasses back up her nose and peered down at the phone. "Oh, yes, that's March's van," Tilly said. "I haven't seen it for a long time, I'm surprised it's even road legal now. This means the three people will most likely be String Bean, Bruiser, and Rooster. They certainly are a bad bunch; if they're involved then they are up to no good."

"Are they their real names?" Lola asked.

Tilly chuckled. "No, they all had nicknames."

"You said they were a bad bunch. What can you tell me about them?"

"Well, nothing was ever proven, but they were suspected of stealing high-end cars back in the day when you could steal them much more easily; it's all electronics now. The thefts probably stopped about 5 to 7 years ago. Let me think back to then." Tilly took a sip of her tea, her eyes far away as she tried to recall the details. "One thing I do remember, they were friendly with our pal, Brent Burton!"

Lola felt a shiver run down her spine. On her previous case, it appeared that Brent was one for the ladies and he liked them young. How old was the buried body? Could Brent have killed her? Part of Lola hoped so for she wanted this man in jail. Another part of her hoped not, she hoped the rumors about Brent were just that.

"There were young ladies at the garage but nothing was ever proven. I tried to find ways to shut them down, but they were clever and they never got caught as far as I know."

"Do you think it's possible that this girl, the one they found buried at the garage, was one of Brent's lady friends? Perhaps something went wrong and he killed her?"

"I wouldn't put it past him. I don't remember any girls going missing, but she doesn't have to be local. Things were different back then too, so if no one missed her, no one would be looking. I will tell you what I can about the others. Let's hope I can finally see Brent behind bars." Tilly took another sip of her tea and her eyes drifted off once more.

CHAPTER FIVE

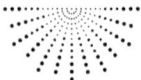

THE SUSPECTS

*L*ola sat quietly while Tilly gathered her thoughts. It was hard, she had that sense of excitement that came when a lead presented itself. Lola had long been a woman of action, and to sit still was against her nature. Every part of her wanted to hunt these men down, to find the evidence, and to send them to a place where they would never hurt another person again. However, she knew she had to be patient. Tilly was her best bet to get a lead and she must give her time to gather her thoughts.

"It was all so long ago," Tilly said. "But maybe I should start with the easy things. Let me have another look at the photos."

Lola scrolled through her phone to find them once more and passed it across to Tilly.

"Yes," Tilly said tapping the screen. "You can't really make him out but that one has to be String Bean, sometimes called Beanie. He got that name because he's tall and thin, around 6 foot 2 I think. A gaunt-looking man with an angular face and thin brown hair. Brown eyes if I remember rightly but I might be wrong. However, I digress, he got the nickname String Bean because he always wore green overalls. Being tall and thin and frankly, I believe he stood about a lot, the guys said he looked like a string bean hanging off the shelves."

"Can you tell me anything about him, what he might have been involved in, what he does now?" Lola asked.

"Well, like all of them he worked for Mick Beecham at the time at the garage, the one that was where your property is now. I'm so sorry about getting you involved in that."

"Don't be, it will be fine, and if I hadn't I wouldn't have taken any notice and they would have got away with this. No doubt, they were moving the body in case it got found during my renovations. They were foolish, I had no intention of digging that area up!"

"Maybe some good came out of this then," Tilly said. "Right, I don't know how much Mick knew about the err... well.... the goings-on there. I guess he must've known something. However, he was not the brightest button in the box. I've said before, Mick was not a very nice person, not well-liked but I don't think he would've been involved in the really nasty things. Of course, I could be wrong."

Tilly looked so worried that Lola reached out and took her hand. "It's okay, if he is innocent this will help prove it." Lola knew that Tilly and Alice, Mick's sister, were good friends. It would be hurting Tilly to say anything against him. But she had to steer her back to the conversation. So far, she hadn't been able to find anything out about Mick. He was still at the home, but she didn't know what the police knew. Until she heard from Wayne she wouldn't find out anything else.

"String Bean, what is his real name and do you know what he's doing now?" Lola asked gently.

"If I remember right, his real name is Paul... now, what was it? Oh yes, Norton. I've not heard much about him, he doesn't live in the village but I believe he works for March's Motors. We will get to March soon enough."

"What can you tell me about March's Motors?" Lola asked, feeling her excitement churn inside.

"Well," Tilly flicked through the other pictures. "I don't see March here, but you said the van drove off very quickly so he could have been driving. March or Marty Stevens is one of the worst of them. He got his nickname because he was jittery, with a full head of red hair that tended to stand on end. The man could never stand still. If anything happened he bolted like a hare. The police raided the place a few times back in the day and Marty was always the first to be gone. So, they called him mad as a March hare, which became March. Unlike most people, he didn't mind the nickname; in fact, I think he loved it hence when Mick closed his garage, March opened another one, it's two villages down and he called it March's Motors."

"What does he do at the garage?" Lola asked. Whatever it was, she imagined it was a good place to start investigating.

In the corner, Sassy began to snore. They both looked around to see her lying on her side, eyes closed, her legs galloping as if she was chasing after some imaginary bird. A combination of yips, barks, and grunts came from her. It lightened the mood and both Lola and Tilly let out a chuckle.

"I wish I could sleep that easily," Tilly said.

Lola had to agree, to be able to sleep like a dog would be an amazing thing.

Looking back at the photos Tilly nodded her head. "From the size of this man, I would think he's Bruiser, also known as Larry Floyd. Larry was the muscle, I had him down at the time as the enforcer. Keeping everyone in line. He's a bulky man, works out a lot, and always looks as if he has no neck. I think he was around 5 foot 10 and from what I've heard he has no morals. To look at he was thickset, with short brown hair, and a big chubby face lined with red veins, I can't remember much more about him and I haven't seen him for some time."

"That's good, I can probably find out where he is now and go to speak to him. What about the third person? Do you recognize him?"

Tilly peered at the photos, flicking back and forth and concentrating so hard that her nose seemed to twitch. "I can't work it out from the picture, but I would have to imagine it would be Rooster, also known as Gary Thomas. Rooster was a real lady's man, he worked closely with Brent. I could never prove anything but I think he was the one who supplied the ladies for Brent. He had red hair and always seemed to have a red face. The men said he strutted around like a Cockrell and liked the sound of his own voice so, in their words, he crowed a lot, hence the name Rooster. I believe he still has ties to Brent but I don't know how to prove it."

"That is amazing, thank you so much for helping me with this. Can you tell me any more about the garage, March's Motors?"

"It's a bit of a rough sort of place and out of the way so I don't know how it gets any business," Tilly said raising her eyebrows to suggest that it was probably into criminal activities. "I had heard that Brent has their company cars serviced there. I don't drive anymore so I can't go out and have a look, I guess I kind of gave up on catching Brent." Tilly looked so sad.

Lola was surprised that Sassy was instantly awake. The little Frenchie came up to Tilly and sat at her side rubbing her head against her leg.

Tilly scooped her up into her arms and nuzzled her head against Sassy's. "Oh, aren't you such a little treasure."

Lola had to agree.

For a few minutes, they chatted and ate cake while Lola thought about all she had heard. The excitement inside her was building. On her last case, she had wanted to put Brent Burton away. The man was a highly respected businessman who ran a successful architect company but she knew he was bad. It was something about him and though she had a video of his business partner saying things that were bad for Brent, they weren't evidence; well, not enough. Maybe this time she would get him and her thoughts drifted to Sam Smith. The young man who had come so far, the young man who thought Brent was his father.

If she could link Sam's mother, Beccy Smith, to Brent would she be able to get the man locked away?

CHAPTER SIX

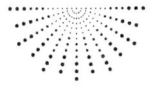

SHUT OUT

When Lola left Tilly's shop she tried calling Wayne again, and this time he answered.

"Hey, Lola, look, I'm sorry but I can't discuss the case with you," Wayne said and even down the phone, she could tell that he was either stressed, tired, or angry. Possibly even a combination of all three.

"Can you at least let me know what is happening with Mick... Mick Beecham?" Lola waited and she could hear Wayne let out a breath. Something had changed, something that he wasn't telling her. Before, he had always helped her out and she felt as if she had an asset. Was it because she owned the garage?

"Why are you asking?" Wayne asked, his voice curt.

"Alice, his sister, has hired me to help him out. Do we know if it's murder?"

Wayne let out another sigh. "I can't tell you much. The autopsy will be back later, then we will know what we're looking at. Still, he looks good for this. There were rumors about that place for years and now a body has been found... it was his garage, he had to have known."

"Maybe," Lola said, "but his health, how could he be arrested?"

"We are waiting for the judge to rule on his suitability for questioning and for standing trial," Wayne said. "At the moment, he is still in the home, we are just asking that they keep him there."

"He's not been arrested?" Lola asked as she was sure that was what Alice had said.

"No, not yet, maybe never. Alice might just be panicking, I'm sure the home let her know we are talking to him."

Lola was pleased that Wayne seemed to be opening up to her and she wondered if she could push it. "Do you have an identity on the body yet?"

"I can't talk about that... look, I have to..."

Lola cut him off. "I may have a lead for you."

"Okay... we can talk tonight. I don't want to be seen talking to you too much; after all, you are involved in this as you own the property where the body was found."

Lola understood, of course, that was why he had pulled away from her. Why he had shut her out. Offering her thanks, she let him go.

Lola went back to Tanya Buchanan's lovely house. It was where she had been staying since she arrived in the United Kingdom from the USA. Tanya was a friend she had met many years ago. They had hit it off and kept in touch. Tanya was also Wayne's girlfriend so she would see Wayne that evening, she hoped.

Back at the house, Lola heard *Princess* in her mind and so she put the bulldog's tiara on.

Sassy stared wistfully at the back door. Lola opened it allowing her into the garden. Sassy would normally bound out and chase birds, butterflies, or if she was really lucky, a squirrel. Today she sat with her back legs stuck out in front of her and her bottom lip protruding a little.

"What's wrong?" Lola asked.

"Princess Portia Ebony Blaze is not there."

Lola bit back a chuckle, Sassy was desperate to have the cat acknowledge her new tiara. "Maybe she is, why don't you go have a sniff around?"

Sassy looked around her eyes wide. "You think?"

"Yep, she could be hunting in the bushes."

A feeling of joy flooded Lola's mind and Sassy raced off into the garden sniffing at all the bushes. Lola wanted to stand and watch her but she decided to do some work.

First, she rang the nursing home where Mick was staying and confirmed what Wayne had said. Sure enough, Mick was in his room as normal. The staff said he had been questioned, but not formally, and that the police had not really got any sense out of him.

Next, Lola rang Alice.

"Hey, Alice, it's Lola."

"Oh, my, have you found anything out yet. Is Mick safe?"

"I want you to know that there is no need to worry. Mick is still at the home. I might want you to come with me and talk to him sometime. He's not under arrest, they may want to talk to him but it is nothing to worry about at the moment."

"We can go now! We need to keep him free." Alice said.

"No, not just yet..." Lola didn't want to talk to Mick until she had worked out the right questions to ask. If he did understand and she went in unprepared he could hide things. She wanted to take him by surprise, and if she could, get him to implicate Brent Burton. However, she didn't want Alice to know that. "He is not under arrest; the police are just asking him some questions." Lola didn't mention them seeking a judge's approval to arrest the man. It wouldn't help for Alice to worry until that was a given, or not!

"Are you sure? I'm so worried."

"You do not need to worry about Mick, I have some leads I am chasing down, just leave it to me and I will be back in touch once I know some more."

"Will it be today?" Alice asked. "I won't go for my bike ride if I need to wait for you."

"No, I doubt very much that it will be today. You go out on the bike and enjoy yourself. Don't worry, I will do all I can to find out the truth."

"Thank you so much," Alice said. "Toodles."

With that, she was gone.

Lola went through the evidence in her mind and felt a little sad. There was every chance that Mick knew something about this. Every chance that he was involved. Of course, with his dementia, there was every chance that he wouldn't remember." Lola hoped she wouldn't hurt Alice by finding out that her brother was a cold-blooded killer.

CHAPTER SEVEN

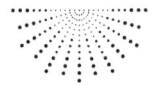

A HELPING HAND

*L*ola decided she wouldn't go out and visit any of her suspects until she had spoken to Wayne. After all, she didn't even know for sure that this was a murder. She also felt that giving Wayne this information before she had dug too deeply would act as good faith, or at least she hoped so.

She spent the rest of the afternoon researching the suspects. March's Motors had no online presence. That was not just strange but unheard of. What business didn't have an online presence. Next, she did a deep dive on the internet on the four men. They all had some social media content except March, Marty Stevens, himself. The one with the largest online presence was, Larry "Bruiser" Floyd.

No matter how far she searched, Lola couldn't find anything about Larry that pointed to him being a hardened criminal. His Facebook page had him as a retired mechanic who loved his family. It was prolific, there were lots and lots of photos and videos of Larry with his daughter. Nicole Floyd had long brown hair and big doe eyes. She was very skinny, almost verging on anorexic, and looked like the sort that wouldn't say boo to a goose. She lived with her dad and the house looked tidy and well cared for as did her children. The two children, Larry's grandchildren, were delightful.

Looking around Facebook, Lola found out that Larry junior was a six-year-old cheeky-looking boy with spiked brown hair and the biggest smile. He liked nothing more than to laugh and to giggle. A few videos had him playing pranks on his granddad. Sometimes, he would sneak up on Larry senior who would be looking the other way. Little Larry would pinch something off the table. Larry senior would then pretend to look back and be astonished that it was gone. Larry junior would laugh so much that sometimes he dropped to the floor holding his belly with tears running down his face. The relationship between Larry "Bruiser" Floyd, and his namesake was charming. There was nothing but kindness in the older man and even though he still was bulky and looked as if he could manage for himself, there was nothing to suggest that he had once been a dangerous enforcer.

His second grandchild, Sabrina, was 5 ½. With long brown hair, she longed to be a dancer. There were many videos of her dancing in various styles. A particularly cute one showed her wearing a pink tutu as she tried to pirouette around the garden. In the background, Larry could be seen laughing and smiling.

Could this really be the man that Tilly had described? There was nothing to point to him being a criminal. Lola found nothing to point to him being anything other than a loving father and grandfather.

Lola searched and searched to see if she could find any old news reports of his dastardly behavior. Way back, he was arrested for assault outside a nightclub. Reading the article, it was hard to tell who was at fault. A gang of drunken lads had started a fight. Though this may point to his character, it was hardly damning. Of course, if he had been investigated and not enough evidence was forthcoming, that wouldn't be something she could find.

Lola started to search for Gary "Rooster" Thomas. His social media was much more sparse and much different in content. There were pictures of him drinking with other men who didn't seem involved. Though his hair was thinning, it was almost exactly as Tilly had described. There were some videos of him strutting around pretending to be the said Rooster, others showed him with various women. It never seemed to be the same woman twice but there was nothing concerning about his dates! If anything, they were older than him, and all looked a little tired. His face was still red, his hair still wild. The pale blue eyes that stared out of that face were disturbing. There was something dead about them. Or was Lola just imagining that?

What she wanted to do was find something that linked him to Brent Burton. There was nothing. The two were not friends on Facebook or any other social media platform that she could find. Was it true that he still received money from Brent? And if so, how did she find out what it was for?

That was when she remembered Wayne telling her, during her last case, that Brent regularly withdrew £10,000 and that there was no way to find out where it went. If Gary was receiving that money he wasn't spending it. Though his life looked comfortable it was not opulent. There was no flashy car; in fact, his car was six years old. His house looked like an ex-council house.

After a little more research, Lola found out that it had been his mother's council house.

Lola did some more research and found out that council houses were available to people who couldn't afford to buy or rent. They were looked after by the local council and rented out at affordable rents. There had been a scheme, some years ago, where if you had lived in the house for so long, you could buy it at a discounted price. Lola found that his mother had bought hers for cash, which could have looked fishy. However, the house had only sold for £12,000, less than a lot of cars, even back then. Now it would be worth £150,000. It had been a good investment. It was not beyond the realms of possibility that his mother could have saved that money by legitimate means. Lola was all but certain that wasn't the case, but she had no proof. So far her research had led her nowhere.

It was time to stretch her legs. She got up and reached to the sky arching her back and easing out the strain of sitting for too long. Deciding it was time for a coffee she headed to the kitchen. While the kettle boiled she stared out the window. Sitting in the middle of the garden, in Portia's favorite spot, was Sassy.

The little Frenchie looked quite sad and so Lola made herself a drink and wandered down the garden to see her.

"What's wrong?" Lola asked.

"Portia won't come play," Sassy said. "Have I done wrong?"

Lola sat down and placed her coffee out of the way. Patting her knee she waited for Sassy to come and join her. The Frenchie curled up into her lap and snuggled against her. "No, I think Portia is just jealous."

"Maybe I give her my tiara," Sassy said.

Lola chuckled, the Frenchie had wanted the tiara so much and yet now she was prepared to give it up. "You are such a gorgeous little girl," she said holding her tight.

"Lovey love you," Sassy said, and then she curled up and fell asleep on Lola's lap.

Lola was back at her desk when she heard Wayne come in that evening. Tanya had a late night at the gallery she worked at and had already told them she wouldn't be home until 10. Lola had continued her research but had found very little out on Paul, String Bean, Norton. His Facebook page was two years out of date. There was little on it, just a few trips abroad. It looked like he liked Spain. Sun, sea, and drink seemed to be his favorite pastimes. If he was still working for Marty Stevens, there was no mention of it.

Lola felt a little bit nervous about seeing Wayne. It was silly, they had always got on so well, but she could understand him wanting to keep details of this case from her. However, she was hoping that she could persuade him to share, at least a little.

Wayne dropped his case on the table as Lola walked through.

"How are you doing?" she asked for he looked tired and had not come home the previous night.

Wayne ran a hand through his dirty blond hair and his eyes opened wider. "It's been a long two days."

"I have some information for you, have you got anywhere?" Lola turned from him and set about making him a coffee. Once it was ready she put it on the table and Wayne slumped down into a chair.

"Thanks for this," he said as he opened his briefcase and pulled out a file. "What information do you have?"

"I know who owns the van," Lola said.

"Really, that is very useful."

"I'll share," Lola said giving him her best cheeky smile. "If you will help me out a little."

"I can't do that," Wayne said. "However, I need a shower. If I left this folder on the table, I wouldn't know what happened once I left the room."

"Thanks."

"Don't know what you mean," Wayne said and turned to leave. At the door, he stopped and looked back. "It looks like buying the garage may not have been such a good idea after all!"

With that, he was gone and Lola could only hope that the property wouldn't be tied up for years to come.

Sassy was suddenly at her side. "Hungry" appeared in her mind.

Lola got up and got the dog her meal.

"Why sad?" Sassy asked as she sat waiting for her food.

"Not really sad, just a bit worried."

"I know something that will help," Sassy said.

"Oh, what's that?"

"Socks."

Lola laughed and put the bowl on the floor. Sassy stared up at her, her eyes bright, her body hardly able to keep still as she sat waiting for the word to let her eat. She was such a good girl and always waited to be told. "Okay," Lola said and Sassy leaped onto her bowl, snuffling the food down as fast as she could.

If only life could be so simple that socks could make it better.

CHAPTER EIGHT

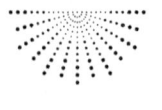

SNEAKY THIEF

When Lola heard the shower start upstairs, she picked up the folder. Feeling a little guilty she flipped it open. There was a photo of a young woman; was this the victim?

The woman didn't look too young, Lola suspected early to mid-twenties. She was attractive in a harsh way. Long blonde hair, big blue eyes, and impossibly thin. She was smoking in the photo and had the air of someone who knew life.

Lola turned over the page and found out she was Kirsty Kelly, the only daughter of Vicky Kelly. She was 25 at the time of her disappearance and it was put down as a runaway.

Lola read on and on, feeling a little sad. Vicky Kelly had not been bothered about her daughter's disappearance. It had been her friends that had reported her missing. The friends' names and details were listed. Lola wrote them down for later.

Jennifer Moody was the one who had reported her missing and she hassled the police for over a year. It looked like Kirsty had disappeared on Saturday night, 18th June 2011. Kirsty, Jennifer, and another girl, Susan Tring, had been out drinking. Jennifer and Susan had left with a man, Kirsty was still there. That was the last they saw of her. She never came home that night.

Jennifer said she was wearing jeans and a black top with a small gold shoulder bag she had borrowed from Jennifer. It was her favorite and it was never found. Lola skipped through the file, there was no mention of it in the items found at the scene. Could it be a clue, could they find it after all these years?

Though she didn't have a criminal record, there were rumors that she was assisting in a ring of car thieves. She was also known to frequent certain pubs. The main one mentioned was not a nice place, it was one that Tilly knew all about. One that Brent Burton used to frequent!

How was she involved with March's Motors? What happened to her? Could she tie this to Brent?

Lola heard Sassy running up the stairs and for a moment she thought about following her. Still, she didn't know how long she would have with the file and the Frenchie never did any harm.

The next document was the autopsy. It looked like Kirsty had been hit in the stomach, but what killed her was a blow to her head. The file said it was caused by something hard, with a 90-degree imprint. The coroner thought it was concrete. From the angle of the wound, they posited that she fell rather than being struck.

Could this be an accident?

If so, why had she ended up buried where she was?

There was DNA under her fingernails but they were still waiting on the results. Could it be Mick's? If so, was this all over? Had she died by accident and afraid they would be found guilty of murder they buried her and hoped it would all go away?

Lola hadn't heard Sassy come back down the stairs when she felt a tap on her leg. She looked down to see the

Frenchie sitting before her, holding a pair of men's black socks.

Lola found herself giggling and she reached down and took the socks.

"There, told you you'd feel better," Sassy said in her mind and Lola had to admit, she did.

"Sassy! Have you stolen my socks, again?" Wayne shouted from upstairs.

"Sorry, Wayne, you know how she loves them. I can bring them up for you."

"No thanks, they will be all wet now!"

Lola found she couldn't help but laugh at the thought of this big brave detective having his socks stolen by the little bulldog and then the thought of him putting them on and having soggy feet.

Controlling her laughter, Lola skipped through the rest of the file. There wasn't much else there. They had no other leads than Mick and it looked like they were doing no more until the DNA results came back.

Wayne came back to the table dressed in a grey jogging suit and rubbing his hair with a towel.

Lola closed the file, she had all she needed.

"Why don't I order a takeaway and you can tell me what you know?" Wayne said.

While they waited for a Chicken Tikka Masala for her and a Rogan Josh for Wayne, Lola filled him in on the van and the men Tilly had recognized.

"Does she know the registration of the van?" Wayne asked.

"I don't think so, she said she was surprised it was still running."

"That makes sense. They could use a van that was off the road with no plates and we have no way of tracing it back to them."

Lola chuckled. "They obviously didn't factor in Tilly!"

"No, they didn't. I will see if I can get a warrant to search for the van but I doubt it will be easy to find. Marty Stevens is a wily one. He would use that van knowing it could never be traced back to him. There are several scrap yards around here and I imagine it's already been crushed."

"Does this help to exonerate Mick?"

Wayne shook his head. "Quite the opposite, they all worked together at the time of the disappearance. If anything this makes Mick look even more guilty. I'm sorry but until we get the DNA results I won't be able to do much more. I am going to interview the friend…."

"Jennifer," Lola supplied for him.

"That's the one. We will see what she has to say but for now, I think it is a pretty easy case. You may as well leave it to us for now."

Lola hid her disappointment. This was not the news that Alice wanted to hear.

CHAPTER NINE

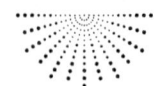

THE MORNING GAME

The following morning Lola woke later than normal. She asked the smart speaker to read the news. Instantly, Sassy pounced on her. The Frenchie was very good and hardly ever disturbed Lola until she asked for the news each morning. Sassy understood that meant it was time to get up and would launch onto Lola, nuzzling and licking to make sure she was fully awake.

After five minutes of cuddles, interspersed with Frenchie groans and grunts, Lola was ready to get up. Once out of bed, she went into the shower room and peeked around the door waiting for Sassy's little habit.

Lola always got cold feet when she first went to bed, and so she wore fluffy bed socks. During the night, she got too hot and would strip off the socks and tuck them behind her pillow. Poised behind the door, she controlled her giggles and kept as still as she could.

Sassy jumped onto the bed and slinkily stole up to the pillow. Once there she checked around the room for she knew the game well. She knew that Lola couldn't be watching or she would lose her prize. Convinced that she was alone, she pounced on the pillow and then gently walked over it sniffing as she went. There was a little grunt of satisfaction and her head came up, the socks proudly clamped in her mouth. Throwing them up in the air she jumped and caught them and then scampered off the bed.

Lola had left the bedroom door open this morning, so Sassy could escape with her prize. With her hands over her mouth, Lola tried to stop her giggles, still hidden behind the bathroom door. She heard the little Frenchie grumbling and groaning as she strolled off with the socks held before her.

Once Lola was showered and dressed she made her way downstairs to find that Wayne had already left. Tanya sat at the table with coffee and scrambled eggs on toast already waiting for Lola.

"I thought you might need this," Tanya said.

"Thank you, I do." Lola sank down into the chair and felt like collapsing forward onto the table. Instead, she had a sip of the coffee and began to eat her breakfast. Once she finally moved out, she was going to miss this. Tanya was so organized and always had everything ready for her. It was almost like living back with her mother.

"How was Wayne this morning?" Lola asked for she knew he had been burning the midnight oil.

"Tired and a little depressed," Tanya said. "His boss thinks this is an open and shut case and doesn't want him working on it."

"Well, I will continue to work, maybe I can find something."

"I hope so, Wayne trusts you despite him not being able to help all the time. However, he's asked if you will wait until the DNA results come back. They won't move on Mick until then. Can you do that?"

Lola understood and she didn't blame Wayne or Tanya for his reticence. "Of course."

"I'm off to the gallery soon but I have a couple of hours if you want to go for a wander around town?" Tanya said. "Lincoln has what they are calling the Imp Trail on at the moment. They do these most years and they are such fun. In the past, we have had the Barons and the Knights. I loved the Knights; they were so wonderful. The colored statues of a knight on a horse."

"The what?" Lola asked, totally confused by what seemed like a foreign language.

"Oh, sorry, let me explain. They are these wonderful hand-painted sculptures, this year of the famous Lincoln Imp, and are placed at various venues around the city. If you remember, the Lincoln Imp is a stone carving in the cathedral, we must go see it sometime."

"Yes, that sounds great."

"Right, where was I?" Tanya asked. "Oh, yes, they are placed all around the city and you can walk to all of them. I think it would be fun if you want to come?"

"I would love to," Lola said. "Unfortunately, I have a new client to meet this morning. I think it's going to be another divorce case and I nearly didn't take it but the lady sounded so desperate. Once I'm finished, I'll give you a call and see if you're free. If not, we must go another time."

"That sounds good, I look forward to it, Tanya said.

* * *

Lola took a short drive to the car park close to Betty's Tea Room. That was where she planned to meet her new client. Getting out of the car, she attached the service harness to Sassy before they made the walk up to the tearoom.

They went across the car park and down the narrow street before turning left to walk up Lincoln's famous Steep Hill.

It was a steep walk and Lola was puffing; however, Sassy was enjoying herself and romping along at quite a pace. Lola was almost having to jog to keep up with her.

They got to the bench called The Rest and Lola longed to stop for just a few minutes; however, Sassy had seen a little dog up ahead and was once more pulling.

"Friend, friend," Lola heard in her mind as Sassy let out her Frenchie scream of excitement.

A few eyes turned towards them, possibly thinking that Lola was murdering her dog; however, they soon looked away and carried on with their own days.

Lola let Sassy lead the way and followed her to say hello to the people with the little brown Staffy who were walking toward her.

Lola asked Sassy to sit and she did so. "Can they say hello?" Lola asked.

"Of course," the woman said. "Oh, isn't she cute?" The woman reached down to fuss the two dogs.

Lola joined her and stroked them both. In her mind, she heard Sassy say, "Chicken, she had chicken for breakfast. I like chicken, can I have it for breakfast?"

Soon they were on their way again. "Maybe if you're very good," Lola said.

"Always good."

Lola had planned to meet her client at Betty's Tea Room. It was a beautiful Tudor building that sat just below the square that housed both Lincoln's magnificent cathedral and castle. As she approached the entrance, she could see that there was a queue outside. It was being managed by Gerald Munro in his exceedingly smart tuxedo. Lola had met him before, and last time the man, who reminded her of the quintessential English butler, had not been too impressed.

He had looked down his aristocratic nose at Sassy and had originally refused Lola's entrance. Luckily, the establishment's owner, the famous Betty, had come to her rescue. Betty was a delight, like everyone's favorite grandma. She managed the tearoom with almost military precision and yet still made it seem both quaint and a special treat.

Lola settled into the back of the queue and checked her watch. She was 10 minutes early, there was plenty of time. However, Gerald waved her to the front of the queue.

Seeing his gaze upon her Lola felt a little inferior. Her hand went to her chest and she mouthed the question, me?

Gerald nodded and waved her forward. "Good morning, Miss Ramsey," Gerald said with his plumb in the mouth accent. "I believe you are here to see Mrs. Claudia Barnes. She is waiting for you and Sarah here will show you to your seat."

"Thank you," Lola managed, astounded at the man's change of opinion. Perhaps Betty had put in a good word for her.

"Follow me," a young woman said giving Lola a big smile. The woman was dressed in black trousers and a white blouse, like all the servers. Smart, and practical. As she led Lola into the restaurant Sassy trotted along at her side.

The place was buzzing; as always it was very busy and the conversation seemed to reverberate around the room. Filled with white linen-covered tables and the famous ornately painted china tea sets, you felt like you were walking into a different era. Lola followed Sarah as they weaved their way through the tables.

They arrived at a table quietly tucked away in a window alcove. Claudia Barnes sat waiting. Lola put her in her mid-50's, she was slightly plump with an anxious smile and shoulder-length hair. It was a dark brown color but the roots showed a touch of grey. Claudia had a pleasant face, but there were deep bags beneath her eyes, and as she smiled it looked tight and a little forced.

"Miss Ramsey?" Claudia asked as she held out her hand to shake.

"It's nice to meet you, Mrs. Barnes," Lola said, taking her hand before sitting down.

"That's a very cute dog," Claudia said, and as if on cue Sassy went around the table and sat in front of the woman. Claudia reached down and rubbed her behind the ears. Sassy groaned in appreciation and settled down at the woman's side.

On the table was a three-tiered cake platter and a large pot of tea with 2 cups and two plates.

"I ordered a cream tea for the two of us," Claudia said. "However, if you require something else I can get it now?"

"No, this is fabulous," Lola said and she nodded to Sarah who left the table.

Claudia's hand shook a little as she poured Lola a cup of tea. "I don't know how this works," Claudia said. "Do you take milk?"

"No, black is fine," Lola said as she took the cup. "The easiest thing is if you tell me what your problem is and I will see if I can solve it for you."

Lola bit back her sigh, another divorce case, she was sure of it.

CHAPTER TEN

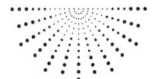

THE BEST MEETING EVER

*L*ola took a sip of her tea and waited for Claudia to speak. The woman swallowed noisily and picked up her own cup, sipping her tea before putting it down. Her mouth opened and closed and then shaking her head she selected a sandwich from the platter.

Taking a bite, she then waved her hand and the sandwich in the air as she began to speak. "My name's Claudia Barnes and I'm married to Marvin Barnes," Claudia said waving her hands about with such force that a piece of the sandwich dropped to the floor.

"Yummy in my tummy," Lola heard in her mind.

"We've been married for 37 years and I believed we were so happy."

"Ooohh, salmon, me likes salmon."

"I know I'm getting a little bit older, but it never occurred to me that Marvin would stray." Claudia paused, eating the rest of the sandwich and then selecting another.

"Well, let's not jump to any conclusions," Lola said. "Perhaps there's another reason for whatever is happening. Explain the situation to me. Well, as much as you can."

Claudia took a bite, chewed and swallowed, and then began to wave her arms once more.

It was obvious that her arms were as much a part of her conversation as her words and Lola was fascinated by the fast and dramatic gestures.

"We never had any children, do you think that could be the problem?"

Lola shook her head, she could see that Claudia was struggling. That this was painful for her. The sandwiches she was eating were simply swallowed, she was hardly even tasting them. The food was just comfort and Lola knew she had to be gentle with her. "Go through everything to start with and then I will ask you some questions. But, as I said, don't jump to any conclusions just yet." Lola offered her a reassuring smile and nodded for her to continue.

"I could never have children," Claudia said with her arms going out in a big expansive gesture. Another piece of sandwich dropped to the floor.

This time, Lola felt Sassy move. The bulldog pounced on the morsel and was chewing noisily. "Cheesy," Lola heard in her mind and had to almost bite her lip to keep her face from breaking into a grin.

"We spoke about it over the years, even considered adopting, but we both felt that it was never meant to be and I thought we were happy." Claudia had finished her sandwich and picked a piece of sponge cake off the platter. "Please, help yourself," she said.

Lola sipped her tea and wondered if she should stop meeting people at this famous tea room. When she arrived in England, she had been a little too thin; she had already put on a little weight and felt right with where she was. If she kept this up, that wouldn't last for long.

"Thank you, please go on," she said picking up a cream cheese and cucumber sandwich.

"Well, we are comfortable, we take 3 to 4 holidays each year and sometimes go away at the weekends as well. Marvin has always been a wonderful husband, caring, kind, supportive, and loving. He even watches Strictly with me, I know he secretly hates it but he watches it every week."

"Strictly?" Lola asked.

Claudia's eyes narrowed. "Strictly Come Dancing... the ballroom dancing show... You must know it!"

Lola was still confused and it must have shown on her face.

"The show where couples dance for a prize... each week one couple is eliminated. I love it, the gowns, the fun, the dancing, the floor, I love how the floor can be anything. I vote every week and I'm very good at picking out the winner. Never mind, I digress I was just saying how he supports me and watches it though he hates it. He can't dance, of course, he has two left feet and has no interest at all. Anyway, I love him dearly, and I couldn't ask for any more..." Her hands went up in the air in a dramatic gesture and a piece of cake dropped to the floor.

"Yummy yummy," Lola heard in her mind.

Claudia put down the cake and pulled out a cotton handkerchief, dabbing at her eyes. "Please forgive me."

"There is nothing to forgive," Lola said. "Take your time, tell me what you need to tell me, and do not worry, I am here for you."

"That was cake. Cake is the best ever," Sassy said.

"Well, it will soon be our 37th wedding anniversary and just a couple of months ago is when things started to go wrong. Marvin has a good job. He doesn't work long hours anymore, he doesn't need to. This was to be our time. The time to relax and enjoy all we've worked for." Claudia faltered and stared at the elaborate and colorful platter of cakes, or through them.

"His employer is all right with that?" Lola asked wondering if there was pressure from the man's boss.

"Oh, of course. It's a company he started himself. A little accounting business that provides all we need. However, for the last few years, Marvin has near enough left the staff to do all the accounting work and he just oversees things. It has meant he can come home early most days. We're not even going into year-end and yet he's going out early in the morning and coming back later at night. I'm so worried that he has found another woman."

Claudia finished the sponge cake and picked up a toffee éclair. As she took a bite Lola could see that the pastry was crumbly. Lola swallowed. It was so hard to keep her face neutral.

Sassy sat staring up at the table, her little body quivering in anticipation as she waited for the next treat to drop.

"Mine, mine, mine," Sassy said in Lola's mind. "Wow... look at that."

"Have you asked him about it?" Lola asked. "Is he less affectionate?"

"It's gonna drop... drop, please!"

Claudia's arms flew out to the side in a big dramatic gesture and her eyes went wide, a little bit of éclair fell. Lola watched it fall. Sassy jumped into the air and caught it before it even hit the floor.

"Crumbly, creamy, coffee; wow, the best ever," Sassy said in Lola's mind.

It always amused Lola at how so many things could be the best ever. It seemed that dogs, especially her little

Frenchie, enjoyed every moment to the full.

"I couldn't possibly ask him about it," Claudia said and it was clear that she was close to breaking.

"I understand, has his demeanor to you changed... at all?"

Claudia stilled for a moment and stared straight at Lola. "No, now you come to mention it, no, not at all. He is still my loving Barny Bear." Claudia blushed at having used her pet name in public.

"That is a very good sign," Lola said. "It points to there being a reason other than infidelity to Marvin's altered behavior. I can do some investigating but I need you to promise me that you will not find him guilty just yet. Perhaps he has found another woman." Lola really hoped he hadn't for she knew it would crush Claudia, and even in this short time, she found she liked this woman. "But perhaps there is another reason, an innocent reason. Tell me about your husband, what he does, where he goes, if you have a picture that's great and I will start to investigate for you."

For the next half an hour Claudia provided Sassy with lots of yummy treats as she told Lola about Marvin while waving her hands as she spoke. The man was short, 5 foot eight, of medium build, and with graying hair. He had what she described as an attractive if slightly chubby, and boyish face.

"For a man of his age, he looks so young, it's one of those faces that elderly aunts always wanted to pinch the cheeks of," Claudia said before pulling out a picture.

Lola nodded, the description was perfect. The man looking back at her looked like such a nice person. It broke Lola's heart to think that he was cheating and she almost wanted to walk away. However, she reminded herself that there could be many reasons for the change in routine. Could there really be, though?

Soon, the meeting was over and Lola spent a few moments assuring Claudia that she would do her best and that she mustn't worry.

They were on the way back to the car and Sassy was strutting out in front of her as they headed back down the hill. The journey gave them beautiful views of the ancient streets and was much easier than the climb up, though a touch hard on the knees. Lola didn't know how the little dog did it, she was feeling bloated and stuffed from the cakes and sandwiches she had eaten and yet it didn't seem to bother Sassy one bit.

"That was the best meeting ever," Sassy said in Lola's mind. "Can we see her again?"

Lola grinned at her dog.

"Why sad?" Sassy asked picking up on her emotions.

"I hate to hurt Claudia, and I get the feeling I'm going to have to."

"Could smell man, not smell anyone else," Sassy said.

Lola hoped that the Frenchie was right and that Marvin had a good reason for his early mornings and late-night excursions.

Just as they got back to the car Lola's phone rang. It was a landline and not a number she recognized. For a moment, she almost canceled the call. It would probably be a telemarketer and she wasn't in the mood. However, she hit the green button. "Lola Ramsey," she said.

The voice on the other end of the phone was difficult to understand. It was a woman, and she was crying and talking about being arrested.

"Slow down, who is this?" Lola asked.

CHAPTER ELEVEN

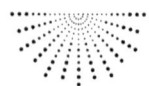

HELP ME, PLEASE

"It's me, Alice, please help me... help me, please, I don't know what I'm going to do." The words were coming so fast that they were jumbled up together and Lola could hardly make them out. Then it came to her!

"Alice, is that you?"

A sigh of relief came through the phone. "Yes, yes, it's me. I've been arrested as an accessory to murder. How can this happen?"

Lola felt her pulse kick up and her heart began to race. There had to be some mistake. No one would believe that little Alice could ever hurt someone. Lola doubted she ever said a cross word. Being an accessory to murder was plainly ridiculous. How could Wayne do this? "Of course, I'll help you."

Over the next five minutes, Lola listened to Alice and questioned her. She found out where she was being held and what was happening and that Wayne was not the officer in charge. Alice had refused the offer of a solicitor. In her words, she was innocent, why would she need one? They were holding her overnight which seemed wrong to Lola and she was going to do her best to have that changed and to get Alice home. The one thing Alice was adamant about was that she needed her diary. Apparently, she filled it in every day and she said that Tilly had a key.

Lola promised her that she would bring the diary and ended the call with a heavy feeling in her heart.

Rather than going straight to Tilly, as Alice had asked, Lola rang Wayne. The phone rang for ages and then went to voicemail. Lola hung up and called again. This time Wayne answered.

"Have you heard?" Lola asked her voice dripping with anger.

"I'm in court, I've just come out for a recess, what am I supposed to have heard?" Wayne asked and there was a sense of weariness in his voice.

"Oh, I'm so sorry, Wayne. Alice has been arrested as an accessory to murder. I'm really worried about her and I think this is the most ridiculous thing I have ever heard."

Wayne let out a sigh. "Really, I got taken off the case, we have a new detective, *Daniel Peterson*."

Lola picked up on the way Wayne said that name. He didn't like this new man.

"Well, our Danny boy was questioning Kirsty's friends last night. He's a little naïve and sees the worst in everyone... you didn't hear this from me but I think he's a bit of a bully. I guess he jumped to the wrong conclusions. I will give the station a quick call and see what I can sort out. It might be a good idea if you can find out what they told him. I know I asked you not to... but have you spoken to them yet?"

"No, I had a new client this morning and I only just left her. I will nip back and go see them next."

"Great!"

"Daniel visited the men you told me about; Marty, Paul, Larry, and Gary. He thinks they're innocent," Wayne said.

"What do you think?" Lola asked.

"If Tilly is right, they have to be involved but leave them until last. If you go there and Danny finds out it will be trouble. Also, if I was you I'd let them stew a little first."

"Okay, good. Can I go see Alice; she wants her diary?"

"Sure, give me a couple of hours and I'll make the arrangements."

Lola heard Wayne being called in the background.

"Gotta go," he said, "but I will sort this first."

Lola hoped that he would.

Lola drove back to pick up her notes. On her way, she passed the village playing field. Walking across it was Sam Smith. Lola had really come to like Sam and they often walked Sassy together at night.

An idea came to her and she pulled up in the parking lot and clicked a lead on Sassy's service harness. Getting out of the car she called to Sam.

The boy turned and even at this distance she could see the big smile that came across his face. He waved and ran towards them. Dropping to his knees and hugging Sassy as soon as he arrived.

"Hello, my little friend," he said as he rubbed her belly. Sassy was lying on her back waving her legs in the air and enjoying every moment of it. Grunts and groans of sheer joy came from the Frenchie and when Sam stopped she pawed at his hand to force him to continue.

Sam looked up, his hair was still spiked to perfection, as it had been when Lola first met him. However, the grin on his face was natural and relaxed. He was happy, no longer bullied by a boy who turned out to be a murderer.

"How are you doing?" Lola asked and then wondered if she should've done that because Sam loved to talk about his new career route and she was short of time.

"Did I tell you I got accepted into the policing college?" Sam's brown eyes were wide and brimming with excitement.

Lola chuckled. "You did. Did I tell you how proud of you I am?"

Sam's cheeks colored and he dropped his head. The first time she had met him he couldn't meet her gaze because he was ashamed and embarrassed. This time, the embarrassment was a good embarrassment. "I guess you did, sorry, I just get so excited."

"Don't be sorry, and we can talk more about it another day, but today I'm in a hurry. You know Alice Beecham?"

"The nice lady on the bike?"

"That's the one. She's been arrested as an accessory to murder."

Sam's jaw almost hit the ground. Pulling the ball out of his pocket he stood up and tossed the ball for Sassy before turning to Lola. "That's crazy, can I do anything to help?"

Quickly, Lola filled him in about the body at the garage. For a moment she stopped should she say more? Then she told him how she wondered if Brent Burton was involved.

With the mention of Brent, a cloud crossed Sam's face. Even so, without thinking he picked up the ball that had been dropped at his feet and tossed it for Sassy once more.

Sam was sure that Brent was his father. His mother had been a teenager when she had him and even though Brent denied it, Sam believed Brent was his dad. "If we can prove it was him... I will be so happy," Sam said, the tightness in his jaw evident in his voice.

Lola felt a little bit ashamed. She should've thought more before mentioning this to him. "Well, we don't know that yet. At the moment, I don't need your help on that case but I would love some help on another one... if you have the time?"

Sassy had dropped the ball at Sam's feet. He raised his hands in the air and shrugged his shoulder. Sassy sat to attention staring at his hand.

"No cake!" Sassy said. It seemed the Frenchie thought that all hands produced food when they were waved in the air now.

Sam picked up the ball and tossed it again. "I would love to help, just tell me what to do."

Lola filled him in on Marvin and also explained that she hoped that the man wasn't cheating and that they had to be very sure, even if he was meeting a woman, that he was meeting her for reasons of infidelity and not for other reasons. Once she had finished Sam nodded.

"I can do that, no problem," he said.

"I'm sure that this is not dangerous," Lola said. "However, you be very careful and keep me informed of how things are going. This is not an urgent matter, so do what you can but don't put yourself in any danger."

Sam took one last look at Sassy. "I'm thinking of working with police dogs," he said.

"You will make an excellent K-9 officer. I can't wait to see you out on the streets."

With a big smile on his face, Sam grabbed the file.

"Do you need a lift?" Lola asked.

"Nah, I can hop a bus at the end of the street. Probably be there just as quick. You go help Alice and I'll keep you informed."

Lola handed him some money. "For expenses." She was blinking rapidly. Her pride in the boy had caused a tear to form in her eyes. He had come so far since she first met him.

As he walked away she had a feeling of dread. Not that she thought that Sam was in any danger, it just seemed that everything was going wrong at the moment. Who would have thought that Alice could be arrested? All she had to hope was that she could find a way to get her out and prove her innocence.

CHAPTER TWELVE

A GOOD FRIEND

"*L*et's go see Tilly," Lola said.

Sassy stared after Sam for a moment and then headed back to the car, Lola had to run to keep up.

"Moley, love Moley," Sassy said. "Treat."

Lola got back to the car to find Sassy sitting waiting for her. She had truly come to love Tilly and their visit to her shop. Sassy called Tilly Moley, not in a mean way, because she looked a little like a mole peering out of her round glasses. It wasn't just the gravy bone treats that Tilly provided, everyone loved Tilly.

Soon they were at the shop and Lola tried to gather her thoughts. She had a lot to get through.

The shop door opened and Tilly came out, blinking at the bright sunshine. Taking Sassy's lead she pulled the bulldog into a hug and carried her inside. "I'll get the kettle on," she called to Lola who was still getting out of the Jeep.

Lola smiled, part of her wondered if she had time but she also knew that Tilly could help her.

Once in the shop she went straight through the door into Tilly's private quarters and sank down into a seat at the table. Sassy was lying on a new dog bed with her treat, chomping away and making yum-yum sounds in Lola's mind.

"She looks happy, but you do spoil her," Lola said with a big smile.

"Nonsense," Tilly said putting tea and cake on the table in front of Lola. "You look exhausted."

Lola quickly filled Tilly in and it was the first time she had seen her lose her smile. "Oh, my goodness. That will not do at all. Mick... now I can understand them arresting Mick but Alice! That makes no sense whatsoever."

. . .

"Well, it seems that the officer in question might not be the best."

"That is a shame but there are good and bad in all walks of life. What can I do to help?"

Lola took a sip of tea and relaxed. "I need to get Alice out and... now, what did she ask me for?"

"Her diary, no doubt," Tilly said. "She fills it in every day, has done for years. I can get that and as soon as Wayne lets you go see her I can take it to her."

"Thank you... but maybe I should take it."

Tilly reached out and touched Lola's hand. "Let me help. Alice would be better served if you find proof she didn't do this. I know a brilliant solicitor, Patricia Darnell. Bright as a button and caring too. I will organize that for you."

A wave of relief came over Lola. "Thank you."

"Patricia is good but we may need bail money. I have some but would not be able to get it quickly. I'm not sure what Alice has."

Lola shook her head. "I have a trust fund... I don't touch it, but for this, I would. Just let me know if it's needed and I will transfer the funds."

Tilly nodded. "I guess it depends on how much?"

"I should be able to cover it," Lola said. "You are such a good friend."

"Oh, don't, you'll make an old woman blush."

For a moment Lola relaxed and nibbled her cake and drank the tea. It was nice to settle for a minute and let her thoughts catch up with the day.

"Do we have a name for the victim yet?" Alice asked.

Lola explained about Kirsty.

"Oh, I hate to speak ill of the dead, but that one was bad to the bone."

"You knew her?" Lola asked.

"Yes, she came up when I was investigating Brent Burton and The Bustard Inn public house."

"The what?!" Lola asked, wondering if she had really heard that right.

"The Bustard... oh, B U S T A R D Inn, it's a type of big bird and I've no idea why that place was named after it."

"I see, it is unusual."

Tilly smiled. "There were many rumors that she was... how should I put it... well, keeping men engaged while their belongings and cars were stolen. It was all tied to Mick's garage but I'm not convinced Mick knew about all of it. He was never the cleverest of men. Kirsty, now she was a nasty piece of work, hated me and Alice for trying to help her. I have some files on the men I suspected of being involved. I can dig them out for you, for later."

"That would be great," Lola said. "Now I have to go, call me if you need anything and let Alice know I believe her, and I will prove her innocence."

Tilly stood and pulled Lola in for a hug. "I will do, you are so kind."

Lola felt heat creeping up her cheeks as she said her goodbyes. Just before she opened the door Tilly stopped her.

"I may have an idea, do we know when Kirsty died?"

Lola shook her head. "It was too long ago to get an accurate date of death. They think it was around the time she disappeared but can't be more specific. She disappeared on Saturday 18th June, 2011. It will be nearly impossible to prove where anyone was that far back. It means circumstantial evidence, witness testimony, and the DNA evidence will make this case." Lola felt quite depressed once she had said this. She felt sure that Kirsty's friends must have dammed Alice, how could she prove them wrong?

"Nothing is impossible," Tilly said. "Leave it to me."

If it had been anyone else Lola would have laughed off such a comment but with Tilly, she almost believed it, almost.

CHAPTER THIRTEEN

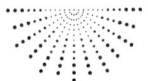

NOT THE NEWS SHE WANTED

*L*ola reviewed her notes and knew her next move had to be to find out what information the police had on Alice. Her best bet was to visit Kirsty's friends. Susan Tring was the closest. She lived in a rough area of town that was just 15 minutes away.

Taking a breath to calm herself, Lola set off.

"All okay," Sassy said in her mind. "Not bad place."

Lola reached over and rubbed between the Frenchie's ears. Her little pal was sensing her stress and just wanted to remind her that she was not back in Afghanistan. The current news from that place was not helping with Lola's PTSD.

Lola sat back and took a breath, she could do this.

A high-pitched squeal came from Sassy and Lola looked over to see the Frenchie straining on her harness and pushing her nose against the car window. On a wall high above them, a squirrel was hopping along hunting for hazelnuts.

"It's getting away," Sassy squealed. "Have to stop it."

"I'm sure it's just after food," Lola said.

"No, planning, takeover." Sassy snorted and pushed against the glass. Sitting back, her body shaking with anticipation, Lola could see she had left some impressive dog art on the window. Sassy whined, she was convinced that squirrels had evil intent and that if left alone they would plan some heinous crime.

"Don't worry, it saw you and won't come here again," Lola said as she put the jeep in gear and drove off. "Now, sit down and be safe."

Sassy grumbled a little but curled up and settled on the seat.

Soon, they arrived at Susan's house. It was scruffy outside with a number of children's toys lying broken in a rough front yard. There was also a swing set but the ropes had been cut. Lola had a bad feeling. Somehow she didn't think that Susan would be up for helping them.

Before she stepped out Lola heard her phone notification that she had received a text. It was Tilly messaging her to say that Alice had been released, for now. Lola let out a breath of relief, it looked like Tilly's solicitor was quick and efficient. That at least was good news.

Attaching Sassy's lead they walked to the door. A doll's head lay on the path, the eyes poked out and a red scribble across its face. Lola shuddered and had to push down the urge to walk away. Children did this sort of thing, it meant nothing.

"Wow, toy!" Sassy said tensing to pounce.

"No, leave it," Lola added quickly.

Sassy let out a long sigh and eyed the head as they passed it. Lola had an image of her chasing around the small yard with the head in her mouth and it released some of her tension. "You can have a new toy soon."

"Really?"

"Yes"

"When? Now!"

"Soon."

"Soon is often forever," Sassy grumbled.

Giving a loud knock on the door, she heard a woman shouting inside. The words were hard to make out but the sentiment was not. She didn't like cold callers.

Lola put a smile on her face and hoped that Sassy would be able to work her magic.

The door opened to reveal a woman in her late thirties wearing a pink fluffy dressing gown and Mickey Mouse slippers.

"What d'you want?" she asked not removing the cigarette from her mouth.

Lola stopped her jaw from dropping and smiled. The woman's long brown hair was up in a messy bun. At around 5 foot 2 she was carrying a little extra weight but the thing that struck Lola the most was how tired she looked. Deep blue smudges sat beneath her brown eyes. "Hi, I'm investigating the death of Kirsty Kelly, can I ask you a few questions?"

"Listen to you, not a local are you?" Susan said, her eyes opening wide and her voice rising in a most unpleasant way at the American accent.

"No, I'm from the...."

"Come in then." Susan opened the door to a messy home. There were clothes and toys everywhere and a child in diapers ran across the hallway and into a room. "Liam, get your brother," Susan called as she led Lola the opposite way. "Cops have already been, can't you ask them?"

Lola found herself in a kitchen, where pots and dishes that needed washing were everywhere she looked. A small table with a dirty green cloth was in one corner. "Sit, I ain't gonna make you a tea."

"It's okay, I just had one," Lola said suddenly unsure how to start.

Sassy was sniffing at some cereal hoops on the floor. "Ah, ah," Lola said warning the dog to leave them.

Sassy sighed and moved back from the treat. It may be tasty to the Frenchie but Lola didn't want her eating everything she found. Sassy sat staring at the treat, but Lola knew that now she had been told she wouldn't touch it. However, that didn't stop her from giving Lola a touch of side-eye.

"Them dogs are worth a pretty penny, you wanna sell it?" Susan asked.

"No, thanks, she's my therapy dog."

"Oh, lardy da."

"What can you tell me about Kirsty and when she went missing."

Susan sat at the table and blew out a big ring of smoke. "We all hung around with Mick and his mates at The Bustard Inn. He bought us drinks if we talked to men, you know."

Despite her bluster, Lola could see that Susan was not too happy about that time in her life. Lola couldn't help but feel sorry for her. Sometimes circumstances put you in a place that was hard to escape from. What could this girl have been if she had been given a chance?

"What do you remember about the night Kirsty went missing?"

"Not a lot really, we drank in those days." Susan sucked on her cigarette and then stubbed it out in a cup on the table. "She was talking to men, I can't remember who, you know it all swirls into one mess back then."

Lola asked more and more questions but there was nothing to help or hinder her case. At last, she got around to asking about Alice. "Did you know Mick's sister?"

"Yeah, horrible lady. Treated us like dirt. I wouldn't be surprised if she was in on this."

Disappointment and shock went through Lola. This was not what she wanted to hear.

"She mad at Alice, but mad at herself too," Sassy said in Lola's mind.

Lola had no idea how the dog could discern emotions to the level she could but she was very reliable. The only problem was interpreting the true meaning. Was Susan mad because she hadn't reported Alice at the time? Could Alice be guilty? No, that made no sense. There had to be another reason. Why was she angry at Alice and what did it mean?

Lola continued with her questions but Susan was determined to make out that Alice was involved. Though she had no actual evidence she insinuated that Alice was mean and hurtful to them. Though there was nothing concrete it was damning.

Lola left the house feeling more and more confused. How was she ever going to prove Alice was innocent.

"No cake," Sassy said as they got back into the car. "Nice smells, lots of poop but no cake." Sassy sat in her seat, her legs out in front of her and her bottom lip protruding. It was such a funny expression that it cheered Lola up a little. However, she knew she would have to do better if she was to get Alice off. Looking at her watch she had time for one more visit. Quickly, she pulled a sachet of food out and fed Sassy in the bowl kept in the car for just this purpose before they set off to see Kirsty's mum. Hopefully, she would have more luck there.

CHAPTER FOURTEEN

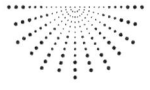

BAD PARENT

Lola pulled up outside a mid-terrace house. It was neat and tidy with a small front garden laid to blue slate. A few red begonias made a merry display in a small circular border in the middle. The lights were on inside, the curtains not drawn, but Lola couldn't see anyone moving.

"Do you need to go yet?" Lola asked Sassy as she attached her lead.

"Noooo, not a puppy!" Sassy shook her head as if this question had been an insult.

Lola chuckled. "Good to hear. This will be the last call tonight and then we can go home."

"Do I get my toy, tonight?"

"How about we go to the store on Saturday."

Sassy tilted her head to one side. The days meant very little to the dog who lived in the now. Her face dropped a bit in confusion.

"Just a couple more sleeps," Lola said.

"Okay, I can choose?"

Lola laughed and rubbed her between the ears. "Yes, you can go in the store and choose, one toy and one treat."

"That will be the best day ever. How many sleeps?"

"Just a couple, you ready?" she said to Sassy as they walked up to the white door.

"Sniffy sniffs all ready," Sassy said a big grin on her face.

Lola knocked on the door and waited as a wave of exhaustion came over her. It had been a trying day, both mentally and physically. She had been on the go for most of the day and had very little to eat other than cake. For Sassy, that was a day to dream of, but it made Lola tired and part of her couldn't wait to get back for some real food.

The door was opened by a slim woman who looked to be in her early to mid-60s. Her eyes were narrowed, her face all cheekbones and covered in freckles. Though attractive, the lines around her eyes showed through the heavy makeup. A cigarette stuck out from thin bright red lips.

"What d'you want?" the woman asked.

"My name is Lola Ramsey. And I'm looking into the disappearance of your daughter. I wondered if I could ask you a few questions?" Lola felt an instant dislike for the woman and she heard Sassy snort at her feet. It was easy to read the meaning behind that. Sassy didn't like her either.

"Oh, I suppose you can come in if you must."

The door was opened and she stepped back to let Lola in. For someone of her age, she was incredibly thin, wearing skinny jeans and a yellow tight-fitting T-shirt. Her blonde hair was long and fastened up in a high ponytail that swung behind her as she moved. There was a touch of grey at her temples that suggested the hair had been dyed. A bony hand took the cigarette from her mouth and as she beckoned Lola in her arms looked almost skeletal.

Lola wondered, was her ultra slim condition because of her worry over Kirsty? Had she spent a lifetime of fear wondering what had become of her daughter? For a moment she felt a touch of shame at judging her so quickly.

The door opened straight into a small living room. It was nicely furnished and well looked after. There was a pink Chesterfield sofa and two matching chairs. One wall was papered with huge damson-colored flowers on a white background and the other three matched the plum coloring of the flowers. It was incredibly hot and Lola noticed that the gas fire was lit.

"Take a seat. Did you have to bring the dog?"

"Don't like, smells acidic, like a lemon that's gone moldy," Sassy said in Lola's mind.

"She's my service dog," Lola said taking a seat on one of the chairs.

"Your what? Never mind." Vicky sat down. "What d'ya wanna know?"

"Tell me about Kirsty."

"Well, she was a one," Vicky said and the look on her face was something that Lola couldn't quite understand. It was a cross between disgust and guilt.

"How do you mean?" Lola asked.

"Kirsty was a bully. She knew how to play men and she loved nice things, fast cars, and money. She had this scam going with them at the garage. She would keep the fools busy and the men would steal their fancy cars. I know she was my own daughter, my own flesh and blood, but she got what was coming to her. I'm almost glad it's over."

Lola felt a flood of adrenaline and her blood ran cold. It was hard to fathom how a parent could talk this way about their own child, especially one who had been murdered.

A flood of warmth filled her mind and she felt Sassy leaning against her leg. The feel of the little Frenchie grounded her and let her know that there was always good in the world.

"You say the garage, do you mean Mick Beecham's garage?" Lola asked, even though she knew the answer. It was best to be sure.

"That's the one. It's closed now. I heard that was where they found my Kirsty." Vicky made a display of rubbing at her eyes but Lola couldn't see any real emotion.

"Do you know who she dealt with at the garage?"

Vicky shrugged and reached across to a small table. On it, was a cigarette packet. A gaudy picture of a heart operation decorated the packet. It was designed to stop people from smoking, but seemed to have no effect on her. Flicking a gold-colored lighter, she took a long draw and then blew out a puff of smoke. "You want one?"

Lola shook her head. "No, thank you."

"Well, at the garage, Mick was never the brightest. Though I guess he had to be the one who organized it all. Maybe he was like Colombo, you know, pretending to be thick."

"That could be it," Lola said. "What about the others there? There was String Bean, Bruiser, and March. Do you know how much they were involved?"

Vicky took another long pull on her cigarette and nodded her head. "I reckon all of them were. The one they called Bruiser, well, he had quite a rep. No one crossed him. I reckon though, that March was the brains behind the operation. He treated my girl right though. Bought her things, looked after her."

Lola kept her mouth closed even though she could feel her jaw wanting to hit her chest. How could any parent think that a man such as that, one who was using her daughter to steal from the men, looked after her? So far, everything she had heard confirmed what she knew.

"What about the men? You said she kept them busy; what men were they, and were they any trouble?"

"Well," Vicky said and smiled a sickly smile. "There were two types of men. They were all there at that place cos they liked the girls, young girls. My Kirsty looked so young even though she was in her 20's. Very mature for her age but looked like a teenager. There were those who dated the girls and looked after them for it. Gave them jewelry, bought them drinks and clothes, some might have even paid. I don't know and I wouldn't have allowed that."

Lola swallowed for hearing this from the girl's mother was making her feel ill. "That place, you mean The Bustard Inn?"

"That's the one," Vicky said. "Then there were the ones who the girls, my Kirsty, Susan, and... oh, what was her name? Thinks she's better than us now... Jennifer something. Well, there were the ones that the girls found and lured there, and then they kept the men busy and handed their car keys to the gang."

"Did you tell this to the police?" Lola asked thinking that if she did why had they only arrested Alice?

"Don't be daft. I told them the girls partied there, nothing else."

Sassy got up from her seat at Lola's side and wandered over to Vicky, sniffing at her feet.

"Keep that mutt away," she almost shrieked.

"Here, girl," Lola called and Sassy trotted back.

"Smells bitter, horrid," Sassy said, and with a cross between a grumble and a growl she curled up at Lola's feet. Vicky eyed her nervously.

"Do you know any of these men?" Lola asked.

Vicky put her head back and closed her eyes taking a long draw on her cigarette. Opening her eyes she let out a puff of smoke. "Not really, well, there was that snooty guy, Bruce... no, Barton... no, what was it? Oh, yes, Brent Barton. He really liked my Vicky and treated her so well.

I even hoped they might end up an item. It's such a shame it was not to be."

Lola smiled as her excitement kicked up a notch. "Do you mean Brent Burton?"

"That was him. Oh, I wish he and my girl had ended up together. He would have looked after me right."

Lola couldn't believe both the naivety and the selfishness she was hearing but she hoped that she could find evidence to incriminate Brent. He was one man she would love to see behind bars. Now she had to ask the million-dollar question and she felt her heart kick up a beat. What if her instincts were wrong? What if Alice had been involved?

"What do you know about Alice Beecham?" Lola asked.

"Kirsty hated her," Vicky said. "Said she was mean. I guess she was in on it."

"Is that what you told the police?" Lola asked with a sinking feeling in her stomach.

"Yeah."

So this was where the officer had got the information from. "Did Kirsty say how she was mean?" Lola asked.

"Mean is mean. I guess she forced my girl to do things."

"Did Kirsty tell you this?" Lola asked, hoping beyond hope that she hadn't.

Vicky raised her head and sneered. "Kirsty never told me nothing. But I know she hated that Alice. Why else would she hate her?"

Lola asked her a few more questions. But Vicky didn't seem to know anything, it was almost as if she didn't know her daughter at all.

"Thank you for your time and I want to offer you my deepest condolences on the death of your daughter," Lola said.

Vicky simply shrugged and pointed at the door. With her loyal Frenchie in tow, Lola showed herself out.

Once they were back in the car Lola leaned back in her seat and blew out a breath of air. There was something incredibly draining about talking to someone like Vicky Kelly. It was as if the woman cared about nothing but herself and Lola knew that she had to take every word she said with the proverbial pinch of salt.

"What did you think of her?" Lola asked.

"No like," Sassy said.

"Why?"

Sassy let out a huff. "No wear socks."

Lola thought back and realized that Sassy was right. Beneath her skinny jeans, Vicki had been wearing open-toed sandals and no socks. "Maybe she sometimes wears them, is there anything else?"

"Never wears them, must be bad," Sassy said.

If it wasn't so serious, Lola would've found this funny but so far she had done nothing to help Alice and it left her feeling so tired.

Sassy pawed her arm and Lola turned to look into the little bulldog's amber eyes. They were so beautiful and so full of love.

"Smells bitter too," Sassy said. With that, the Frenchie cuddled up on her seat and was almost instantly asleep.

Lola guessed that Sassy had had a long day too. There was nothing more they could do today, she just hoped that tomorrow would bring them better luck.

Quickly, she called Alice and Tilly, both seemed okay for now, and pleaded with her to find out who had done this. They believed in her. What was remarkable was that both of them were more concerned about finding Kirsty's killer than Vicky had been.

Lola hoped that she could live up to the trust her friends had put into her.

CHAPTER FIFTEEN

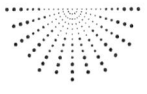

THE PROTÉGÉ

*T*he following morning Lola rose early but Wayne had already left. When Lola followed Sassy down, she fed the Frenchie and found a note from Tanya; she too, had already left for the gallery.

While Sassy ate Lola made a quick breakfast of egg and bacon. Just in case it was another busy day she wanted some protein inside her to keep her going.

Sassy sat in her bed staring up at her tiara. "Do you want to see if Portia is there?" Lola asked.

"Yes, must show her my princessness again," Sassy said before spinning in a circle and leaping in the air.

"Here you go." Lola fitted the tiara and let Sassy out. She could see Portia stalking a bird at the end of the garden. Sassy saw her at the same moment and letting out a squeal of delight as she set off down the garden like a missile. The noise scared the bird and Portia turned around giving Sassy such a look that would have frozen Lola on the spot. Sassy, however, was too excited to show off to her friend and ran down so fast she almost skidded into the cat.

Portia leaped into the air landing 2 feet away, her spine arched her hair on end.

"You stupid dog, you scared away my breakfast," Portia said.

"That's Princess Stupid Dog to you," Sassy said, sitting down on her butt with her legs stuck out in front of her.

Portia hissed once more and then ran across the garden scaling the fence and disappearing.

Sassy came trotting back up the garden. "She saw me."

"Yes, she did." Lola chuckled. "Just let me finish my coffee and then we will take you for a walk."

"Can I wear my tiara?" Sassy stuck out her bottom lip and Lola could feel that she expected her to say no.

"Sure, why not?"

Lola finished her coffee and sent Tilly and Alice a message that she was working on the case and would update them later or tomorrow.

Just as she finished Sam messaged to say he had some information and he was at the park. Lola sent back that she would see him in five minutes.

"Wanna go see Sam?" she asked as she cleaned the kitchen.

"Yes, Sam throws the best bally, he will love princess me."

It took them just a few minutes to meet Sam.

"Hey," he said to Lola before dropping to his knees and pulling Sassy into his lap. "Well, look at you, my little Princess," he said before rolling her over and rubbing her tummy.

Sassy groaned and grumbled enjoying every minute of the fuss. "Me lovey Sam," she said in Lola's mind.

"She's enjoying that," Lola said. "I'm sure you're her favorite."

"She's been just great for me," Sam said getting up and pulling a ball out of his pocket. He threw the ball and as Sassy ran off to fetch it he sat next to Lola on the bench and pulled out his phone. For the next 15 minutes, he threw the ball and told Lola what he had discovered. He had followed Marvin Barnes to a house on the Lakeside estate of Burton Waters. The photos showed Marvin going inside and a tall, slim woman in her early fifties at the door. She had short black hair and an aristocratic face. The way they greeted each other looked more business-like than if they were lovers.

"Is this enough to say he's cheating?" Sam asked before picking up the ball and throwing it again.

In Lola's mind, she heard, "Yeaaaaaaaaaah." As Sassy turned and chased after it.

"Normally it would be but his body language is all wrong and I really want to make sure that this is what it looks like. What do we know about her?"

"Oh, I never thought about that," Sam said and scratched his head. "I guess I'm not much of an investigator."

"Hey, don't run yourself down. There aren't many people I would trust with this and you have done really well."

"How do I find out?"

Lola thought for a moment. Burton Waters was a small close-knit community. "You could google her address and see if anything comes up then I would go to the café and ask if anyone knows her. Keep it casual, say you're asking for a friend, and see what you come up with. Did you see anyone else going to see her?"

"I didn't stay, I followed Marvin."

"I hate to think that he might be having an affair but something just doesn't feel right."

"What, exactly?" Sam asked.

"It's just an instinct, what do you feel about it?" Lola didn't want to admit that it might be the fact that she didn't want to break Claudia's heart.

"Well. I've watched Brent a time or two when he sees his... women. He looks much greasier than Marvin did."

"I agree, you have good instincts. Are you okay to do a bit more work?"

Sam threw the ball again. "You bet, I'm loving this and want to help you as much as I can."

"Great, save any receipts for anything you spend and here," Lola took out her purse and gave him some cash, "grab yourself a meal and coffee while you're working."

The smile on Sam's face made her day. It was so nice to see his enthusiasm and she hoped even more that she could put Brent behind bars. This young man deserved a father much better than that one.

Sassy dropped at their feet not letting go of the ball. This was her signal that she had done enough. The tiara sat on her head at a very jaunty angle and her long tongue was hanging out almost to the floor.

CHAPTER SIXTEEN

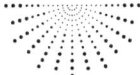

THE ONCE BEST FRIEND

*L*ola's next stop was to visit Jennifer Moody, the girl who had reported Kirsty missing. After their visit to the park, they dropped Sam at Burton Waters and took the Lincoln bypass to the turn-off for the Birchwood Estate. Jennifer lived in a house that backed onto Hartsholme Country Park.

As Lola turned into the estate Sassy let out a wheezy whistle of appreciation. It was such a strange sound that Lola found herself laughing but somehow the little dog had summed up her thoughts exactly. Jennifer was living a life far better than the friends she had left behind.

"Need me some socks from here," Sassy said.

"Don't you dare." Lola chuckled. "Besides, they will be so clean they won't smell nice." The houses were all immaculate and Lola imagined they would be as nice inside as they were outside.

"Socks always smell lovey, no matter how much you try to cover it with that smelly stuff."

"Smelly stuff?" Lola asked.

"When you put them in the roundy roundy thing with the horrid smelly stuff."

"Oh, you mean fabric conditioner, that smells nice," Lola said biting back another chuckle.

"Not as nice as sweaty feet," Sassy said, "or smelly butts."

"Really!" Lola was trying hard not to laugh.

"Why you not sniff butts when you meet someone?" Sassy asked.

"Why would I?"

Sassy's head went back and her mouth dropped open. "You can tell so much, what eaten, where been, how healthy, what feeling. Why not learn all that?"

Lola glanced over and she could see by the intense expression on Sassy's face that the little Frenchie really wanted to know. "I hate to admit this, but my nose is not as good as yours. I could probably smell sweaty feet but all I could smell was sweaty feet and I don't even want to talk about what I would smell if I sniffed butts."

"Hmmm." Sassy cocked her head to one side. "Feel sorry for you. Must be hard to be so inadequate. I give cuddles later."

"Thanks, that will make up for a lot."

They pulled up outside an impressive detached house with a beautiful, but very minimalistic, front garden. A brand new Mini Cooper in blue with a Union Jack roof was parked outside.

"It looks like she landed on her feet," Lola said.

Sassy's eyes opened really wide. "Maybe she's a cat!"

Lola knocked at the door and it was opened almost immediately by a woman with a big smile. She looked down at Sassy. "Oh, aren't you the cutest?"

"Hi, I'm sorry to bother you but I wondered if I could have a talk about Kirsty Kelly?" Lola asked. The smile dropped off the woman's face and for a moment Lola thought she would slam the door in their faces.

"Are you Jennifer Moody?"

"No... well, I was, now I'm Jennifer Walker... look I don't want to get involved." Jennifer flicked her long straight black hair over her shoulder and narrowed her brown eyes, she started to close the door.

"Please, just talk to me," Lola said, but the door closed a little more. "You must've cared for her at one time, surely she deserves justice?"

The door was pulled open and Jennifer seemed to shrink in on herself but she shrugged her shoulders beckoning Lola to follow her inside.

The house was immaculate and very nice. Jennifer led her down a champagne-colored corridor lined with pictures of two cheeky boys. In all of them, they were smiling, in some playing with a ball, or sitting with Jennifer and there were a few of a tall, handsome man, obviously the boys' father. Lola understood. Jennifer had left her old life behind and she didn't want it crashing into this new life.

They took a right turn into a bright and modern kitchen. The units were a deep rich grey and highly polished, the walls white and the view out into the garden was beautiful.

"Can I get you a drink?" Jennifer asked and pointed at a table.

Lola took a seat and Sassy sat down beside her. "Not very smelly," Lola heard in her mind; she could understand why. The house looked immaculate. "A coffee would be lovely," Lola said.

"Lady smell good, nervous, but good," Sassy said.

The nerves could be because she didn't want her family to find out or they could be from guilt. Lola wondered if the Frenchie could distinguish nerves from guilt and decided that she must do some experiments when they had some free time.

Jennifer plugged a capsule into the coffee machine and pressed a few buttons. Soon she was bringing two cappuccinos over to the table. When she sat down, it was as if she was afraid, that she was trying to avoid this. Once sat, she stared down at the cup in her hands, her hair a curtain between them.

"Thank you," Lola said and took a sip of the coffee. She needed to allow Jennifer time to relax. "You have a beautiful home."

"Thank you." Slowly she raised her head. "I love my family very much and I don't want to do anything that would involve them in my old life."

"I understand totally," Lola said. "All I'm asking of you is some information. We can keep it between you and me and your family never needs to know. I know you cared about her, you were the one who reported her missing and you chased the police diligently for a long time. Now we have found her I want to bring whoever did this to justice. Will you help me?"

Jennifer nodded. "I will do what I can. But I don't know what I can do, after all, it was all so long ago."

"Thank you," Lola said. "Tell me what you remember of that night."

Jennifer sighed and then took a drink of her coffee. "I was very different then. I drank too much, I stayed out late, and... well... You know there were the men. That night is just a blur, we drank way too much and Kirsty was talking to some men, me and Suzi left to go clubbing, but Kirsty was talking to some guys and didn't want to come."

"Do you remember anything about the men?"

"Not really, I did tell the cops who was there but I can't remember. There were a few regulars Tommy Smith, Robert Kennedy, Dean somebody, and Brent Burton."

Lola felt excitement bubble inside her at the mention of Brent's name.

"They all treated us pretty well. Treated us like a girlfriend." The flush that reddened Jennifer's cheeks gave as much away as the words.

"Were they with you that night?"

"No... well, not that I remember. Oh, there was one man we didn't like, Peter... Buck I think."

"Peter Bucknell?"

"That was him. He was nasty, had a real temper."

"Did he hurt any of you?" Lola asked.

"He would pinch us, or twist our arms, if we didn't do what he said," Jenifer said.

"Was he there that night?"

"I don't know whether he was there that night but it was around then that he slapped Kirsty for taking money from his wallet. She was good at that. Take the man's wallet, remove some but not all of the cash, and put it back without them noticing. Most never mentioned it, I think they thought they had spent it."

Lola felt her excitement climb. This man could be the killer. "Was there anything else you can remember?"

"There was a car that March wanted. A Mercedes or maybe a Jaguar because he kept saying it was like a great big cat slinking around the streets, but it could've been any posh car, I didn't know car makes very well then. They wanted us to get close to the guy and take his keys. I know that Kirsty was the guy's favorite and she was working on him. I think he might have been one of the men she was talking to but I'm pretty sure he left before we did, though."

"Do you know the name of the man whose car it was?"

Jennifer shook her head and there was genuine sadness in her eyes. "I'm sorry, I had this all written down and I kept it for years but when I met Paul, I just knew I had to let it go. I have a great life now. I work at the dentists down the road, I have two fabulous children and a husband who loves me. I don't want him to know what it was like... what I was like. I don't want to get too involved."

Lola asked more questions about the man and about the operation and how the girls were handled. It seemed that March was the one who dealt with them and that Jennifer didn't think that Mick was that involved.

"Could Mick have killed Kirsty?" Lola asked.

"Mick was a creep, but I don't think he killed her. He was not as smart as March and I don't think he truly understood what was happening. I think he just liked us girls around... to gawk at."

Lola asked a few more questions about the men but there was very little that Jennifer remembered. Not enough to help at all.

"What about Alice Beecham?" Lola asked and couldn't help but hold her breath.

Jennifer took a sip of her coffee only to find the mug empty. She let out a sigh. "At the time I thought Alice was a meddling old busybody. Not that she was much older than we were, she just seemed old. She was much younger than Mick, I always wondered about that." Jennifer stopped and seemed to be staring into the past.

Lola knew she had to push her a little bit further. "You said at the time you thought she was meddling, what do you think now?"

Jennifer smiled. "She was trying to help us. She was trying to get us away from the garage and away from the life we had. I wish I had listened to her earlier than I did."

"The police think that Alice murdered Kirsty," Lola said.

Jennifer's eyes opened wide and she shook her head. "No, no way. I know she didn't do it. She never came to the pub. I don't think she even drives; she would not have been there."

"What about Mick, do you think it could've been him?"

"No, I'm pretty sure Mick wasn't there at the time. He used to go away a lot and was never at the pub with us. I'm not sure how you could prove it though."

Lola asked a few more questions but she could see that Jennifer was getting nervous. She was constantly checking her watch and glancing around, Lola had enough and it was time to let her go. "Thank you for your help, if you can think of anything else this is my number." Lola handed her a card with her number on it and a cute picture of Sassy to make it easy to recognize.

"Oh, I just remembered something, Kirsty had my favorite gold clutch bag. It was one of the reasons I knew she hadn't run away, she wouldn't have taken it from me."

"What did it look like?" Lola asked.

"I have a picture," Jennifer said and stood and left the room.

"Get a good smell of her in case we come across something of hers later," Lola said to Sassy.

"Got it already, feet not smelly enough, but I know her scent now." Sassy sat staring up at Lola with such adoration and a touch of pride. It was so cute she wanted to scoop her into her arms and just hug her for hours.

Jennifer came back and showed them a picture of three young girls dressed for going out. It was easy to recognize all three of the friends and in Jennifer's hands clutched in front of her was a gold sequined purse. It was about 4 inches deep and maybe 8 long and had a gold-looking chain strap.

"Thank you," Lola said.

"Was it found...? Not that I want it back... it would just sort of confirm to me that it was her."

"No, but I'm sorry the identification was solid; it is Kirsty without a doubt."

"I really hope you find out what happened, but I don't want to get involved," Jennifer said.

Lola and Sassy got back into the car, she had some new information and she understood why the others hated Alice, but did she have enough to prove her innocence? Maybe not, but it was a start.

Now, how could she find out about the cars going missing and could they be involved in Kirsty's death? What happened to the purse? Would any of these questions ever be answered?

CHAPTER SEVENTEEN

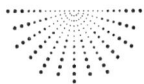

A SPOT OF LUNCH

*L*ola made a quick call to Wayne and explained about the car thefts. Though he wasn't sure he could find much out he agreed to look into it for her. She asked if she could visit the men from the garage. Wayne was quiet for a long moment.

"Not just yet, something is going on with Danny Boy. I don't want you involved until I have worked out what it is. Okay?"

"Okay, but I will have to talk to them at some time."

Wayne agreed but asked her to wait a little longer. She also told him about the purse and he confirmed that it hadn't been found. "It was probably thrown years ago," he said.

With that done Lola decided to go see Tilly. The shop owner would hopefully be able to fill her in on Kirsty and the men. In the past, Tilly had been keeping a file on The Bustard Inn, and hopefully, she had dug out the information.

When Lola arrived at the shop it was empty and as always, Tilly invited her into the back room.

"I was just about to have some lunch," Tilly said, "would you like some, it's chicken salad?"

At the mention of her favorite word, Sassy gave a little squeal and jumped into the air. "Me love chicken," she said in Lola's mind before sitting down in front of Tilly and almost blocking her way.

"Well, I think I might be able to find you a little bit of chicken," Tilly said with a chuckle, bending to stroke the Frenchie's head.

At the mention of food, Lola heard her stomach grumble and Tilly gave another chuckle. "Before you say no," Tilly said, "I can tell you're hungry and I have plenty, so take a seat." With that, she waved Lola to the table and began to prepare another salad.

"You are so good to us," Lola said as she sank into the seat. "Can I help?"

"No, it won't take me a moment." Tilly had already got the salad prepared and was slicing chicken. Some of it was going on to the plate for Lola and there was a little plastic dog bowl that she was preparing for Sassy. It was pink and in the shape of a heart, and was the cutest thing that Lola had ever seen. It was also new, Tilly was certainly spoiling little Sassy.

Tilly placed the bowl on the floor for Sassy. The little Frenchie reached up and kissed her cheek before diving into the chicken. Lola could hear all sorts of mumbles and moans and grumbles inside her mind; it almost sounded like the Frenchie was going nom, nom, nom and it made her want to smile. Tilly then put two plates on the table, one for her and one for Lola. It was a beautiful salad with plenty of chicken.

"Would you like a drink?" Tilly asked.

"Sit, and eat up, we can have something later," Lola said feeling a little guilty that this old lady was running around after her while she sat here resting.

The salad was delicious. The lettuce was crisp and refreshing on this hot summer day and the chicken was melt in the mouth and still warm. Once they were finished, Tilly made a glass of homemade lemonade each and sat back down once more.

"I wondered if you managed to dig out the files?" Lola asked.

"I did." Tilly pointed to a box in the corner that Lola hadn't noticed before. It was like the ones that copier paper came in and a little dusty. "I went back through my notes as well. I did try and close that place down. The police just thought I was an old fuddy-duddy. That Alice and I were just interfering. Now, I wish I had tried harder."

Sassy had finished eating and she went across and leaned against Tilly's leg. It was amazing to see how just a touch of the little Frenchie brought her comfort and her hand reached down and rubbed the spot between her ears that Sassy loved the most.

"Don't go blaming yourself. At least you tried."

For the next 30 minutes, Tilly explained about some of the men. About the ones she knew. There was Brent Burton, no more needed to be said about him. Whenever she mentioned him, Lola noticed that Tilly's jaw tensed.

How she hoped she could put this man away. How many lives had he destroyed?

"We will get him," Sassy said in Lola's mind. "He smelled bad."

Tilly also knew a number of other men and she had details on some of them. As they spoke, Lola took notes. She would go through the full files later but for now, the condensed version would do.

"How is Alice doing?" Lola asked.

"She's fine. I think it was a little bit of a scare but she's more worried about Mick. She shouldn't be, the man never worried about her... but I guess family is family."

"That it is."

Once they were finished, Lola left Tilly's with some good suspects. There were four men that Tilly suggested she look into along with Brent Burton. She suspected these men had been conned by the gang, three of them had reported vehicles stolen and one hadn't. They were Dean Banks, Christopher Jones, and Robert Kennedy and all had reported cars stolen, and Peter Bucknell who hadn't. Had Peter been conned in some other way? Lola wondered if one of them had taken the matter into his own hands.

Tilly had been so excited and so happy to help that Lola hid her own feelings of despair. How would she ever prove Mick and Alice were innocent? After all this time what evidence could there be?

CHAPTER EIGHTEEN

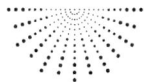

DOWN ON HIS LUCK

*L*ola quickly checked the map and found that Dean Banks lived the closest to her current position. Though she had no idea what to ask these men she decided it was best to go see them and see what she could find out. As she was driving a call came through and she hit the hands-free button. "Hello, Lola Ramsey."

"Hello, Lola, it's Claudia Barnes here, I wonder if you had any information on my husband yet?"

Lola felt her stomach turn a little and she knew she must not say anything to Claudia just yet. Though it looked like her husband was cheating she had to be sure.

"Hello, Claudia. We are still investigating at the moment but I don't want you to worry."

"Oh, that is fabulous, are you saying he's not cheating on me?"

Lola gulped. "I have found nothing at the moment that says that he is. I promise I will get back to you as soon as I know more and I have my best person on this for you." Lola didn't know why she added the last part. Perhaps she wanted to give Sam the credit he deserved.

Claudia was delighted and hung up leaving Lola feeling even more guilty. What would she say to the woman if she found out that her husband was cheating? And why else would he be seeing another woman in the daytime? Oh, how she hated spousal cases.

By the time she had hung up, she had arrived in front of a small tower block where Dean Banks lived. Lincoln didn't have many tower blocks, probably because they would obscure the view of the magnificent cathedral and castle. It would be such a shame if the city was blighted with ugly modern architecture that would hide the treasures of the past. This one was just four stories high and didn't look too bad.

Lola quickly fastened the lead onto Sassy's harness and they stepped out of the car. "Do you want a walk before we go in?" Lola asked.

Sassy sniffed the air turning her head from side to side. "Too smoky," she said.

Lola chuckled, they were in a very busy part of the city and the little dog preferred to walk where the air was sweeter and there was more chance of squirrels.

Lola soon found the apartment and knocked on the door. It was opened by a man in his mid-50s. He was small, probably 5 foot five with hardly any hair and small brown eyes lined with blue smudges. The man looked worn out and run down. His clothes were dirty, the knees of his brown trousers ripped and tatty. This was not what she expected. In the file, it said that Dean was very rich and at the time of Kirsty's disappearance he drove a Mercedes sports car. Probably the one that March wanted to steal. What had happened to him?

"What d'you want?" he asked.

"Is it Dean, Dean Banks?" Lola asked.

"Yeah, can I help you?" he said looking down at Sassy and smiling. "That's a cute dog."

Lola put on her biggest smile and was so pleased that Sassy often won the day for her. "I was wondering if I could have a chat with you about a young girl." Lola had been about to explain about Kirsty's disappearance and then she decided to change her tactics. "She was involved in a ring stealing expensive cars, we believe she may have stolen yours."

Dean nodded, a smile coming across his face as he opened the door. "Come on in."

"When did your car go missing?" Lola asked as the door opened into a dingy and smoky living room. The curtains were drawn closed and it was lit by a single lamp and old-fashioned lightbulb. It was probably barely 40 watts and left the corners of the room in the shadows.

"It was summer, 2011. I know it was that lot from the garage at South-Brooke. Bunch of crooks the lot of them and those girls, I'm sure they paid those girls to rob us." He chuckled and shrugged his shoulders.

Lola was not expecting that. She had expected anger, bitterness, that he would resent the people who had taken from him, and yet he seemed to find it amusing.

Dean sat down in an armchair facing a large TV. He pointed at the sofa opposite him. It had once been cream but was stained and darkened with age and time. Lola didn't want to sit on it, but she needed to keep him sweet. Gently, she lowered herself to perch on the edge. Leaning forward as if to question him.

"Do you remember any of the girls?" she asked.

Dropping Sassy's lead she watched as the Frenchie wandered around the room sniffing here and there.

Dean shook his head. "Not really, they all tended to blend into each other. They were young, naïve, just looking for a bit of fun and so was I! I have to admit that was a time of booze and drugs, I was always partying and don't remember a lot." He stopped talking as if he had realized that he might incriminate himself.

Sassy was sniffing the corners of the room and working around toward him. "Been micey's here," she said and continued on sniffing, her little tail upright and wagging as she enjoyed the scent of the mice she had sniffed out. Lola moved her legs away from the sofa a little. Surely, the mice could not be hiding under it?

"Was your car ever recovered?" Lola asked.

"No, the coppa's never seemed interested. I got the insurance money, did well out of it really," he said and he looked as if he was reminiscing a good memory from the past. However, his phone buzzed and he picked it up, glancing at the clock on the wall. Something changed, he was eager, restless. "You need anything else, I've got an appointment?"

Lola noticed how his eyes flicked from his phone to the TV and he no longer seemed to want to talk to her.

"Just a couple more questions," Lola said. "At the time, back in 2011, you lived up close to the cathedral. It seems your circumstances have changed, do you mind if I ask what happened?"

It was as if the air had been let out of him and he sunk in on himself, deflating before her eyes. Placing his phone on the arm of the chair he bowed his head for a moment and then looked up at her. "I like the ponies," he said. "That's what I'm waiting for, I have a sure thing on the next race at York." Then his eyes widened. "You're here because of that body they found, aren't you?"

Lola nodded, there was no point denying it. "She went missing around the time your car was stolen." Lola could see that Sassy was close to him now, sitting just in front of him and sniffing the air. "If something happened, if you caught her and it was an accident you should tell me now. The police will find out the truth."

He put his hands on his knees and bowed his head once more, lifting it a few seconds later and letting out a big roar of laughter. "As I said, I did much better out of the insurance than I would if I'd kept that car. It was a ringer, it cost me a lot of money, and it was forever breaking down. Whoever stole it, well they got what they deserved," he said with a chuckle. "Back then, I liked to party. I had plenty of money and that's what the girls wanted. I never did anything illegal… well, drugs… it was accepted back then. There was none of this woke nonsense. You gave a girl a compliment and she liked it then. We had fun, we partied, we all knew what we were in for. It wasn't me who killed her, I had no reason, I didn't even know it was the girls at the time. I found out about a year later."

Lola nodded. "How did you find out?"

"Oh, that should be your next stop. You should look at Peter Bucknell, that one had a temper and it was him that told me they were a gang working together with the man from the garage… what was his name?"

"He telling the truth," Sassy said in Lola's mind. Lola knew that the Frenchie's intuition or probably scentuition wasn't always reliable but her gut told her that on this occasion Sassy was right.

"Do you mean Mick Beecham?"

"Nah, not him, he was just a fool… the other one, the one that was always so jittery. I can't remember his name."

"March," Lola said.

"That's him." Dean clicked on the TV and stood. "I need you to go now, I have an important race."

Lola showed herself out, she couldn't help but feel sorry for the man. From what she had read at one time he had it all and it seemed he had lost it by no doubt betting on a sure thing.

She was pretty sure that Dean wasn't the killer but maybe Peter Bucknell was. Her only problem was that so far she hadn't been able to find an address for him.

CHAPTER NINETEEN

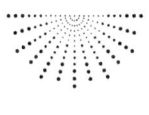

A QUICK STOP

Lola knew that Peter Bucknell was one of her best suspects. Tilly had told her that the man had a temper, that he had several arrests for assault and other even more unsavory crimes. Lola suspected these were for soliciting but she hadn't pushed Tilly on the matter.

Suddenly feeling thirsty she decided to try the Lakes Garden center. It was not far from their current position and she had heard it did lovely meals and had a café by the lake where you could sit outside with dogs. It was very popular and it would give her time to do some research and to see if she could find out anything more about Peter.

Pulling up at the garden center Sassy stood up and

looked out the window. She was securely strapped in but liked to be nosy on occasion. As they drove around the back a small flock of geese waddled across the path in front of them. Sassy let out an excited whine. "Big birds, must chase."

"They're bigger than you; what will you do if they chase back?" Lola said as she pulled into a parking space on a nice open field.

Sassy turned and looked at her, her eyes open wide her mouth open. "Birds don't chase me! I chase them!"

"Are you sure?"

Sassy sat back down and let out a harrumph. "They looked like nice birds, I not chase them."

"Good idea." Lola clipped her onto an extender lead and unclipped the seatbelt clip. Sassy climbed over onto her knee and sat waiting for the command to leave the car. Lola opened the door and looked around. The geese were eating grass about 50 yards away, honking and fluffing out their feathers. The field had a few other cars in it but most people had parked closer to the doors on the tarmac. When she could see it was all clear she said, "Okay."

Sassy leaped out of the car and instantly began sniffing the grass. Her little tail was high and wagging incessantly showing that she had found something delicious to smell.

Lola grabbed her purse and got out. Sassy was keeping an eye on the geese as she sniffed back and forth over the field. It was something that one of the farmers had told her was called quartering and was a way for a dog to cover all of the ground so they didn't miss anything. It amazed Lola that Sassy, a French Bulldog, with a tiny nose could still sniff and find out so much, never missing a thing.

"Lovely smells, me want," Sassy said as she pulled Lola away from the car.

Lola was happy to follow. Letting her pal have a few minutes and a toilet break and this was the perfect place for this.

Sassy surged forward and dived on the grass in front of her. Lola knew what she was about to do. "No," she shouted and Sassy turned around and gave her the stink eye. She had been about to roll in a big pile of geese poop.

"Don't you dare!" Lola said.

"Oh, want to," Sassy said digging in her claws and resisting the pull of the lead. "Easier to chase birdies if smell like birdy..."

"I understand." Lola began to chuckle. "But you're not coming back in the car if you roll in that."

Sassy took one more longing look at the pile in the grass before trotting back in the direction they had come. "Lots to sniff," she said as they did a quick walk around the field. Lola noticed that she kept her distance from the geese and was relieved. Though she was sure the geese would run, she didn't want the Frenchie chasing them away from their meal.

Lola approached the sliding doors of the garden center and not quite sure what to do, she hadn't put Sassy's jacket on because she didn't think she would need it. Tanya had told her that dogs were more than welcome but for a moment she wasn't sure. Then she watched a couple with a Golden Labrador walk through the doors. It looked like dogs were allowed in the whole place so she followed shortly behind them.

Inside it was almost like a barn with a translucent roof. The floor was carpeted with brown serviceable carpet. This area was filled with furniture and brick-a-brack.

There were a lot of fake flowers and trees and some lovely items that she wondered about coming back sometime and doing a bit of shopping. Once her property was complete she would need some new furniture. Of course, as a body had been found on it, that might take some time.

Lots of people were browsing and as she walked further along there was an area selling clothes. It all looked so nice but she didn't have time to look and kept walking as they entered another area, this one filled with bedding plants. At the end of the lead, she felt Sassy stiffen and turned to see the Frenchie face to face with a live chicken. The little bantam had silver-white feathers lined with black and as Sassy stared at it wide-eyed it raised onto its toes and spread out its wings. Sassy backed away until she bumped Lola's leg. The chicken shook itself and strutted away secure in the fact that it had chased the dog away.

"What was that?" Sassy asked. "Smelled like chicken but was scary."

"It was a type of chicken and I think it was just protecting its home."

"Oh, I won't mess with it, looked angry."

As they stepped out into the plant area a brightly colored cockerel crossed their path. Sassy stepped back and around it walking behind Lola and coming around the other side. "These birds don't run," she said and Lola could feel her confusion.

"They are pets and they are used to people and dogs, don't worry."

A little girl was pointing at the cockerel and laughing then she saw Sassy and came running over giggling. Her parents came rushing up behind her just as she reached Sassy.

"Jeannie, come here," they called.

"She's friendly," I said and they smiled.

"Jeannie, be nice to the doggy."

Jeannie knelt down and Sassy crawled onto her lap. The little girl giggled as she cuddled her close. "Cute doggy," she said.

Sassy groaned and rolled over so that her tummy was in the right place for stroking. She was so funny and when the little girl stopped she used her paw to pull her hand back to stroking.

"I'm so sorry," the mother said. "Come on now, Jeannie, we have to go."

Jeannie bent and kissed Sassy's head before standing and walking away.

"Like it here," Sassy said as they made their way to the café. With a cappuccino in front of her and a biscuit for Sassy Lola searched for information on Peter Bucknell. There was nothing recent and she couldn't find an address. A few newspaper reports came up of his crimes, GBH – grievous bodily harm, assault, armed robbery. For a small-town crook, he was pretty vicious. This was definitely someone who could have killed Kirsty. However, no matter how she tried Lola couldn't find out where he lived.

In the end, she called Wayne and filled him in on her investigation so far before asking for help.

"I don't know," he said. "This could get me in trouble."

"I'm not asking for much, just for an address if you can find it," Lola pleaded.

He sighed. "Let me see what I can find. I have to tell you something. The judge has ruled that Mick Beecham is mentally capable and can be prepared for trial."

"What?!"

"I know, don't say anything yet as it isn't official. They won't be releasing the news for at least a day and I will let you know once you can tell Alice. However, if you can find anything out to exonerate him you need to do it now."

Before she could say anymore he had hung up.

Would he help her and when the news hit, what should she tell Alice?

CHAPTER TWENTY

A CASE SOLVED

*L*ola sat for a few minutes and savored her drink. She had to decide what to do next. There were two more men to interview as well as Peter. Or should she go see Alice and work out if there was a way to exonerate her brother? Or should she start on the men from the garage?

Closing her eyes she relaxed a little and a loud bang jerked her back in time. Sweat ran down her back, her heart rate rocketed, and her body shook. The smell of gunpowder made her want to cough but instinct told her to both hide and search out the danger.

Sassy scratched her leg and a feeling of love and warmth filled her mind. "Here, good place," Sassy said to her.

Feeling her heart start to slow Lola reached down and rubbed the little Frenchie between the ears. She was safe. Looking around she could see a group of five teenagers laughing as one of them had knocked over a chair. They were just kids having fun, it was nothing to worry about.

Her calm had gone now and she decided to leave when her phone rang. Looking at the I.D. it was Claudia. Lola had no new news and so she ended the call. It would be best if she didn't speak to Claudia until she had something concrete to tell her. Should she call Sam?

As if on cue her phone rang again and this time it was Sam.

"Hey, do you have any news?" she asked.

Sam laughed and she could tell he was excited. Her stomach cramped, was he excited because he had found evidence of an affair or evidence of no affair?

"I did what you said," Sam was talking fast and she had to concentrate to keep up. "Sally at the coffee shop was so helpful, she told me that lots of people go see Miss Antonia Simpson."

Lola felt her heart break a little, was this woman some form of escort?

"She's a ballroom dancing instructor. A real nice lady by all accounts. Marvin had even been in the coffee shop and he is planning a big surprise for his wife for their anniversary. She's a big Strictly fan."

"A what?" Lola asked.

"Strictly Come Dancing, you know, the show on telly where celebrities and famous people dance and the audience votes for their favorite. It's his wife's favorite program."

Of course, Lola remembered Claudia telling her as much.

"Well, for years she has made him watch it and she dreams of dancing but he couldn't dance. He is planning on taking her dancing for their special day but as I said, he couldn't dance. Hence, the trips out and the secrecy. I think he's a really nice guy."

Lola had to agree. "You have done a great job for me. Would you like to help out on a more permanent basis?"

Sam was quiet for a moment and she thought he was about to refuse her.

"Really?!" he asked. "I would love to."

"That's great, I will sort things out and we will sort out remuneration for you," Lola said and she heard him cough down the phone.

"What, you mean I will get paid for doing this?"

"Of course," Lola said.

"Wow, maze balls," he said. "I mean that is just great, thank you."

"You deserve it," Lola said. "I have to go; I will talk to you soon."

"Thank you, thank you again."

"You happy now," Sassy said. "Tis good."

"Yes, it is," Lola replied before she rang Claudia. "Hi, Claudia, it's Lola Ramsay."

"Oh, Miss Ramsay I've been so worried, it's bad news isn't it?"

"No," Lola said. "You have nothing to worry about. Marvin is not cheating on you; in fact, he is arranging something special. Know that he loves you very much and trust him."

"Can you tell me what he's doing?" Claudia asked, her voice sounding much brighter but still a little pleading.

"Trust me, the surprise will be better if I don't."

"Thank you, thank you so much," Claudia said. "I will send you a cheque."

With that, she was gone. Lola chuckled, Claudia didn't even know how much to send but Lola didn't worry too much. This case had been worth doing for free. It felt so good to have a positive outcome for once.

As Wayne hadn't gotten back to her Lola decided to visit another of Kirsty's men. The closest was Robert Kennedy. How she prayed that she could find something to clear both Alice and her brother and yet in her heart she doubted she would. It was too long ago for anyone to remember much, let alone for there to be any evidence left.

CHAPTER TWENTY-ONE

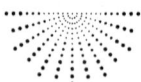

THE SCENT OF GUILT

*A*s Lola drove she questioned Sassy. "How easy is it for you to tell different emotions?"

"Know when sad, when happy," Sassy said.

"Can you sniff out guilt?"

"What guilt?"

Lola thought for a moment. Did Sassy mean what guilt specifically or was she not sure what guilt was? "Say, for example, a person hurt someone and they felt bad for it, could you smell the changes in them that would cause?"

Sassy gave a little harumph. It was a way of letting on that she was confused. Long sentences and some concepts were difficult for her to understand and she did much better with short easy sentences.

"When you do something wrong and you feel bad that is guilt," Lola said.

"When do something it done, why feel bad?" Sassy asked.

Lola wondered if she could give herself an emotion and so she thought of something that she felt guilty for. It was easy. When she joined the army her parents had been hurt, they died while she was deployed and that guilt had never left her. Then there was survivor's guilt; she came home when many of her good friends didn't. Lola concentrated on the two feelings and felt her stomach churn, the hair rose on her arms and her throat tightened. "What do I smell of?" she asked.

Sassy sniffed quite dramatically and then sat back confused. "You had this before. Not scared but... like lemons, bitter, and a little sweaty. Me don't like."

"That was guilt," Lola said. "Would you be able to smell it on someone else?"

"Maybe, but different people, smell different emotions."

Lola understood, Sassy was saying that the same emotion would smell different on different people, still. it had been worth a try.

"Here we go," Lola said as the sat nav announced that they had arrived.

Robert Kennedy lived in a rural property set back from the road. Lola pulled through the gates and drove up a tree-lined drive to an impressive detached property. It was 2 stories high and had 4 windows on each level each side of the door. It was a little boring looking almost like a brick box. The gardens were extensive and simply mown grass with a few trees. As they drove up to the house they passed a robot lawnmower. Sassy pressed her nose against the glass. "What that?"

"It cuts the lawn."

"Can I chase it?" Her legs were shaking and her tail was high and wagging ten to a dozen.

"No!" Lola almost shrieked and Sassy turned around and gave her a look that said Drama Queen. "It's dangerous and could hurt you."

Lola felt a flush of love fill her and Sassy smiled. "You always look after me."

"You look after me too," Lola said. "Right, ready to sniff out some clues?"

"Yes, will there be socks?"

"I doubt it," Lola said.

"Treats?"

"I don't think so."

"Me still work, like a slave." Sassy sat on the seat her bottom lip protruding.

"You'll get treats later," Lola said as she pulled the car to a stop.

"You're the best," Sassy said jumping up ready to get out of the car.

* * *

Lola knocked on the door and waited, part of her expected a butler to open it instead, it was opened by Walter White or at least a man who looked like him. Lola felt her jaw drop open and the man glared at her.

"Yes?" the man with the bald head, goatee, and wire-framed glasses asked.

"I'm sorry, my name's Lola Ramsay and I'm investigating... a ring that stole cars many years ago," Lola said twisting the truth a little, but it seemed a better opening than did you kill Kirsty Kelly! "Are you Robert Kennedy?"

The Walter White look-alike nodded. "You'd better come in." As she crossed the threshold she noticed he was wearing an ice blue Ralph Lauren polo shirt and matching pants. On a rack near the door was a fedora hat. She guessed he knew who he looked like.

The house was plainly but expensively furnished. A polished wooden floor complimented the oak-paneled walls of a large entrance hall. Twin staircases led up to the next floor and a crystal chandelier lit the room. He led her through and into a drawing room where a desk sat in one corner and across from it in front of an unlit fireplace was a burgundy sofa and two armchairs.

"Need to find socks," Sassy said and Lola had to bite back a chuckle.

"Take a seat, can I offer you any refreshments?"

"No, thank you, I'm fine."

Lola unclipped Sassy and let her go and the little Frenchie began to sniff around the room. Before walking over to Robert and sniffing at his feet. A grin crossed his face and he reached down and stroked her.

"Tell me all that you remember," Lola said.

"Well, it was a long time ago. I had left the car on the street in Lincoln. I can't remember where and had gone to a few pubs. I can't remember which ones when I came back my car had gone. The police were not a lot of help. I didn't realize it was a gang of thieves. I just thought it was an opportunist."

"Did you still have the keys?" Lola asked.

The man's jaw tensed but he smiled. "I believe so, but I really can't remember. Is that important?"

"He smells nervous," Sassy said.

Was he nervous because he had killed Kirsty or was it because he felt guilty that she had taken his keys, that he had been duped?"

CHAPTER TWENTY-TWO

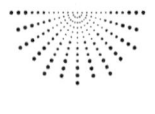

LOVELY FEET

"We believe that a group of girls was playing men and that they were paid or bribed into doing it for this gang."

"What do you mean?" There was a rush of emotion to his face and she could see that his fists were clamped by his side. Had he really not known?

"We believe that the girls kept men busy and either took their keys and sometimes their wallets or just got them out of the way while the gang took the cars. Do you remember any of the girls? Their names? What they looked like?"

"I don't think I lost my keys." The way his eyes couldn't meet hers contradicted his words.

"He smells more nervous but has lovely feet," Sassy said.

"I have to admit, I'm not sure I can remember that far back," he said.

"Do your best. The girls, tell me everything you remember about them." Lola had been careful how she phrased that question. If she asked him if he could remember it would be easy for him to say no.

Robert stood, his hands flexing in front of him and he paced to the fireplace and leaned against it before turning back to her. His face was a lot calmer now, he had himself back under control. "I don't remember much about them. I think they were in their mid-20s, attractive, fun to be around. There were so many girls that it's hard to remember. Back then, I drank too much and I played around a lot but it was nothing out of the ordinary for a bloke out on the town."

"You met the girls at The Bustard Inn?" Lola asked. "Is that where the car went missing from?"

Robert was nodding his head, Lola got the feeling it was giving him time to think.

"He nice man," Sassy said. "He worried but don't think bad."

"That's right, I'm pretty sure it was The Bustard, but we had another name for it, we changed one letter. I guess it was a little childish." He chuckled and shrugged his shoulders. "I really apologize, I can't remember much about the girls."

Lola noticed that there was a picture of him with a burgundy Jaguar on the mantle behind him. He looked very different with a full head of hair and a big smile on his face. From the angle, she wouldn't be able to see the license, the registration plate but it was pretty obvious that this was one of the cars that had been stolen.

Sassy was now sniffing around the office and Lola asked a few more questions. If he could remember anyone else who visited the pub anything else he could remember. She asked about the men he drank with, about March and the others from the garage but he was keeping things pretty generic now. However, he seemed like a nice man and willing to answer all her questions. That one point he had been nervous, she wondered if that was because he was ashamed of his awkward behavior.

"Do you have any more questions, I have a call in 20 minutes and I would like to prepare?" he asked.

"No, you have helped me a lot, but if you remember anything else would you give me a call on this number?" Lola handed him her card and stood to leave.

Where was Sassy?

As if on cue the Frenchie came running down the stairs and Lola shook her head hoping that Robert hadn't noticed.

"Couldn't find any socks," Sassy said as they left the house.

As they walked back to the car Sassy backed off, straining on her lead as the robot mower came towards her. "Get away, get away," she barked frantically.

"Don't worry, I'll chase it off," Lola said and stood in front of the mower just at the edge of the lawn. Lola had seen these before and knew there was a perimeter wire that would turn the mower around. It came towards her and she could feel Sassy pulling on the lead but then the mower turned and set off in a different direction.

"Wow! You chased it off good."

Lola chuckled and picked Sassy up. Robert was still a possible suspect but she had no evidence on him. It was time to go and see the next suspect.

CHAPTER TWENTY-THREE

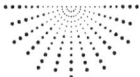

A DIFFERENT KETTLE OF FISH

Lola went through the evidence in her mind as they drove to their next suspect. Well, what little of it there was! March and Bruiser both had criminal convictions but they were minor. They were suspected of much worse but nothing had stuck. The only person with a hard criminal record was Peter Bucknell. Lola was pretty convinced that it was either him or one of the men from the garage; Bruiser had to be her favorite but March seemed clever. However, it was always better to follow through and talk to everyone involved. So she was on her way to see Christopher Jones, who ran an accountancy practice around 6 miles from their present position.

The drive didn't take them long and soon they were pulling up outside of a business called Number Crunch. From her research, Lola had found out that this was a franchised business and that Christopher had owned it for over 20 years. It seemed profitable and there was a gleaming gull-winged silver-grey Mercedes parked outside in the spot reserved for Christopher.

Lola walked into the office with Sassy trotting at her heels to be greeted by a smiling redhead who looked to be in her early 20s. She was very pretty and the badge she wore said, Brittany.

"Good morning, how can I help you?" Brittany asked peering over her glasses at Sassy. "Oh, I'm sorry but we don't allow dogs in here."

"Good morning, I believe as a service dog she is allowed everywhere," Lola said.

Brittany giggled. "Oh, I'm sorry, I've never seen one that looked like that."

Sassy grunted. "Cheeky monkey."

Lola bit back a chuckle. "My name is Lola Ramsey and I was hoping to speak to Christopher Jones on a matter of some urgency," Lola said and gave her brightest smile.

"I'll see if he's available, what exactly is it about?"

Lola had hoped she could get away without explaining, as her instinct told her that Christopher would not want to play ball. "I'm investigating some car thefts and I believe that Christopher may have been a victim."

Brittany buzzed on the intercom. "Mr. Jones, I have a Lola Ramsey at reception, with her little service dog. She wants to speak to you about some car thefts that you may be a victim of. Should I show her in?"

"Little!" Sassy squared her shoulders and stretched up as tall as she could.

"Yes, show them through."

Brittany stood and led Lola across the reception area before knocking on the door.

"Enter."

Brittany pushed open the door and waved Lola through. "Would you like refreshments?"

"No, the lady won't be staying long," Christopher almost barked out the words.

Lola walked into a plush office with a big picture of Christopher on the wall behind him. The man stayed sat at his desk and for a moment Lola felt threatened.

"Me save you," Sassy said and rubbed against her leg.

It was enough to push back her fear, Lola had faced much worse than him when she was in Afghanistan. The man leaned back in a large burgundy chair. Thick black hair and thick black glasses tried to make his plump face look distinguished; it didn't work. To Lola, he just looked mean and there was a coldness to his pale brown eyes. This one was a different kettle of fish, she would have to be careful.

"So, you're investigating car thefts from way back... just when a body was found at the garage that we all believed was behind the thefts," he said with a smirk on his face.

"Even from here, he smell bad," Sassy said and blew out as if she wanted to get the scent out of her nose.

Christopher glanced at her but didn't offer Lola a seat. Deciding she may as well rattle his cage a little Lola sat anyway and crossed her legs, taking her time, before looking over at him.

"Did you know the young lady who was murdered?" she asked.

"Why would I?" There was amusement in his eyes, he knew she had nothing. All she could hope was that she could trip him up by sparking his anger, but she doubted it.

"I have several witnesses that place you talking to her at the time of her disappearance."

"Maybe it's time for you to go."

"Then you agree, you were there?" Lola kept her face neutral.

"I didn't say that…"

"You can't deny that you were at The Bustard Inn," Lola said, though she had no proof he was there that night she pushed to see if he would break.

"I used that place for meetings. I wasn't as…" He glanced around the office at the gaudy pictures and an expensive-looking bust of Caligula. "That place was cheap. Was I there when she went missing? I have no idea but if I was, I was working."

"I see, so the young ladies that say you... took advantage of them are lying, are they? All of them?" Lola knew she was pushing this too far but she also knew such an accusation would damage his business if it were to get out. This man was a snake, she was sure of it and she would push him as far as she had to. It would be worth it to make sure Alice suffered no more and to find Kirsty's killer.

He laughed but it didn't reach his eyes and he paled a little. "Well, now you're insulting." His hands rose in front of him and then floated down his body. "With this, I don't need to take advantage, the girls love me."

Sassy snorted, loudly.

Lola simply raised her eyebrows. Did he really believe that? Well, maybe his money did the talking.

"It's time for you to go." Red had crept up his neck and colored his face. He was rattled. "You will be hearing from my lawyer and if you spread any vicious and untrue rumors about me then I will sue you for every penny you own. You won't even be able to feed that mangy little mutt when I'm done with you."

He stood, his fists clenched, pushing back his shoulders and glowering at them. Lola could see that he was barely controlling the urge to leap at them.

"Mangy, little! What wrong with people?" Sassy said bristling so much that her hackles made a dark line down her back as she barked at the man. It was a strange high-pitched bark but Christopher jumped back, no doubt startled more than afraid. Sassy bore her teeth. "That showed him," she said.

"Thank you for your time." Lola grinned at him as she stood and slowly and calmly left the office.

Christopher was a good suspect. He had demonstrated that he had a temper, he had the opportunity. Motive! Well, if Kirsty had pushed him too far or he found out she was involved in stealing his car then he had that too. Even back then he had been driving a Mercedes so his excuse of being too poor to afford a nice meeting room didn't hold much water. However, Lola knew all of this was mere speculation. There was no evidence. How could she get some?

CHAPTER TWENTY-FOUR

WHERE NOW

*A*s Lola made her way back to the car her phone rang, it was Wayne.

"Hey," she said hoping for some news.

His, "Hey," in return sounded pretty depressed.

"What is it?" Lola asked.

"We are arresting Mick," Wayne said. "I thought I'd let you know."

"Has the DNA come back yet?"

"No, but Susan Tring and Vicky Kelly both gave another statement and said that they saw Mick being rough with Kirsty that evening. They say she left with him."

Lola felt her heart tumble. Could it have been Mick? It was possible, people changed a lot over the years and anyone could lose their temper and yet her gut said no. Also, Jennifer didn't think it was him. How could she prove this?

Well, for now, it didn't matter, she needed to see Alice before she got the news.

"Ok, I will go see Alice now, will someone ring her and give her the news? Mick's solicitor will no doubt tell her. I have one other bit of information… Peter Bucknell…"

Lola felt her excitement build, would this help free Mick? She could hear Wayne checking his notes.

"Peter was stabbed and killed in Manchester two years ago in a believed drug-related incident." The sound of shouting could be heard in the background. "I have to go, I've been taken off this case and I'm not happy with the guy who's on it. I would have been doing things very different but my boss is on my case."

Lola heard the call end and her hopes with it. What could she tell Alice? If only they could prove Mick was not the killer.

"No sad," Sassy said in Lola's mind.

"I'm not really sad, just sorry for a friend."

"I give them lovings, make everything good... or let smell butt if really sad."

Lola chuckled, she wished it could be that simple.

The journey back to Alice's took them just a few minutes. Lola had never been there before. It was a small bungalow with black metal railings around a well-trimmed lawn. Flowers grew all around the lawn in an abundance of color. Lola thought they were mainly begonias but she wasn't sure. Leaning against the wall of a conservatory was Alice's bike. She could see Alice sitting inside at a little table writing in a book.

Lola pulled up and picked Sassy up, unclipping her from the seatbelt harness. She knew Alice would be happy with her running around and it was not worth putting her on the lead. As she climbed out of the car Sassy wiggled in her arms excited to have the chance to cheer Alice up.

Alice raised her head and smiled. Beneath her short and curly blonde hair, her eyes looked tired and her smile was not as broad as usual. Rushing to the door Lola could see she was dressed in a purple shell suit that Jane Fonda would be proud of. It was not as exuberant as some that Alice had, but still had black stripes across each leg and forming a V on the top.

"Come in, come in, do you have good news?" Alice asked as she opened the gate. She scooped Sassy from Lola's arms and cuddled the little Frenchie close while smothering her in kisses. "Aren't you just the sweetest?"

"Pleased someone noticed," Sassy said in Lola's mind.

"Come in, I will make some tea," Alice said, putting Sassy down and rushing into the kitchen through the conservatory."

Lola followed her and could see that her hands were shaking. "I'm so sorry but Mick is going to be arrested," Lola said.

Alice froze for a moment with her back away from Lola, then she picked up the kettle and filled it from the tap. Once it was on she turned around. There was something strong and proud in her eyes. "I know he's not guilty, what can we do?"

Lola nodded and noticed that Sassy was rubbing against Alice's leg, offering what comfort she could. "I am still working on it, don't worry, I won't give in."

Alice nodded and made the tea. She carried a tray through to the conservatory and they sat at the table. On the surface was a large diary that she had been filling in. She picked up her pen and wrote in it in strange squiggles.

"What is that?" Lola asked.

"Oh, it's my diary, it's shorthand; I used to be a secretary in the days before dictation. I write everything in my diary... am I still a suspect?" Slowly, she raised her eyes to meet Lola's.

"I don't think that will be a problem and I think I have a witness that can cast enough doubt over Mick's involvement that he won't be found guilty," Lola said hoping she was right. She was sure that Jennifer's testimony, which contradicted that of Susan and Vicky, would be enough in a court of law but would it be enough for the police? Jennifer would be a much better witness too... if she could persuade her to get involved.

"Oh, okay."

"Too sad," Sassy said and went and stood in front of Alice turning to face away from her. "She can sniff my butt, tell her, make feel better."

Lola had to bite back a most inappropriate laugh.

"See, worked with you," Sassy said.

Alice reached down and stroked Sassy.

"It's just so long ago I guess no one can remember anything," Alice said.

Lola swallowed and looked around the room. On one side was a bookcase lined with books, no, not books, diaries. They must go back years, decades. Excitement filled her.

"How long have you been keeping a diary?"

"Oh, since I was 10," Alice said and a smile came over her face as they both realized what this meant.

Alice stood and walked to the case. Her fingers scanned across the spines until she found the one for 2011. "Here we go." She plucked it out and returned to the table opening it up in front of them. Quickly they skipped through it to June. Alice skipped through and found Saturday 18th. She scanned down the page and found it. It was all in squiggles incomprehensible to Lola but she read it out. "Mick at Cadwell Park, racing, came 3rd in his class."

Alice turned to the previous page and scanned again. "Mick left for Cadwell today, early start, he was on the road by 7 am, he's there until Monday morning." She looked up a big smile on her face. "This is proof."

Lola smiled too. She hoped it was enough but the squiggles could say anything.

"Oh, don't worry, the police will be able to find someone who can read my shorthand. They don't have to believe what I say."

"What is Cadwell Park?"

"It's a racing circuit. Mick used to race there, it's mostly for bikes; however, he raced bangers. Someone, somewhere will have the results and as he was placed that has to be incontrovertible evidence, doesn't it?"

Lola hoped so and took the diary straight to Wayne.

CHAPTER TWENTY-FIVE

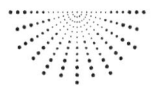

TIME TO THINK

The following day Mick was released from prison and later that morning Lola got a call from Wayne telling her the DNA had come back. It wasn't Mick and it wasn't Alice but they didn't know who it was. However, at least they had it for when they found a suspect.

"Does that mean all suspicion is off the two of them?" Lola asked.

Wayne didn't answer for the longest time. "Well, the diary was read by one of the older officers who understood shorthand. It gave Mick an alibi... unfortunately, Daniel still likes Alice for this..."

"What?!"

"I know," Wayne said. "I feel the same way. I know you have Jennifer's testimony but we don't and they will only go on what they have. To be honest I think it's lazy policing at its worst. Young Danny Boy thinks he knows it all. A criminology degree and he's fast-tracked up the ranks, but he has no feel for people, no empathy. I will keep pushing but it may get nasty for Alice before this is resolved."

"What can I do?" Lola asked feeling her heartache and her anger sparked.

"Find me an alternative suspect or get Jennifer to come in. That would help."

Lola sighed, she would push but she was unsure if the woman would be prepared to do so. "What about the other guys from the garage? Surely, they are good suspects?"

"Susan Tring and Vicky Kelly said they weren't there, that they weren't involved in anything, that they just worked at the garage." There was a pause and she could almost see Wayne running his hand through his hair." Look, I believe they were involved and I don't believe Alice had anything to do with this. I think it is sour grapes but it's all we have to go on," Wayne said. "My hands are tied and I'm so busy with this court case that I can't do too much for at least a week. I'm hoping to get to the fete for my lunch tomorrow but then I'm straight back to court."

"The fete?" Lola asked.

"It's a church fete, for charity, if you have time you should go."

Lola doubted she would have time, she had to make sure that Alice was kept safe and that the real killer was found. "Are they going to arrest Alice?" Lola asked.

"No, well, not yet. They are after more witnesses but the thing is, Danny Boy is likely to lead those witnesses to say what he wants to hear. But we have a bit of time, he is on a sensitivity course for the next two days.

Lola felt a wave of exhaustion come over her after Wayne ended the call. The last thing she wanted to do was tell Alice that she was still a suspect; still, she had to go see her.

With a heavy heart and a mind that kept going over all she knew, Lola went to see Alice and was surprised to find she already knew and was in remarkably good spirits.

"Don't you worry about me. I'm just so pleased that the cloud has been lifted from Mick," Alice said as she sipped on her tea stroking Sassy who sat on her lap. Each time Alice stopped stroking, Sassy used her paw to guide Alice's hand back to her chest. "I can pay you, don't you worry, I'm not even worried about me. It is just ridiculous and this will all come out in the wash but I want to know the truth."

"I understand," Lola said, "but I'm only worried about you. For the rest, surely, the police will get to the truth."

The postman walked past the garden and Sassy jumped off Alice's lap. She didn't bark but went to see if he would come and give her strokes, she loved the postie like she loved everyone.

Alice smiled, closed her diary, and patted the cover. "It's not that I don't trust the police, I know I will be exonerated; it's after that... I don't think this will be a priority for them. Mick and I, we are easy targets. I feel for that poor girl. I feel I let her down and I know Tilly does too and so I want to find out who did this. I want to see them get their just desserts."

"Okay, I will do what I can but from now on there will be no more charge."

Alice's mouth dropped open and she raised her hand but Lola shook her head. "That is my condition. I will investigate but I will do it on my dime."

"Oh, I do love to hear you talk," Alice said. "Okay, I will agree to this but I owe you. Anything you ever need, you come to me."

"Need tummy rubs," Sassy said in Lola's mind and she rolled on her back in front of Alice and waved her paws in the air. "And chicken, lots of chicken."

Letting out a joyful little laugh, Alice bent down and rubbed the Frenchie's tummy.

"Paid in full," Sassy said. "Oh, no, forgot chicken, get chicken."

"Tilly and I were going to walk up to the church fete tomorrow," Alice said. "It's on the field and the garden behind the church and we wondered if you'd like to come?"

"I don't think I should take the time out." Lola had intended to review all her notes and decide what her next step in the investigation was to be.

"You need a break," Alice said. "Half a day won't hurt and who knows if Tilly has come up with anything. Rest, recuperate and let your mind have a bit of freedom, maybe an idea will come to you."

Lola nodded, she had no new cases and it wouldn't hurt to take a few hours off. "We'd love to," she said and then blushed a little as she had included Sassy.

Alice clapped her hands in front of her. "Excellent. Great, we'll call for you at 10 am."

"That would be great."

"We normally have a cream tea so don't eat too much breakfast."

"Cakes, me loves cakes," Sassy said, jumping up and giving a squeak of excitement as she spun around on the spot before flopping back down on Alice's feet.

"Sometimes, I think that dog can understand me," Alice said.

"She has amazing intuition where her stomach is involved," Lola said. "Okay, I will get off and I will see you tomorrow."

"Thank you so much," Alice said as she showed her to the door. "Toodles," she called as Lola walked away.

"Me get cream tea?" Sassy asked.

"I'm sure we can share."

"Lovey love you, you the best."

Lola couldn't help but smile. The feeling of love that the little Frenchie gave her just made everything seem better.

She spent the rest of the day collating her notes and going over everything she had on the case. Instinct told her she was missing something, but she didn't know what. Maybe she could go back over it all tomorrow morning. Maybe, taking a few hours off would allow her brain time to work out what she had missed.

When she went downstairs she found Tanya doing some washing.

"I'm sorry, I didn't hear you come in," Lola said. "Are you here for the night?"

"No, I have to nip back and meet Louisa."

Lola felt a jolt of worry and she hoped that Louisa was all right. It must have shown on her face because Tanya smiled and reached out and patted her shoulder.

"Don't worry, Louisa is fine; in fact, she's better than fine, she sold out of her paintings once more. I need to persuade her to price them at a higher level and I know she's not going to like it."

"Well, she's making a good enough living and she's selling everything she paints... so why does she have to raise the prices?" Lola asked.

"I understand what you're saying but the gallery needs paintings to be there all the time. As soon as one of her paintings goes up it's sold and then we are left with an empty space until she can paint another one. If she's not careful she's going to run herself into the ground. In my opinion, she needs to at least double and maybe triple her prices. That way, she will make an excellent living and she will give herself time to breathe."

Lola supposed that made sense for she knew Louisa, and if people wanted more of her paintings she would paint until she dropped.

"Do you want me to talk to her?" Lola asked.

"No, it's okay, I've got this. However, I'm sure she'd love to meet up for a coffee sometime... as would I!" Tanya raised her perfectly manicured eyebrows and gave a mock angry expression. "We seem like ships that pass in the night at the moment, however, it's good we're both busy. How is the case going?"

Lola filled her in and told her how she was having tomorrow morning off and was going to be church fete.

"Oh, it's always a great day out," Tanya said. "I'm hoping to meet Wayne for an hour, he has been so busy I've hardly seen him. We hope to see you there. At least nothing can go wrong and we can all have a breather," she said, giving a little chuckle as she left the house once more.

Lola picked Sassy up and rubbed her face against the bulldog's head. "Let's hope she hasn't jinxed it."

Sassy grumbled and groaned before licking her cheek. "I keep you safe."

CHAPTER TWENTY-SIX

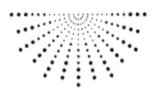

A BIT OF HISTORY

At 10 am precisely there was a knock on the door. Lola grabbed her purse and opened it to the smiling faces of both Alice and Tilly. They were a strange pair. Alice was in her mid-40s and Tilly must be at least 60 if not older. Tilly had neat, short, flat grey hair and sensible clothing. Today she was wearing a white blouse, a long blue cardigan, and a long blue skirt. With dark brown eyes and a small nose, she looked like a mole as she peered intensely at you, her nose almost twitching. Sassy had even taken to calling her Moley. There was no malice, it was just how she saw her.

Alice was so different, with her tight curly blond hair, open smile, and brightly colored shell suits. One stood out and one melded into the background and yet they were the best of friends.

"Are you ready?" Alice asked.

Lola grabbed Sassy's lead and instantly the little Frenchie ran to the door and sat. She was squealing with excitement in her high-pitched and over-exuberant way and desperate to go on her walk. Her whole body quivered and shook, however, she knew that if she didn't sit still they wouldn't go and so she did her best to keep her bottom on the floor while Lola put on her harness and clipped on the lead. Putting a harness on an excited Frenchie was not the easiest and Lola could hear "Hurry," in her mind as her fingers fumbled with the clips. At last, they were ready and Lola opened the door. Sassy sat, squeaking a little in anticipation she looked at Lola waiting for the word.

"Okay," Lola said and Sassy trotted through the door.

The walk to the quaint and beautiful village church only took them a few minutes.

"Do you know much about the church?" Alice asked, her eyes bright once more.

"No, not really," Lola said as Sassy began to tug on her lead a little. She had probably got the scent of food.

"Well, it's really interesting," Alice continued.

"Now, Alice, don't bore our guest." Tilly wagged a finger and chuckled.

"No, it's okay, I would love to hear all about it."

"Oh, goody," Alice said. "I do love history. Well, the west arched doorway, which is now the main entrance, dates back to Norman times. That's when the original church was built."

"When was that?" Lola asked feeling a little silly for not knowing. She was trying to slow Sassy down a little. "Steady, Sassy."

"Hungry, smell sausages."

"There are no records as to when exactly it was built but somewhere between 1066 and 1075." Her face was lit with excitement and the exhaustion of the previous days seemed to have dropped from her. Lola hoped that this would last.

"Wow, that is old."

"Yes, the rest of it was built over various generations, the current tower was built in 1678. In 1795 a new church was constructed using the remains of the old one. At that time there was the nave, chancel, a gallery, a three-deck pulpit, and box pews. It really must have been something. The vestry on the north side was added later, in 1925 I believe."

"How do you know all this?" Lola asked.

"Faster, get to sausages," Sassy said in her mind.

"I love history and when I go out on my bike I visit historical sites and learn as much as I can. I travel to the library a lot too and research all I can. It just fascinates me."

"I can understand."

Tilly chuckled. "Sorry if we're boring you." Her eyes flashed at Alice who simply shook her head and continued.

"Did you know that the church has chairs used at three coronations?"

Lola was quite stunned and wondered what it must have been like to be at a coronation. There would have to be another one sometime in the future though she would hate to see Queen Elizabeth go. It was both exciting and incredibly sad. "No, I didn't."

"Yes, yes," Alice said, her words rushing out of her. "They were used by Lord and Lady Monson at the coronations of Edward VII, George VI, and Elizabeth II. They keep them in the gallery now. I will see if you can see them sometime."

"Thank you." Lola found it so hard to get her head around such history but somehow it made her feel part of the community to learn some more about it.

"Oh, good, we're here," Tilly said as they walked in through the church gates. The beautiful sand-colored stone building was an impressive site with its colorful stained glass windows and impressive tower. The churchyard was a scatter of gravestones nestled amid trees and flowers. They were all different sizes, shapes, and colors ranging from grey stone, through browns to black slate. At the back, they seemed to be arranged haphazardly but at the front of the church, they were in orderly rows. It was quaint and felt so peaceful and yet you could hear a buzz of conversation.

THE BULLDOG AND THE BURIED BODY

"The fete's in Father Jackson's garden, come this way," Tilly said and led them through the churchyard.

Lola had met the vicar on a few occasions and she attended service most Sundays. He was a nice man, open and easy to talk to. He believed that God was a loving God who wanted the best for all of His children. There was no fire and brimstone in his sermons but acceptance and love.

As they walked around the side he was waiting at the gate into his private residence. The archway was covered in balloons and the extensive garden was filled with people talking and eating. The smell of a BBQ made Lola's tummy rumble.

"Tilly, Alice, and Miss Ramsay," Father Jackson said and reached out and took all their hands.

"Please, call me Lola," Lola said.

"Come on in and make yourself at home," Father Jackson said. He was in his mid-50's, around 5 foot 10, with short salt and pepper hair and a kindly face. Big expressive brown eyes always seemed to be looking into you, listening to you. "This is all for charity. There is a BBQ, cakes, stalls and a tombola and we will be playing some games later. Enjoy and if you need anything let me know."

Lola was about to agree when she noticed that the smile slipped off his face and his eyes drifted away from them. His jaw had tightened and he was staring at a swarthy-looking thickset man to one side who was eyeing up a group of youngsters.

"Excuse me," Father Jackson said and walked purposely across to him.

Lola couldn't see what was going on but she could see that the man was not happy that the vicar was coming over. He squared his shoulders and stood his ground. Lola wondered if she should go over when her mind was filled with a whine. "Hungry!" Sassy said.

Lola glanced down to see the Frenchie in her pouting pose sitting on the base of her butt with her back legs stuck out. Her chin was down and her bottom lip stuck out.

Lola glanced back at the vicar to see that the man had walked away and Father Jackson was watching him. Then he shook himself off and turned, the smile back on his face once more. Lola decided she must ask him what that was about but it would wait. First, she must get the Frenchie a bit of sausage.

As they wandered over to the food Lola tried to keep her eyes on the man. She wanted to ask Tilly who he was but he seemed to have gone. She guessed it wouldn't matter for now.

CHAPTER TWENTY-SEVEN

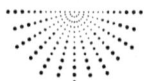

TROUBLE IN THE GARDEN

*L*ola bought a sausage for Sassy and cut it into pieces. There was too much for now but she could save some for later. She always carried bags in her purse for just such an occasion.

They wandered around talking to a few people but Alice was making a beeline to a marquee. Inside, it was filled with beautiful tables and tea sets that Lola recognized. The tent was run by Betty's Tea Room. Gerald, in his butler-like splendor, was at the door. Seeing Lola, he smiled.

"Miss Ramsay, Sassy, a table for three?"

My, how he had changed. Lola smiled in return. "Please Gerald."

He bowed slightly and led them to a corner table before leaving them with a menu.

"You are very honored," Tilly said. "How do you know Gerald?"

"I use Betty's for my meetings." She didn't explain that her first meeting with the man who looked just like a butler was less than congenial. He had thought that Sassy was not up to being a service dog and was about to prevent her entry. Luckily, the Betty of Betty's intervened. Since then Gerald had been nothing but cordial.

They picked a cream tea for three and sat and chatted waiting for it to arrive.

"Who was that when we came in?" Lola asked.

"I didn't see anyone," Alice said.

"Will you make the food fly?" Sassy asked in Lola's mind just as she was about to take a sip of tea. She choked back a laugh and had to put the cup down quickly.

"Do you mean the swarthy-looking man that Father Jackson went over to intercept?" Tilly asked.

"That was the one. I felt some tension between them."

"He's Alexander Petrov. There have been some rumors that he is peddling drugs around some of the bigger schools. We don't want him around here and the vicar has had to chase him off on a number of occasions."

"What do you know about him?" Lola asked as the food and tea arrived. The platter looked scrumptious.

"Yummy, yummy," Lola heard Sassy say so she passed her a little bit of sausage under the table.

"Not cake but good."

"He's from a very rich family. His father, Borya Petrov, is well known in the city. Though he has a legitimate business, it is believed that he started in the Russian mob. He moved here with the fall of the USSR and fell in love with Lincoln. He has a financial business now and tries to keep his sons on the right side of the law. Alexander does very little but his brother, Uri, has his own warehouse. I'm not sure that he does that well though."

Lola was, as always, amazed at Tilly's knowledge. She decided it would be worth looking into the Petrovs and keeping an eye on Alexander.

Sassy sat looking up at Alice, her bottom lip stuck out as Alice was so engrossed in the wonderful Victorian sponge cake that she had eaten it all without thinking of the bulldog at her feet.

Lola chuckled and snuck a piece of her own cake down. Sassy nuzzled her hand in appreciation.

Once they had eaten they left the marquee and were about to walk over to the tombola when Sassy let out a shriek of excitement.

"Goodness!" Alice said and stepped away, scared she had trodden on her.

Lola followed the dog's gaze to see her staring at a big brindle boxer.

"Don't worry, she's just seen another dog."

Alice put a hand to her chest. "Oh, yes, that must be Tony's new dog. Wow, it's big."

They wandered over to intercept Tony Munch and the big brindle boxer. Tony was of average height and had always been a little overweight. With his brown hair cut in an old-fashioned way, he had been teased by some of the local youths for years. The more horrid of them used to call him Munch Munch. Lola noticed that he had lost some weight. Maybe the new dog had got him out walking?

"Sit nicely," Lola said as they reached him. The boxer was a beautiful brindle. Expressive brown eyes sat beneath big velvet ears giving him a friendly and impressive face. Sassy sat before him, her bottom polishing the grass as it wiggled with such excitement.

"Hey, Tony, can she say hello?" Lola asked Tony Munch.

"Of course, Tyson is friendly."

"My new friend," Sassy squealed.

"Okay," Lola said and Sassy squirmed up to the dog that looked huge beside her. While the two became friends Lola saw Alexander skulking in the background. There was something about him that raised the hairs on her neck. Maybe it was his dark eyes or maybe the way he was staring at the youngsters. Maybe she should chase him off? Before she could move she saw Father Jackson appear once more and she could see that they were having sharp words causing a few people to look in their direction. Alexander towered above the vicar and Lola began to move, but before she could get far Alexander turned, and throwing his plate of food at Father Jackson, he stormed off.

It looked like this was over, at least for now.

CHAPTER TWENTY-EIGHT

MY NEW FRIEND

*L*ola turned her attention back to the dogs in front of her. The boxer was a tiger-striped brindle with a coat of stripes of dark brown and red. He was stunning, with a big, soft looking head with hardly any white. His eyes were brown and expressive and he was staring at Sassy with wonder.

They walked around each other sniffing butts and Lola almost laughed as a vision of her meeting someone the same way was put into her mind. She wasn't sure if Sassy had done that or if it was just because they had spoken about it.

"You be my friend," Sassy said.

"Sure."

"I like Tony," Sassy said.

"Me too. It's nice to have food and be warm. Have you ever laid on carpet? Wow, it's so soft."

"You should try beds or the sofa," Sassy said.

"Really, you can go on them?"

Lola pulled her eyes and mind away from the conversation and back to Tony.

"I took your advice," Tony said.

Lola had met him on her last case. Tony Munch was a nice man who had been a suspect as he told his neighbor he would prevent him from drowning by taking his foot off his neck. Tony's brown hair was cut into an old-fashioned style, greased over to one side. With his new figure, he was wearing jeans and a grey T-shirt and as normal his face wore a smile. He had the habit of losing his temper and saying things he didn't mean but Lola knew he had a good heart. After all, he helped out at the church on many weekends.

"What's your name?" Lola heard Sassy ask.

"I'm Squishy Face the Noble but Tony man calls me Tyson. He says it's because I'm a boxer which I don't understand but he feeds me delicious things and gives me treats. He even strokes me, it's just so wonderful."

Lola bit down a lump in her throat; she had suggested Tony get another dog as he had been lonely after losing his previous Labrador.

"He looks great," Lola said. Tilly and Alice had wandered off and were speaking to someone Lola didn't know.

"He's a rescue, starved and beaten when they found him but good as gold," Tony said. "I call him Tyson as he didn't have a name."

"He looks really nice."

At that moment Alexander stormed past Tony and pushed the boxer out of the way.

The dog looked at him but not in a nasty way. "Excuse me!" Lola heard the boxer say in her mind.

"You keep that cur away from me or I'll wring its neck." Alexander raised his fist as if to hit the dog and at the same time drew back his leg. He was wearing sandals and no socks and there was a tattoo of a scythe on his left foot. Tyson cowered down and Tony stepped in front of the Russian blocking his arm with his own and knocking his leg away.

Lola was amazed at how fast Tony moved and she wondered if he was ex-military, he certainly seemed to know how to handle himself.

"I hate cowards like you who hurt animals. Touch my dog and I'll chop you into little pieces with my ax and scatter you across the fields."

Alexander visibly paled and at that moment Lola noticed that Wayne had just walked in with Tanya. He was close enough to hear and he shook his head at Tony.

"Tony!" Lola said and smiled at him as the Russian walked away.

Tanya shrugged at Lola and followed Wayne as he had been called by Clarissa Gee. Lola was surprised to see that she was wearing her jodhpurs, even here.

"I know, I need to learn to control my temper but he threatened my pal. I won't have that," Tony said. His face had turned bright red with anger but was paling rapidly.

Lola had to agree with him, she wouldn't have let it go if it had been Sassy and she would never have let the man hit either dog.

"He's my hero," Tyson said and Lola bent down and rubbed the boxer under his jaw.

"Nice," Tyson moaned.

"You like that," Lola said and the dog's eyes widened.

"My human is nice too," Sassy said.

Lola was filled with joy.

"Have you had chicken?" Sassy asked.

"Don't know, what's it taste like."

"It's my favorite."

While Lola and her friends enjoyed the fete the two dogs raced around in a quiet area of the garden. Sassy was so good at helping out humans in need and Lola got the feeling that she would help this dog too. Lola hated to think about what had happened to him but at least now he had a good home.

Wayne and Tanya came over when Lola was alone watching the dogs.

"You have to keep an eye on Tony, he can't go threatening people, especially not loudly and in public," Wayne said.

"Hi, Lola, how are you finding the fete?" Tanya asked elbowing Wayne in the side.

The big detective's cheeks flushed pink and he nodded an apology. "It's hard to relax at the moment."

"It's okay," Lola said. "Tony was provoked though. What do you know about Alexan...."

"Stop!" Tanya said raising her hands. "Wayne you have an hour off, no shop talk. Lola, you have worked non-stop for days. Both of you, take a few minutes to unwind."

Lola and Wayne both hung their heads and mumbled, "Sorry."

For the next hour, they wandered around, talking, laughing, playing games, and enjoying the sunshine. There was a raffle for church funds and just as Father Jackson called for everyone's attention there was a great roar in the sky above them.

Everyone looked up, the sky was crystal blue and clear of all clouds, and at that moment the 9 jets of the Red

Arrows aerobatic team flew over in arrow formation. The crowd let out a gasp as they put on their red, white, and blue smoke and made a circle in the sky before racing away across the fields. Lola knew that this was probably a coincidence as the display team was based just a few miles away at RAF Scampton but she wondered if one of the crew was doing Father Jackson a favor. No matter, it was a wonderful display.

"Now, back to the raffle," Father Jackson said and he most definitely looked pleased.

All of the crowd had bought tickets and the prizes ranged from flowers to hand-stitched quilts, a £50 voucher at Tilly's, a months' riding lessons from Clarissa, a visit to the Red Arrows' base. Even Tony had put up a half-day of his labor for anyone, he would do gardening, or joinery.

Wayne cheered when he won the voucher at Tillys and then checked his watch. "I have to run, we will talk tonight," he said to Lola before kissing Tanya's cheek and walking away.

Soon the fete was over and Lola, Tilly, Alice, and Tanya wandered back. She had seen no more of Alexander and wondered if Wayne had any news for her. For some reason, she felt her stomach churn. Had this just been the calm before the storm? Would Alice end up in jail for a crime she didn't commit?

CHAPTER TWENTY-NINE

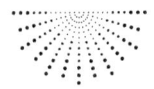

BACK ON THE CASE

After the fete, Lola went back to her room and reviewed everything she had found. She still had to interview the staff from Mick's garage. According to Wayne, the police and Daniel Peterson, were still focused on Mick and Alice. It was apparently because of Susan Tring and Vicky Kelly's testimonies. It seemed so silly. Mick could not have been the one driving the van. Tilly placed the van at March's and yet still it was ignored.

Lola went over and over her notes and she kept being pulled back to the garage and to Brent Burton or to the theft of the cars. One of these had to mean something.

If the garage were running the girls and if that was why Brent had his cars serviced there then he had a motive to silence anyone who might talk. Could it be him?

Was he still involved with March? Was that where the money that Wayne had found missing in his financials was going?

There were so many questions and so many years had passed that it seemed she may never find an answer. Letting out a frustrated huff she leaned back in her chair and put her hand over her eyes. They were sore and she felt so tired.

Sassy pawed at her leg and gave a little whine.

Lola looked down and stroked her between the ears. "No sad," Sassy said.

Lola knew that she was telling her not to be sad not that she thought she wasn't sad. "I'm not sad, there is just... trouble."

"What trouble?" Sassy asked and sat down with a serious expression in her eyes. "I bite it."

Lola wished it could be that easy. "I'm trying to find the bad man who killed Kirsty but I don't know where to look."

"I smell out bad men for you."

"I know you will. Can you remember Kirsty's scent?"

"Hard, maybe." Sassy's bottom lip slipped out. "Tired."

Lola looked at her watch. It was gone midnight. "Me too, Monkey. Let's get some sleep."

Sassy jumped up on the bed and Lola closed her laptop. She would sleep on it and hopefully something would come up.

Lola woke around 7.30, and as always, she placed her socks for Sassy to find but this morning she went straight in the shower. She knew that Sassy would take the socks downstairs and sit in her basket with her treasure waiting for her.

After her shower she came down the stairs. Tanya had left but Wayne sat at the table with a bowl of Weetabix.

"Morning," he called.

Lola murmured a reply and noticed that Sassy was in her bed, the socks covered by her paws. "Do you want to go out, Monkey?"

"I already let her out," Wayne said, "Grab yourself a coffee, it's fresh."

Lola fed Sassy and grabbed some coffee and a muffin from the fridge.

"That's a healthy breakfast." Wayne's eyebrow rose as he eyed the muffin.

"It will keep me going." Sitting at the table she took a sip of coffee. "Is there anything you can tell me on the case?"

"Not really. Daniel is convinced that it's Alice but we have no proof, the DNA doesn't match and no relatives are pushing us to solve the case. It's not going to be a priority."

"What does that mean for Alice?" Lola asked, a frisson of worry dancing in her stomach.

"Nothing much unless the press gets hold of it. I guess she will still be a suspect but the only one interested is Danny Boy."

"Will he hassle her at all?" Lola asked as she nibbled on the muffin.

Wayne let out a sigh. "He might, but I can see that he's kept busy. If he does, tell me and I will have it stamped on."

Lola had been over her notes time and time again.

"Has anyone interviewed the staff from the garage?"

"No, well, a very easy interview and then letting them go. I think they are too much hard work for our Danny Boy, Alice is a much easier target."

Lola could see that Wayne was angry and she felt the same but her anger wouldn't solve this.

"Okay. Did you find any more out about the stolen cars? Who was stealing them? Who's were stolen?"

Wayne nodded and then pointed his spoon across the room. Lola turned to see a box beneath the stairs.

"They are all the old case files. I requested them and brought them home. I've been told to let it go now, but I might forget to take them back this morning. I've been so busy and no one will miss them."

"Thanks. If I find anything I will let you know."

"Great, today should be my last day in court for a while. It will be good to get back to some policing. I will ask about as much as I can but I have to be careful."

"You're the best," Lola said.

"I wish you'd tell Tanya that," he said with a grin.

"You know she adores you."

Wayne laughed. "Yeah, I guess I do. See you later."

With that, he was gone and Lola had a box of files to review. She was going to skip through those first and then start on visiting the guys from the garage. They had to be involved in this somehow. If the van really had been March's it was too much of a coincidence.

Lola took Sassy for a quick walk and then grabbing a big cup of coffee she spread the files out on the dining room table. With her trusty laptop to make notes, she set about going through the files.

The first one was a bundle of five thick folders all on Mick's garage and the staff. There were reports, interviews, officers' notes, lots of conjecture, even a few witness statements but nothing concrete.

Lola went over and over it but they were clever, there was no proof that they were guilty and none that they were innocent. A few people had pointed fingers or said they were in the area but it was not enough. Lola noticed that the three men she had talked to had all pointed to March and two of them to the girls. It was interesting but nothing more. There was no proof. How could she find it?

"What you doing?" Sassy asked after a few hours.

"I'm studying these documents for clues."

"Must be good, can I sniffy them?" Sassy asked staring up at Lola her brows knitted her expression serious.

Lola chuckled and passed a piece of paper down to Sassy. The Frenchie sniffed the page from top to bottom. "I smell you, paper, old skin of old man with dark illness nothing more. Why you take so long?"

Lola swallowed; she knew that dark illness was cancer. Sassy had sniffed it out before from people that Lola knew were ill. For a moment she wondered if she should tell Wayne. She didn't want to but if the man who had handled these files didn't know then she had to.

"Why you take so long?" Sassy asked again. "Better things to sniff outside."

"I'm not sniffing them; these little marks are words. I'm reading them."

Sassy's eyes opened wide as if she was amazed and then she looked again. "You read slow!"

Lola laughed. The little bulldog was right she had been staring at the same page for a long time. "I guess I was thinking." With that, she had a seed of an idea. For now, she pushed it down knowing that if it was anything then her mind would let it grow.

The rest of the files were on the cars that had been stolen. She went through them one by one; they were sparse, and policing had been very different in those days. It didn't look as if anyone had been that bothered. Lola wondered if there had been any corruption. She hoped not, Wayne was a good officer, one of the best and the type that was needed. The last thing she wanted to do was stir up trouble and start accusing the police of wrongdoing. Maybe it was just that the officers didn't have a lot of sympathy for the men, it certainly read that way.

Lola had been through everything and made lots of notes. As far as she could see two cars had been stolen around the night of Kirsty's disappearance: a Jaguar and a Mercedes. She had interviewed both of the owners, might it be worth another look?

CHAPTER THIRTY

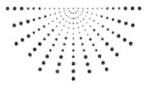

THE GARAGE

*A*fter a quick lunch, Lola decided it was time to start visiting the garage. Part of her had thought about getting Sam to stake the place out. Her worry that it could be dangerous had stopped her. She already knew that Brent Burton had his cars serviced there. That he probably paid them money, but as much as she wanted him to be guilty of this; she was sure he wasn't. There was no one to put him at the scene.

With Sassy in the car, Lola drove the few miles to the tiny village of Dunweld. It was just half a dozen houses and a farm nestled in the crook of an ancient woodland. A beautiful place, and so peaceful. There was a small village square and Lola could see a sign-posted footpath leading into the woods. She decided to park the car there and walk to the garage. Maybe she could watch the place before she went to see them.

With Sassy's service harness on, she attached her lead and let her out of the car. It was pleasantly warm with just a slight breeze. Lola could feel the sun on her skin but still, she grabbed a coat. The sky had been cloudy all morning and the last thing she wanted was to get caught in the rain without a coat. From the back of the car, she grabbed a rucksack. It contained her surveillance kit, then they were ready.

"I smell cow poop and rabbits"! Sassy said standing four square and sniffing the air.

"That's the country for you," Lola said as she locked the door and checked her pockets for baggies. Finding some there she set off in the opposite direction to the one Sassy was looking.

"Best smells this way," Sassy said.

"Where we're going is this way."

"Oh." Sassy looked wistfully along the path that led to the woodland and no doubt to plenty of rabbits but then she turned and trotted off in the right direction.

Lola had checked on Google Earth and knew that the garage was just a few hundred meters out of the village. It was set back from the road and surrounded by copper beech trees.

They walked along, Sassy sniffing at every leaf and tuft of grass they passed. As they came out of the village, Lola saw the copper beech trees that surrounded the garage. They were magnificent, around 25 m high and probably the same in circumference. The leaves were more purple at this time of year, but they would change to a deep copper as the season changed to fall, to autumn. They provided an amazing screen for the garage, keeping prying eyes out and whatever was inside was shielded from any passing traffic.

"Can you smell any people?" Lola asked.

Sassy sat down and raised her head in the air sniffing all around her. "Only you. Though someone passed this morning with a big hairy dog with a bad tummy."

"Thanks."

Sassy rubbed against her leg and they set off walking again. When they reached the trees Lola walked along them until she came to the entrance to the garage. There was no signage outside advertising the business. In fact, if you did not know it was there, the entrance was almost hidden. It looked like March's Motors was not looking to attract passing trade.

Lola walked back a little way toward the village and then slipped under the cover of the trees.

"Where we go?" Sassy asked.

"We're going to wait under these trees and just watch the place for a while."

"Oh, we sneaking up on them ready to pounce when they're not looking."

"Something like that," Lola said and moved further beneath the trees. Under the shade of their leaves, it was instantly cooler, almost cold. The breeze murmured as the branches moved and the leaves rubbed together. It was darker too and Lola had to wait for her eyes to adjust. Looking up she could see sunlight filtering through and it felt amazing to be beneath these amazing and ancient trees.

Lola made her way through until she could see the garage on the other side. It looked pretty run down.

Quietly, she pulled some binoculars from her backpack and an extending seat. It was simply a stick that she pushed into the ground and on the other end was a seat made of a strip of leather on a small frame which she opened out. Tanya had called it a shooting stick and had given it to Lola when she was doing a clear out.

Lola opened the stick, pushed it into the ground, and balanced her butt on it. Hidden beneath the trees she took the binoculars and studied the place. There were a few old cars that didn't appear to have been moved in years on one side of the property. Grass was growing around them and a few blackberry brambles were trailing over the bonnets.

The door to the workshop was open and a Shiny black Land Rover Discovery was parked inside. No one was working on it; in fact, no one seemed to be there. Then she moved the glasses to the front of the building. There was a small pedestrian access door and a window next to it. Inside she could see who she thought were March and String Bean in what looked like an office. The window was filmy and they appeared to be watching TV.

March had a phone to his ear and was waving his hands a little. Lola watched for some time as Sassy sat at her feet. Nothing much happened. No one came, no one worked on the cars. This seemed to be a very slow business. It was all as she suspected but it proved nothing.

Sassy jumped up, her hackles rose and she began to shake in anticipation.

Lola looked at the little Frenchie and followed her gaze. Just 10 feet away a squirrel had come down from the tree and was gathering the nuts from the beech.

Sassy squealed and strained against her lead. The squirrel sat up on its haunches holding a nut and staring straight at her.

"Look what it's planning," Sassy said her voice desperate.

"Don't worry, it's just getting food for the winter," Lola said.

"No, it's planning, takeover, evil, bad."

Lola chuckled as the squirrel darted away. "Look, you scared it off, you saved us again."

Sassy sat back down and raised her head. There was a very smug look in her eye. Lola knew she had to deal with this sometime soon but for now, she would let the Frenchie think that squirrels really did have an evil master plan.

Once they emerged from the trees, Lola heard a car start behind them. She wanted to rush back in but decided that she might be seen. Instead, she pulled out a baggy and bent down pretending to pick up poop. The Discovery pulled out of the garage and headed away from the village. Lola couldn't work out who was in it, but she did see the sticker on the back *Burton's Architectural Solutions*. It was the name of Brent Burton's business now that his partner, Fred Johnson, was dead. What would such a new car be doing at a rundown place like this?

There was no reason for it to be heading in the direction it was. The road that it was on was single track, winding, and headed away from Lincoln. On the map it went nowhere that couldn't be got to easier the other way, this all looked more and more suspicious but what did it mean?

Lola knew it was time to find out. Her nerves kicked up a notch as she realized how remote this place was and how she was here all alone.

"I protect you," Sassy said.

Lola hoped that would be enough.

CHAPTER THIRTY-ONE

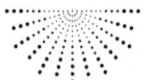

AS MAD AS A MARCH HARE

*L*ola walked along the road back to her car and then drove to the garage. As she pulled in, the door to the office opened and the two men stepped out. The taller skinny one was indeed wearing green overalls. Though he had put on some weight over the years, he could still pass as the String Bean of his nickname.

Lola reversed in and stopped the car. Sassy was still on her lead and wearing her service harness. Putting a big smile on her face, Lola stepped from the car.

"Smell oil, and bad people," Sassy said.

Lola wanted to say that was quick but she could see the face of the two men staring at her. They were not happy that she was there. What had she gotten herself into?

The men came closer, crowding around her and Sassy jumped toward them and barked.

The shorter man backed off for just a moment but in his hand was a heavy spanner. Much too big to be used on a car, this was over 40 centimeters long and the sort of thing for use on heavy machinery. He raised it onto his shoulder, the gesture obviously a threat. A monk's ring of red hair surrounded a pale head. Freckles spotted his wrinkled face and watery brown eyes should have looked weak but they held a menace that set Lola's heart beating faster. This man was the type who liked to hurt people. A coward at heart but dangerous nevertheless.

"What do you want?" March, Marty Stevens asked.

"I was looking for somewhere to service my vehicle," Lola said and put on a big smile. She would play innocent and see where it lead.

"Why'd you come here?" March asked, his eyes flicking at the workshop and then the office. The man looked so nervous that if she were the police she would consider his behavior probable cause.

"I heard a friend of a friend uses you, Brent Burton."

Paul "String Bean" Norton whistled. "Just like Brent to give it up to the dolly birds."

"Shut it," March hissed. "Lady, we only work with certain clients and you're not one of them."

"Yes, but while I'm here you could have a quick look." Lola knew she was pushing her luck but what else could she do.

"You ain't from around here, are you?" Marty asked. "Oh, I've heard about you, the lady detective from across the pond. You don't want to go poking your nose into our business." Marty stood closer and Sassy growled at him.

Lola could see that the Frenchie's courage was rattling Marty but he didn't want to admit it.

"He smells of fear," Sassy said.

Lola wanted to say she understood and that Sassy must be careful. Lola wouldn't put it past the man to swing the big, heavy spanner at the dog. It would not go down well for him if he did. Lola may no longer be in the military but she still had her training and she would not let her friend be hurt.

"What business is that?" Lola said stepping in front of Sassy.

"Let me at him!" she heard in her mind.

"Private business that could get a girl like you into trouble." He swung the spanner up, meaning to let it fall near Lola's face.

With a move quicker than he could see she intercepted the spanner, twisted, and pulled it from his hands. Now she hefted it in front of her. "Careful with this, you could hurt yourself," she said.

March stepped back, his hands flying up to his face and began to chew his nails. Lola could see that both hands were red raw around the fingers. This looked like a nervous habit.

"I'm looking for a van that I believe belongs to you," Lola said.

Paul breathed in like a child caught in a lie.

"Don't say a word," March said to him, and regaining his nerve he turned to Lola. "You're trespassing, Miss. I suggest you take that mutt and get out of here if you know what's good for you. Go, NOW!"

"The van with the snake transfer, where is it?" Lola pushed a little harder.

"I don't know what you mean." March folded his arms and tried to look taller but she could see the nerves in his eyes; he wanted to run, to bolt like the jittery march hair he had been named after.

"A witness recognized you two and your van at the old garage in South Brooke the night that body was found," Lola said.

Paul sucked in a breath and Marty hit him in the stomach.

"I've not had that van for years. I believe it was stolen but the cops never caught the people who did it," Marty said recovering quickly or maybe he had rehearsed this.

"Really?" Lola asked and she noticed that red flushed his cheeks and anger filled his eyes. Would he lose it? Is that what happened to Kirsty?

Just like that, the anger was gone and the color dropped from him. "I'm sorry, Miss, but we have work to do, so if you don't mind." With that, he turned to leave, and grabbing hold of Paul he pulled him away too.

Lola tossed the spanner in the dirt and got back in the car. She was not afraid of the likes of Marty and Paul but the visit had got her nowhere. These men were the type to have committed this crime. They obviously knew something as they had to be the ones trying to move the body but how could she prove it?

As she turned the jeep around she scanned the cars and the garage. Part of her wanted to go into the workshop and around the back to see if she could find the van. It was foolish, as Wayne had told her it would have been disposed of long ago to make sure that it couldn't be linked back to them. Maybe if she hadn't let them know she had seen them that night then the van would still be here but without it she had nothing.

"Don't be sad, I chase bad men away," Sassy said.

"I know you would, my little Monkey." Lola hugged the little dog as she fastened her harness to the seat belt.

"Lovey love you, but not a monkey."

Lola chuckled. "You're my little monkey."

Sassy stuck out her bottom lip but Lola could feel the sensation of love in her mind.

CHAPTER THIRTY-TWO

CROW LIKE A ROOSTER

*L*ola wondered if she would ever solve this case. No matter where she turned it felt as if she got nowhere. The garage had been a bust, it deserved further scrutiny but she doubted that Marty or Paul would give anything up.

Paul had let his emotions show, a sharp draw in of breath was enough for that, but it wasn't something that Wayne could use. There was nothing concrete. Lola knew they tried to move the body, they had to have, but did they kill Kirsty, or were they just moving the body for Mick Beecham's sake, or their own?

It all made no sense. Mick couldn't have killed her so why weren't the police looking into these men?

Would Gary "Rooster" Thomas or Larry "Bruiser" Floyd give her more to go on?

Lola decided to visit Rooster next. She had a feeling that he would be easier to lead. Maybe she could get him to say something. Before she got there she undid an extra button on her blouse and applied a little lipstick. Giving her hair a flick she hoped that she could use her feminine wiles to get something from the Rooster.

Gary lived in a small but nice bungalow on the edge of Skellingthorpe Village. Lola pulled up to see him working on a car on the driveway. It looked like an old Landrover, the bonnet was up and one panel was missing off the driver's rear quarter, the rear wheel on the same side was off. Gary was under the car as Lola walked up.

Sassy went almost up to his face and Lola heard him give a little squeal, the rooster was crowing but not in a brave way. He cursed, before rolling out from under the vehicle on a trolley. He stared up at Lola his eyes wide at first but something changed and he put on a big smile and stood up.

"Scared him," Lola heard in her mind and bit back a chuckle.

Gary was now eye to eye with Lola and he was flirting. The man had to be in his late fifties or maybe even early sixties but he still felt he was a lady's man. His once red hair had receded and pale blue eyes stared out of a pale and wrinkled face. There was something a little ridiculous in the way he licked his lips and looked Lola up and down. Sassy had spotted it too and Lola saw her hackles rise and she felt her bristle in her mind. It was a strange protective sensation and she understood it perfectly. Gary was a bit of a creep.

"Well, what can I do for a lovely lady like you?" Gary said leaning in and touching Lola's shoulder.

Sassy snapped and jumped at him and he pulled back.

"Whoa there, little dog, I was just being friendly."

"Hi, I'm Lola Ramsay. I had a friend tell me all about you." Lola batted her eyelids and watched as his eyes glazed over. It was working. "She said you were a real good guy and might be able to help me out?"

"I'm sure I can help out a pretty lady like you, why don't you come inside?"

"Maybe later." Lola leaned in, there was no point leading him around the garden too much. She had got his interest now she would ask a few teasing questions and then jump in with *the real question* and hope he was too distracted to notice. What she wanted was for him to answer without thinking.

"Well, I'm always here to entertain if you want a little fun," he said, licking his lips, his eyes almost popping out of his head.

"I like a bit of fun," Lola said and giggled. "Is it true they call you the Rooster?"

"You bet." He stood up a little taller and his shoulders went back and he walked around and then gave a big crow just like a cockerel. "You know what another name for a rooster is?" He winked and Lola felt her stomach turn a little. But she managed to giggle.

"I thought you would," he said touching her arm.

Lola put her hand on his and leaned in closer. She could smell his breath and it seemed he hadn't cleaned his teeth in a while. Taking a breath she whispered the words against his cheek. "What you were doing last Friday night?"

"A few friends and I were up to no good." He pulled back, for a moment Gary smiled and then his face crumpled a little as he tried to work out why she was asking, then he turned red as he got the date in his mind. That was a look of guilt, he knew exactly what she meant.

"Why'd you ask?" he asked.

Lola stepped back and removed the flirty look from her face, now she was all business. Sassy gave a little bark as if recognizing that they were winning this. "I have a witness who saw you and took photos of you at the old South Brooke garage. You were digging something up out of the ground and the police later found out it was a body. Did you murder her?"

Gary jumped back. "You can't ask me that."

"I just did, now, did you murder Kirsty Kelly?"

"No, we never murdered her," he said and then realized that he had incriminated himself. "I was not there. You're mistaken," he said hastily changing his mind.

"Look, Gary, I know you didn't kill her. If you tell me who did then I can help you out here. If it's Brent Burton and he's paying you to keep quiet the police will find out." Lola could feel her excitement building. She was gambling on the fact that he was just there to help but it felt good to finally have something.

Gary's face paled and his mouth opened wide. "I won't say any more until I see a solicitor. You can't fool me."

"Then I have no choice but to call Detective Wayne Foster. He will take you in for further questioning."

Gary's eyes were so wide they seemed to fill his face and he froze in place. "You can't do that. I have to make a call," he said, shaking, and with that, he turned and was gone. Lola imagined that he would be calling Marty or Brent Burton. How could she push him enough to find the final piece of the puzzle?

Quickly, she called Wayne and waited for him to arrive. Just as he pulled up Gary came out. "No comment," he said as he tried to walk past them.

Wayne smiled. "Gary Thomas you are under arrest. Come with me."

Before Wayne could read him his rights or say anymore, Gary tried to run. If it hadn't been so serious it would have been funny, for he did look like a startled cockerel fluffing up and then bolting.

Sassy stepped in front of him and grabbed hold of his trousers. He fell to the ground at Lola's feet. Rolling over onto his back he glared up at her. "You will pay for this," he shouted.

Wayne hauled him to his feet, slapping cuffs on his wrists before throwing him into the back of his police car.

"Don't worry, we will get it all out of him," Wayne said.

Lola hoped so but she decided to go see Larry Floyd anyway. Something was niggling at the back of her mind and she just couldn't quite put her finger on it. Before Wayne left Lola took him to one side.

"What is it?" he asked, "You look worried."

Lola shrugged her shoulders. "This is going to sound crazy but when Sassy and I did our training there was a cancer dog being trained at the same time and the trainer taught Sassy to indicate when she smells cancerous cells."

Wayne's face dropped and he paled before her. "Is Tanya all right?"

"Yes, yes." Lola touched his arm and nodded. "It's the files you gave me. Sassy was indicating that she smelled cancer on those files. I know it could be nothing but just in case I thought I had to tell you."

Wayne shook his head, blew out and whistled. "That little dog is amazing, especially as she has no nose. Our Evidence clerk has prostate cancer. He's getting treatment and he should be okay. If she smells anything else let me know."

"I smell his socks, they yummy," Sassy said, looking up with a big grin on her face.

Lola nodded. "I will do."

CHAPTER THIRTY-THREE

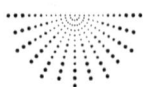

ONCE A BRUISER

Lola soon arrived at Larry "Bruiser" Floyd's property. It was a nice semi-detached house with a neat and tidy front garden set to block paving. There was a 3-year-old Toyota in the driveway and a smaller Renault Clio. It looked well cared for and just your normal run-of-the-mill house. There was nothing to say that a once feared enforcer lived here.

Lola didn't know how to tackle this. Of all the men this one was an enigma. Everything about his current appearance defied what she had discovered about his past.

"Just ask," Sassy said and wagged her little tail as Lola smiled down at her. "I tell you if he lie."

"Sounds good," Lola said as she knocked on the royal blue door.

The door was opened by a man just a little taller than her. He was thickset with a chubby face lined with red veins and a big smile.

"Hey," he said. "Can I help you?"

"I'm Lola Ramsay and I'm investigating the murder of Kirsty Kelly," Lola said.

"You'd better come in. Want a cuppa?" he asked and turned from the door expecting her to follow.

"Thanks," Lola said.

The house was nice and well kept, he led her along a carpeted hall lined with pictures mainly of his grandchildren and daughter. All of them looked so happy, smiling, laughing, and having fun. Larry was in some of them and he was the perfect grandad, there for his child and grandchildren. Lola noticed that there was no father in any of the photos.

Larry led her into a neat modern kitchen with beautiful oak units. He made two teas from hot water straight from an expensive-looking tap. As he fished out the teabags Sassy looked up at him a big smile on her face, her tail wagging.

"Well, you're a cutie; Larry Junior would love you." Reaching down he rubbed her under her chin and then lead them out onto the patio.

"My daughter's out and the kids are at school so it's just us," he said pointing at a table with chairs.

For a moment Lola's nerves activated sending the hairs on her neck to attention. Had that been a threat? Looking at him and feeling Sassy lean against her she knew it wasn't, just a turn of phrase.

As she sat she saw him raise his eyebrows, he had clocked her reaction. The man was still able to read someone, even her who had masked her worry.

Lola sipped her tea and waited for a moment. The garden was lovely and dedicated to the grandchildren. There was a swing set with a slide, a ball pool, a paddling pool, and a trampoline.

"You can see my life is mainly my grandbairns now," Larry said. "They are what I live for."

"They look like amazing kids," Lola said and noticed that he puffed up a little with pride. "I have to tell you that Gary Thomas was just arrested, He admitted that he was moving Kirsty's body on Friday night."

Larry nodded and smiled. "The Rooster was always prone to a little too much crowing."

"Were you there?" Lola asked.

"Nice try, but no, I wasn't. Look, this is off the record and I'm telling you this for your own good. Leave the guys I used to run with alone. They are rough around the edges. Not bad by yesterday's standards but things have changed. You don't want to go there and if you do you won't find Kirsty's killer."

"What do you mean by that?" Lola took another sip of tea to give herself time to think, she had to play him carefully for it seemed he would talk.

"I'm sure you've heard rumors that the guys used to run girls to steal cars. I don't know whether that is true or not. I know the girls were all legal age and they were as much a part of this as the guys. Of course, things have changed. Back then you kissed a girl and if she didn't like it she told you so. Now, well you kiss them and they like it then six months later they change their mind and they sue you for every penny you have. I'm pleased I'm out of the game and happy with my grandbairns."

Lola couldn't believe his attitude but she was going to push it as far as she could. She wished Sassy would let her know what she thought

"Nice feet, fruity," Sassy said in Lola's mind.

That wasn't quite what she meant.

"I knew Kirsty, she was a wily one, knew what she wanted, and went for it. That got her into trouble more than once." Larry said.

"Telling truth," Sassy said. "Bird!"

Lola felt her strain on the lead and she let it go. Sassy flew across the garden and a blackbird disappeared over the fence. Lola knew that she would be back to work soon and would sniff around the place, later she could find out if any of the other men had been there recently.

"What do you mean by that?"

Larry nodded. "This is all off the record. I don't want you coming back and spoiling things for me, I wouldn't like that." For a moment his face was no longer the jovial grandfather but was full of menace.

Lola understood and she nodded her acceptance. Her gut told her that Larry may have been involved with moving the body but he was not the killer.

"Let's just say that if a certain bunny persona was stealing cars, he might use ladies to lure the men into a false sense of security to facilitate that. Now, if Kirsty cheated someone then maybe she brought it on herself?"

"Are you saying that March killed her because she took from him?"

"I'm not saying that. I told you to leave those guys alone. I'm not saying anything, just that maybe she asked for trouble."

"Do you know who killed her?"

"No, I don't, but if we did steal cars then them men might have been angry. Some angry people are like big cats fighting. Sometimes they slink around, others they squeal and strike at each other, who knows if one would go too far."

Lola was both elated that she may have a clue to the killer but sad that a life was worth so little. Part of her wanted to tell him to imagine it was his granddaughter that was dead. Some people could treasure the lives of those they loved but throw aside the lives of others. It was sad, too sad.

"That's all I will say and if you send the cops I will deny any of this. Tread carefully, think like a hunter, and you will find her killer."

As they got back in the car Lola looked at Sassy. "Did you smell any of the men we went to see?"

"Smelled Larry, children, and woman. No men"

"Good girl." Lola rubbed her between her ears and she groaned her appreciation.

"He smells like nice man, had sweeties in his pockets."

Lola had to agree, Larry came across as nice, caring, he had changed his spots. That didn't mean he wasn't the killer, but she had a new theory. One that felt right and her old excitement was back. Her only problem now was how did she prove it?

CHAPTER THIRTY-FOUR

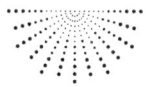

A HINT OF KILLER

*L*ola was sure that Larry knew who the killer was. That he had hinted at it and was hoping that she would solve the case and leave him and his old friends alone.

Taking a quick drive to The Lakes garden center she sat with a latte looking over the lake and going through all the clues. She was sure she had worked it out but how could she prove it?

Sassy sat on her knee looking at some ducks on the lake. A beautiful black swan glided past. Sassy's eyes followed it and she reached forward almost slipping off Lola's knee.

"Need to chase," Lola heard in her mind and she looked up to follow Sassy's gaze.

"That swan is three times your size, are you sure?"

Sassy let out a grumble of excitement.

"That's its home and it's a nice bird; maybe you should leave it alone."

Sassy huffed and looked the other way. "Hungry!" Lola heard in her mind so she reached in her pocket and pulled out a dog treat.

"You're the best."

"We're going to a man's house and I want you to search for any hint that he killed Kirsty," Lola said pretending she was talking into her mobile as the family on the next table were giving her funny looks.

"What hint?" Sassy had jumped off Lola's lap and was looking up at her with her head tilted to one side.

Lola didn't know what she hoped to find if anything. "If I ask him something let me know if he is worried or lying."

"I try."

Next Lola rang Wayne. He answered straight away.

"Hey, Lola, how you doing?" he said.

"I think I have a suspect."

"Who is it, Brent? What evidence do you have?" Wayne was straight down to business.

"It's nothing concrete. No, it's not Brent." She heard a sigh. "I'm pretty sure one of the people I interviewed was hinting that he knew who the killer was."

"That's pretty weak, how are you going to prove it?"

Lola didn't know but she decided to trust her instincts and have faith that the truth would be revealed. It was all she could do, either that or give in and she was no quitter. "I'll get back to you on that. Did you get anything from Gary?"

"No, he called his solicitor, and a very expensive one it was too."

"The same one that Brent Burton used?" Lola asked as she still wanted to get that man.

"Good try but no, still, this man is too expensive for Gary and he had his number in his memory. That's suspicious but nothing more and I don't think we will get enough from him to take this further."

"Are you letting him go?" Lola asked as a wave of fatigue rolled over her. The guy was guilty of something, of using those girls and yet he would walk free.

"I'm gonna hold him as long as I can... just to be awkward."

Lola laughed. "I like your style, actually, that might help me. I will call you if I find anything out."

Lola had an idea. "Come on, Monkey, let's go."

"Not a monkey!" Sassy said.

"Oh, sorry, my little munchkin."

"Not munchkin either! What is munchkin?"

Lola bit back a chuckle. "A munchkin is a wonderful friend, the best ever."

"Maybe am munchkin," Sassy said and trotted out of the garden center her head high her little tail wagging so fast it was a blur.

Lola made the short drive to her prime suspect. All the time her mind was a blur. How could she force him to incriminate himself? How could she coax out a confession? Was there any evidence? It all seemed too much and her mind couldn't come up with any answers. As she pulled up Sassy put a paw on her arm.

"Calm, smile," she heard in her mind and she was flooded with the warm feeling of love.

"I will do my best," Lola said and hugged the little Frenchie before stepping out of the car.

Sassy was instantly on guard as the robot mower seemed to have spotted her and was coming straight at them.

"Must chase it," she said but even though her hackles were up and she was barking that strange Frenchie scream, she was backing up.

"Don't worry, it is just paying its respects. It will turn away before it touches us," Lola said.

The mower came to the edge of the grass bumped a little making it look as if it was taking a bow and then turned away.

"It knows I princess," Sassy said and swaggered up to the house.

Lola just hoped it would be that easy to convince her suspect to back down.

CHAPTER THIRTY-FIVE

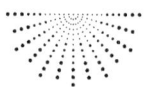

ON THE HUNT FOR SOCKS

"Remember, search for any clues," Lola whispered as she knocked on the door.

"Got it!"

"Miss Ramsay," the Walter White lookalike said as he opened the door. The smile was no longer there and Lola could see that his jaw was tense. He hadn't expected her back. "What can I do for you?"

Lola smiled at Robert Kennedy and used all her military training to read his facial expression. He was anxious, not annoyed. The lines around his eyes were tight, his jaw tense.

"I have some more questions," Lola said keeping it low-key for now.

"Well, I'm sorry but now is not a good time." He started to close the door.

Lola pulled out her phone. "I understand, I will need to report my findings to the police, I wondered if you might have any insights before I do that."

The door hovered, half shut, half open and she could see that he was trying to keep his face neutral as he made a decision on what to do.

The door opened and he forced a smile on his face. "I guess I can spare a few minutes, please come in."

Once more, he led her across the polished wooden floor of the extensive hallway and into a drawing room. Ignoring the desk, he led her across from it to the burgundy sofa and two armchairs set in front of the empty fireplace. Taking one of the chairs he pointed to the sofa.

Lola sat and reaching down she slipped the lead off Sassy.

"He nervous," Sassy said. "I investigate."

Lola watched as the Frenchie went over to Robert and sniffed his feet. She looked back at Lola and gave her a look that was almost a thumbs up. Sassy liked the smell of his socks.

As Sassy began to wander around the room Lola wondered where to start. She had to be bold, she had to push. Sassy was sniffing at the curtains and then the desk before she disappeared out of the room. Lola hoped she wasn't just on a sock hunt, she really needed some evidence and wished the dog had stayed closer. Her input into Robert's mood would have been useful.

"Good smells up here," Lola heard in her mind. "Me hunting socks."

"What can I do for you?" Robert asked again.

"Oh, I'm sorry," Lola said, "It's been a busy day and this is the first chance I've had to sit and rest my feet."

"Well, I am busy, if you wouldn't mind letting me know what this is about." His words were curt, clipped almost. He was desperate to hear what she had to say but trying to be nonchalant. It wasn't fooling her, he was worried.

"I'm investigating the murder of Kirsty Kelly and I have a few questions to ask you. I have a witness that puts you with Kirsty on the night of her murder." Lola had been going to say disappearance as they didn't know the night Kirsty died but on a hunch, she changed it to murder. It was worth it. Robert's face visibly paled. Could it be this easy?

"I... I have no idea what you are talking about," he said covering up quickly. "As I said before I used The Bustard Inn for meetings, nothing more."

"So, you are denying you were there on Saturday the 18th June, 2011?" Lola asked pinning him to the chair with her stare.

"I... I... well, how would I know what I was doing so many years ago?"

"I can assure you, Mr. Kennedy, that a very reliable witness saw you talking to Kirsty shortly before she disappeared. What do you have to say to that?"

Lola heard the sound of Sassy going up the stairs. Luckily, Robert was panicking so much that he missed it. It looked like she would have some of his socks to add to her collection. Maybe a murderer's socks would be a special prize?

Robert shook his head, stood up, and then sat back down. His face was white and his hands were shaking. Sassy had said he smelled like a good man, was she wrong?

Robert recovered. "How could anyone remember so far back. Relying on such a memory, well, it would never hold up in court." There was now a smug smile on his face and he sat back and folded his arms. It almost looked as if he was enjoying this, almost, but not quite.

Lola got the feeling he had been dreading this day for many years.

"The witness made extensive reports at the time, written reports and you know how British bureaucracy is for keeping everything. Of course, back then, because there was no body those reports were ignored, but they are there now, in black and white... well, blue and white as she used a blue pen."

"Maybe I was there, maybe I wasn't, I truly don't remember, but you have no proof that I pu... that I killed her."

What had he been about to say? There was no doubt in Lola's mind now that he was the killer but how could she prove it? Could she force him into confessing?

She thought back to the autopsy report. The coroner had said that Kirsty had been hit in the stomach, but was killed by a blow to her head. Lola struggled to remember the exact wording. Yes, the coroner thought it was concrete with a 90% angle and they thought that she might have struck the object, that she fell or maybe she was pushed. Had that been what he was about to say? Had this all been a terrible accident?

Lola knew that there was a good chance that it would be Robert's DNA under Kirsty's nails but that was not enough to get a sample from him. She scanned the room, there was nothing she could hide in her purse. Maybe she could get Sassy to pinch some socks, would they contain DNA? It wasn't enough, she needed more and then it came to her.

"I understand how angry you must have been. Kirsty was a real player and she made a fool of a lot of men. There is a lot of evidence against you and the police are soon going to put it together just as I did. It will be better for you if you tell me what happened now… before they get here."

Robert shook his head. "I want you to leave now. You are just making this up." Standing he pointed at the door and then looked around the room. "Where's that dog of yours?"

Lola glanced down and raised her eyebrows as if in shock. "I'm not sure. Let me find her."

"No, I want you gone now." There was a threat in his voice and as he closed in, she saw a glimpse of the man who had made the fatal error all those years ago. Lola imagined that his temper had gotten the better of him and it looked like it was about to do the same again. He raised his hand a nasty expression on his face.

CHAPTER THIRTY-SIX

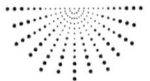

THE CASE IN THE BAG

*L*ola ducked and Robert tilted forward. Grabbing his arm, she pushed him into the wall. "You don't want to do this," she said.

Robert snarled and tried to escape but she was using his own weight against him and had him pinned down tight. "I understand what happened. She cheated you, you got angry, and there was a fight. Maybe her death was not intentional but it happened. We can prove this, it's over, give in."

"Got it," Lola heard in her mind and glanced over her shoulder to see Sassy trotting down the stairs. She was carrying something and Lola presumed it must be some socks. Part of her wanted to laugh, but it wasn't appropriate. Instead, she spun Robert around so his back was against the wall and let go of him.

"You need to tell me the truth," Lola said.

Robert sighed and rubbed a hand across his shaved head scraping his nails over the stubble. "I never meant to kill her. She kicked me and I struck out, instinctively, punched her in the stomach. She screamed and ran at me and I just pushed back, it was self-defense really. I just pushed her and she fell. The sound when she hit the curb... I will never forget it and the blood. I panicked, I just ran. But you can't prove any of this." His eyes opened wide and a tear ran down his cheek, then he looked down. Lola could see Sassy holding a small gold clutch bag. "Where did you get that?" he asked and sank to his knees his head in his hands. "I never meant to kill her, I swear I never meant to kill her, it was just a terrible, terrible accident."

"Hunting socks in big cupboard. Smelt lady faint behind bag of smelly clothes. I dug and dug in boxes and found this."

"You did good," Lola said and took the bag.

It didn't take Wayne long to get there and place Robert in cuffs in the back of his car. "I can't believe you found the clutch bag. I can't believe he kept it. However, you shouldn't have been searching his house."

Lola shrugged, later she would tell him that Sassy had found it on a sock hunt.

She had been surprised that he kept the bag too, but once he had started talking Robert wouldn't stop. He had grabbed the purse during the struggle and after he pushed Kirsty he had run off with it. In his mind, he never thought she was dead and he expected her to come back for her purse. He was then going to bargain with her for his car. Once he found out she was missing he knew she was dead, he just didn't understand why she wasn't found. After all, he had left her body on the street. At that time he was in denial, afraid to move the purse, afraid to throw it away in case it was linked to him but then when there was never a murder investigation it got cast aside. Over the years the purse had been forgotten and now it was there to seal his fate. The DNA could have been circumstantial, his solicitor could have gotten around that but the purse in his house was the nail in his coffin.

"So how do you think she got buried at the garage?" Wayne asked.

Lola shrugged. "I guess we'll never know for sure but I imagine that March or one of the others who stole his car came back and found her there. I guess they thought that if she was found it would bring too much heat on them and their activities. I guess it seemed easier to have her disappear."

"Yeah, that sounds about right," Wayne said. "What brought you back to Robert?"

"It was Larry Floyd. I think he pointed me in his direction, very subtly, but all the same, he gave me the push to come back here. When I did, Robert just looked guilty, nervous, anxious, wanting me gone."

"What did Larry say? It makes me wonder if we could have wrapped this up earlier if Danny Boy hadn't kept away from him."

"I don't know, maybe, maybe not. Jennifer had told me March was after a car that he described as a big cat so I guessed that was Robert's Jaguar. Then Larry said words to the effect of, some people get mad they are like cats fighting. The look he gave me, I'm sure it was a hint."

"Why would he do that?" Wayne asked.

That was something Lola was sure she understood. "With the killer caught the attention is off him, again."

"That makes sense. Now, go home and crack open a bottle of wine; you deserve to celebrate. Tell Tanya I shouldn't be too late," Wayne said and turned to his car. Turning back he said, "At least we should be able to release your property soon, now the case is solved."

Lola was pleased about that. It would be good to have a place of her own, but she would miss living with Tanya and Wayne.

CHAPTER THIRTY-SEVEN

OH OH

The following morning Lola set off for a walk with Sassy. They walked down the hill, along the path next to the ancient yew hedges. The short, spiny leaves were trimmed to perfection and gave off a pungent smell. Alice had recently told her that yew was once called the Tree of Death. It was used to commit suicide during times of war. It was reputed that even food or drink containers made from the wood could be deadly. Taxine would leech from them into whatever they were used to contain and slowly kill the unsuspecting person. Yew trees were also symbolic of everlasting life and for this reason, were often found in churchyards. It was unsure whether this was because they lived so long, to 3000 years old and it was reputed that there was one that could be 5000 years old.

Some believe that the St Cynog church yew situated in a churchyard in Defynnog, in Wales could be 5000 years old. Lola wondered about that. What had that tree been through? It had seen 5 centuries of history and yet was hardly known and left alone.

As they walked Alice was coming up the hill on her bike. A great big smile on her face, almost as bright as the orange and blue shell suit she was wearing. Crossing the road, she stopped next to Lola. Sassy let out a little squeal of excitement before sitting and waiting for strokes.

"What a lovely morning to be free," Alice said. "I still can't thank you enough."

"You don't need to thank us," Lola said.

"I take chicken as thanks," Sassy said as Alice bent down to stroke her. "Cuddles good too."

"Oh, I do. I know they had let me go, but a stain would have always been on me and my family if it wasn't for you."

"It was nothing. Did I tell you they rushed the DNA and Robert was a match to what they found under Kirsty's nails? It nicely ties everything up."

Alice was nodding. "I'm so pleased he will get his punishment. She didn't deserve to die and to be lost like that for all these years. What is the world coming to?"

"I know what you mean. I thought England would be so quiet."

"It has been rather exciting, hasn't it? I must go, I'm visiting Mick at the home. I want him to know he's no longer a suspect but he doesn't seem to understand."

"The main thing is you know," Lola said.

The smile was back on Alice's face. She got onto her bike and rode away. "Toodles," she called over her shoulder.

"Alice gives scrummy cuddles," Lola heard in her mind.

"I'm sure she does." Lola could feel the sun on her face. Even though it was nearly November the sun was warm and made her feel good. With no new cases, she had decided to spend some time exploring the area. Today she would look at some of the gravestones and explore the church and some of the footpaths leading away from it. Tomorrow she was going into Lincoln with Tanya and they would visit the cathedral and maybe the castle if they got time.

Letting out a big breath she glanced over the countryside. The view before her was a picture postcard of green and gold. Green of the grass. Hedgerows, and trees and gold where the corn had been harvested leaving stubble in the fields and where the leaves were starting to turn. It was glorious and once more she was grateful for making the decision to come here.

"Not scary," Sassy said in her mind.

"What's not scary?"

Before Sassy could answer the boom of a fighter jet broke the peace. Lola felt her nerves strum like a fine bow but nothing more. Sassy was leaning against her leg. At one time the sound would have had her diving for cover but she was recovering. Beginning to realize that the world around her was safe.

Above them, 9 red and white jets were flying in a V formation, resplendent against the clear blue of the sky. The Red Arrows flew over, banked right, and flew a circle in the sky, red, white, and blue smoke formed a perfect O, and then they were gone. The smoke distorted and dissipated floating away on the wind.

"Pretty," Sassy said. "Makes me want to jump up and grab it." She did a little jump biting at nothing.

Lola chuckled. "I think you would need to jump a little higher."

"Next time I be ready," Sassy said and then turned and continued on their walk.

As they passed the churchyard Father Jackson was closing the notice board. "Miss Ramsay, how are you this lovely morning?" he asked.

"Good, thank you, Father. Do you mind if I look around?" Lola had been told to visit the churchyard and then follow the path behind it by Alice. The woman knew so much about the history of the place but she suddenly wondered if she should be here.

"No, of course not, be my guest."

"Thank you, have a nice day."

Just inside the wall of the churchyard and nestled in one corner was their own yew tree. Lola wondered how old it was and decided to ask Alice. Walking over she could see that the tree was as wide as it was tall. The branches weeping over the muscular knarled roots. The trunk itself was split down the middle and looked almost petrified. Lola reached out to touch it just as Sassy gave a big whine and strained on her lead.

Lola turned expecting to see a squirrel, instead, she saw Tony Munch shouting and waving his arms as he ran along the path from the field behind the churchyard toward them. "Tyson, Tyson, here," he called.

Lola took an intake of breath as she could see the boxer bounding over towards them. He had something in his mouth. As he got closer Lola realized what it was.

"Oh, oh," Sassy said and approached Tyson.

The boxer was holding a foot, a human foot.

Murder Afoot the next cozy mystery from Rosie Sams will be out soon. Join her newsletter to find out when here

THE BAKERS AND BULLDOG MYSTERIES 20 BOOK COLLECTION - PREVIEW

A BODY, A BLADE, AND AN EARLY BABY

Melody sat down with a big huff of breath. The aching in her back was driving her crazy and she felt like a whale. Almost as soon as her bottom hit the sofa, Smudge, her blue-gray French bulldog appeared and sat in front of her.

With a whine, Smudge laid her head on Melody's knee.

"I can't help it, girl," Melody said as she absentmindedly scratched the bulldog between her ears.

In her normal cute and gorgeous way, Smudge grumbled and groaned as only a Frenchie can. It was a cross between a groan of pleasure and the funniest little froggy snore you had ever heard and it brought a smile to Melody's lips. She tried to lean over and kiss Smudge on the head but the huge bulk of her belly wouldn't let her. For a moment she didn't know whether to laugh or cry; it seemed her emotions were all over the place at the minute.

"I'm bored," Melody said as she sat back and flicked a lock of red hair out of her eyes. Even though she knew she was supposed to be taking it easy, and she had only stopped work three days ago, already she was stir crazy. After all, she was only 36 weeks pregnant and the thought of another four weeks sitting at home doing nothing was driving her mad.

Smudge jumped up onto the sofa and flopped over onto her back. With her paws in the air, her belly was ready for rubs, her pink tongue lolled out between her purple lips. It was a sight that melted Melody's heart and she couldn't help but accommodate the little pup.

"What would I do without you?" she asked as she absentmindedly stroked Smudge's soft belly.

The problem was this could only distract her for so long. Alvin, her gorgeous and wonderful husband, and Port Warren's amazing sheriff wouldn't be home for hours.

Her hand reached for her mobile. There it was sitting on the table beside her. All she had to do was pick it up and speed dial and she could check in on the bakery. It was something she had wanted to do all morning, for her business partners and friends, Leslie Mathers and Kerry Porter Smedley, hadn't been in touch this morning.

Of course, they would be okay. The girls were competent and knowledgeable and they would call her if there was a problem. Melody knew that they were probably just giving her time and space. The problem was, that was the last thing she needed. Melody had owned the bakery for years now. It was hard work, long hours, and she was always on her feet but she was used to it and it kept her fit. She had to admit that she was slightly annoyed that Alvin had insisted that she take her maternity leave now. After all, it could be another four weeks before she gave birth and baking wasn't exactly hard work.

Smudge kicked out her legs to remind Melody that she had stopped stroking her.

"I'm not your personal slave," Melody said with a giggle.

Smudge jumped up and off the sofa, shaking herself as she ran to the door.

Melody laughed. "Point taken, I guess I am your personal slave." Melody got up to let Smudge out into the garden and then decided to take her for a walk instead. The fresh air and a gentle stroll would do them both good.

Grabbing a lead and a thick coat Melody opened the door. There was a chill in the air and she pulled the coat tightly around her. Winter was definitely here. As they set off down the street Melody had no particular place in mind. It just felt good to be moving and to be doing something. Though it was cold, the sidewalk wasn't slippery and she felt quite safe. Traffic was light at this time of year without the influx of tourists but she nodded to a few people she saw walking.

Smudge was enjoying herself too, sniffing at this and sniffing out that, wagging her little stump of a tail as she led the way. Melody wasn't sure if it was Smudge and habit or if her own subconscious had taken over but suddenly Smudge stopped and they stood outside of the Delicately Delicious Bakery, her bakery!

A flush of guilt warmed her skin and she thought about turning around and rushing straight home. If she went in, the girls would think she was checking on them. But then again, if they saw her there and she didn't go in then they might think her ignorant. Before she could make up her mind the door opened and Smudge ran inside.

Melody smiled at the exiting customer and entered the shop to find Smudge behind the counter and already tucking into a butter cookie.

"Hi, Melody," Leslie said from behind the counter, tucking a stray wisp of blonde hair back under her pink hairnet. Then she turned to Kerry, a petite woman with a black pixie bob and dark eyes, who sat on a stool just behind her, and held out her hand. "I told you she would never make the week."

Kerry laughed. "I don't think I ever took that bet. Just like you, I knew Melody couldn't stay away. I'm never sure if it's our wonderful company or if she loves the work too much. Either way, both of us knew she would never stay away for a whole week."

Melody held up her hand in surrender. It looked like Kerry had been on the coffee this morning as her speech was going at 100 miles an hour and no one else could get a word in edgeways.

"I don't even know how I got here," Melody said with a shrug of her shoulders. "I just started off walking Smudge and then here we are."

"I've done that a million times," Kerry said. "When I first started working here the second morning I drove to my old job and it was only when I got there I realized where I was. I think I did it all on automatic."

Leslie ducked under the counter and gave Melody a big hug and it was only then that Kerry stopped talking and came and did the same.

"Why don't you come in the back and share a muffin and a coffee with us," Leslie said. "You can then see that everything is under control and have a break. Then, one of us can drive you back."

"I'll take the coffee and the muffin," Melody said, "but I didn't come to check on you. I have every confidence in you both. And I don't need a ride back, the walk will do me good."

Soon, Melody was sitting in the break room with a lovely raspberry and white chocolate muffin and a cup of hot, strong coffee.

"You should be more careful," Leslie said. "What are you now, 37 weeks?"

"No, I'm only 36 so that is four weeks away from giving birth. I really don't need wrapping in cotton wool."

"I bet Alvin thinks you do," Kerry said. "Besides, I've been looking up some statistics and not all births are at 40 weeks. In fact, the most common time to give birth is anywhere from 37 to 42 weeks and I believe you are now 36 weeks and five days." She raised her eyebrows, wiggling them and smiling before continuing. "So, you are actually just two days before the most common time to give birth."

"Oh, I'm sure I'll go at least 40 weeks," Melody said chuckling at her friend. "You know me, being at home is just... it's just so difficult."

"We know, Leslie said, "it's killing you."

The two partners laughed and Melody couldn't help but join in. They knew her only too well. For the next 15 minutes, they chatted about what the bakery had on and how they were coping. One of the girls would go through to the shop every time the doorbell rang. Melody was proud to see that they were doing so well and she began to relax.

Leslie sat down again and took a quick sip of her coffee. "Come on, Melody, what is really wrong?"

Melody let out a big sigh. "Don't get me wrong, I really want this baby." Her hands absentmindedly went to her massive belly. "The problem is... it changes everything. I loved my life and now it's all going to be different. I loved working here, I loved my time with Alvin."

At their feet, Smudge gave a surprisingly big bark.

"Don't worry," Melody said, "I wasn't going to forget you, Smudge. I love my time with Smudge and I loved solving the mysteries that we ended up getting into... now all that is gone."

"It doesn't have to be gone," Kerry said. "Things will just be different. You will be back working here quicker than you know it. You're lucky, you can bring your baby with you."

That put a smile on Melody's face for Kerry was right, she could.

"Your life with Alvin is only going to get better, you are a real family now and you have other priorities. You may not see them now, but you will do. Your work will be the same but different, your home life will be the same but better, things between you and Smudge are never going to change. You will love that little dog forever."

Melody smiled and nodded but then she realized they'd missed something. "And my mysteries?"

The two girls shared a look and Melody knew they were concerned for her. How many times had she cornered a murderer on her own and nearly paid the price?

"Maybe it's time to hang up your magnifying glass, at least for a while?" Leslie said.

Smudge rubbed her nose against Melody's leg and suddenly she found herself nodding. Maybe it was, at least for a little while. After all, the mystery of birth was about to come her way, maybe that was enough mystery for now.

Read this book and 19 other sweet cozy mysteries with Smudge, Melody, and all the gang for just 0.99 or even better FREE with Kindle Unlimited. Grab The Bakers and Bulldog Mysteries now

ALSO BY ROSIE SAMS

To be the first to find out when Rosie releases a new book and to hear about other sweet romance authors join the exclusive SweetBookHub readers club here.

The Art of Murder

The Case of the Mix-Up Murder

Grab The Bakers and Bulldog Mysteries now. 20 sweet cozy mysteries with Smudge, Melody, and all the gang for just 0.99 or even better FREE with Kindle Unlimited.

To be the first to find out when Rosie releases a new book and to hear about other sweet romance authors join the exclusive SweetBookHub readers club here.

* * *

If you enjoyed this book, Rosie and Lila would appreciate it if you left a review on Amazon or Goodreads. This picture is a hint about their next book.

©Copyright 2021 Rosie Sams
All Rights Reserved
Rosie Sams

License Notes
This Book is licensed for personal enjoyment only. It may not be resold. Your continued respect for author's rights is appreciated.

This story is a work of fiction; any resemblance to people is purely coincidence. All places, names, events, businesses, etc. are used in a fictional manner. All characters are from the imagination of the author.

Rosie is a member of SweetBookHub.com, a place where you can find amazing fun books that are sweet and suitable for all ages. Join the exclusive newsletter and get 3 free books here

Printed in Great Britain
by Amazon

74482998R00169